Chaos in the Green Zone

Chaos in the Green Zone

My Time as an Iraq War Strategist

Tom Mowle

Foreword by John Nagl

University Press of Kansas

Published by the University Press of Kansas (Lawrence, Kansas 66045), which was organized by the Kansas Board of Regents and is operated and funded by Emporia State University, Fort Hays State University, Kansas State University, Pittsburg State University, the University of Kansas, and Wichita State University.

Library of Congress Cataloging-in-Publication Data
Names: Mowle, Thomas S. author
Title: Chaos in the Green Zone : my time as an Iraq war strategist / Thomas S. Mowle.
Description: [Lawrence, Kansas] : University Press of Kansas, [2026] |
Includes bibliographical references.
Identifiers: LCCN 2025047015 | ISBN 9780700641314 paperback |
ISBN 9780700641321 epub
Subjects: LCSH: Mowle, Thomas S. | United States. Air Force—Officers—Biography | Iraq War, 2003–2011—Personal narratives, American | United States—History, Military—21st century | Iraq—Politics and government—2003–| BISAC: BIOGRAPHY & AUTOBIOGRAPHY / Military | HISTORY / Wars & Conflicts / Iraq War (2003–2011) | LCGFT: Autobiographies
Classification: LCC DS79.766 .M69 2026
LC record available at https://lccn.loc.gov/2025047015.

British Library Cataloguing-in-Publication Data is available.
EU Authorised Representative Details: Easy Access System Europe
Mustamäe tee 50, 10621 Tallinn, Estonia | gpsr.requests@easproject.com

Printed in the United States of America

10 9 8 7 6 5 4 3 2 1

The paper used in this publication is acid free and meets the minimum requirements of the American National Standard for Permanence of Paper for Printed Library Materials Z39.48–1992.

Cover design by Karl Janssen
Photograph: Plumes of thick black smoke rise from central Baghdad's Green Zone after a rocket attack on March 27, 2008. Faleh Kheiber/EPA/Shutterstock

To Ann

Contents

Foreword

War is full of contradictions.

It can elicit both the most horrible and most beautiful of all human actions. War can drive human progress and blow it to smithereens. It can create freedom or take it away. War can be cold and calculated or be borne of elemental hatred and fury.

And war can be absurd.

Perhaps the best American writing on the absurdity of war is Joseph Heller's *Catch-22*, which tells the story of Army Air Corps Captain John Yossarian, a bomber pilot in Italy during the Second World War. According to Heller, it asks the question, "What does a sane man do in an insane society?" The book has been taught at the United States Air Force Academy to help cadets there think about the wars in which they may someday serve; while *Catch-22* is a novel, it is clearly based on Heller's service with the Twelfth Air Force during World War II.

America has, sadly, fought many wars since then, wars that have resulted in the triumph of Operation Desert Storm, which liberated Kuwait from a brutal Iraqi occupation, and in the tragedies of American defeat and enormous human suffering in Vietnam and Afghanistan. Those wars produced remarkable pieces of literature, books like Neil Sheehan's *A Bright Shining Lie* and Carter Malkasian's *The American War in Afghanistan*. However, none have captured the absurdity of war as eloquently as did Joseph Heller, until now.

Tom Mowle was an air force major with a doctorate in political science, teaching at the Air Force Academy in summer 2004, when he received an email asking for volunteers to help develop strategy for the then-foundering war in Iraq. Mired in an unhappy marriage and having been passed over for promotion to lieutenant colonel, Mowle committed the one mortal sin in the military: He volunteered.

Three weeks later, Major Mowle found himself corkscrewing into Baghdad International Airport (BIAP) in a C-130 Hercules with two other officers from the Academy, a historian and an economist; they would call themselves "Doctors without Orders," as they had arrived in the combat theater on a "drug deal" that had been brokered outside the usual personnel channels by their new boss, the air force two-star in charge of strategy for the whole war. The general, a fighter pilot, was in over his head and needed what he himself called "the Brainiacs" to help make sense of a senseless occupation.

Tom and his friends lieutenant colonels Mike Davis (the historian) and Neal Rappaport (the economist) were out of their comfort zones, if not out of their depth. An insurgent rocket hit the fuel farm at BIAP not long after they landed; an airman greeted Major Mowle with the salutation, "Welcome to Iraq, Major! If you heard the sound, that means you're not dead!"

It was an omen, and not a good one. America had invaded Iraq on faulty intelligence and under false pretenses that Saddam Hussein had had something to do with September 11. There were enough troops to topple Hussein's government but not enough to secure the peace when an entirely foreseeable, and foreseen, insurgency erupted afterward, and there was no plan for what to do the day after the shooting stopped, before it started again. In a bitter little revolt against the failures of planning that marred Operation Iraqi Freedom, the US Army's Third Infantry Division, which had conducted the "thunder run" into downtown Baghdad that collapsed Saddam's regime, noted that after occupying the capital and having accomplished all its assigned tasks, it asked its higher headquarters for further instructions. The official after action review says baldly, "None were received."

President George W. Bush flew a fighter jet onto the USS *Abraham Lincoln* under a banner proclaiming "Mission Accomplished"; a more appropriate military term for the situation on the ground would have been "FUBAR."

Major Mowle and his buddies find this out for themselves. The SUVs that come to pick them up from a still-burning BIAP are late, having suffered an insurgent attack on the short trip from the Green Zone to the airport—one has a windshield shattered by a rocket-propelled grenade, or RPG. Artillery, rocket, and mortar attacks greet them on their arrival at the supposedly safe Green Zone (so called because it is safer than the Red Zone outside the barricades patrolled by armed guards). These will continue throughout their four-month tour; indeed, the security situation will deteriorate so much that Mowle departs the Green Zone in a helicopter rather than ground transportation for the short flight back to BIAP in 120 days that feel like a lifetime.

During that time span, Major Mowle will become one of the world's experts on disarming militia groups and on the Iraqi political system created by the United States in the wake of Saddam Hussein's rule. He and his friends will play a critical role in developing the campaign plan that is designed to accomplish America's objectives in Iraq—after first figuring out what those objectives ought to be. It might have been good for someone to have thought some of this through prior to the invasion, which was, after all, a "war of choice" initiated by the United States at the time and place of our choosing; as Mowle notes, they were not building an airplane while it was in flight, but after it had landed.

The absurdities multiply. Major Mowle notes that Bush "wanted to stay until the Iraqis stopped fighting us, and the Iraqis wanted to keep fighting us until we left." As indirect fire casualties in the Green Zone mounted, Mowle says, "We were directed to wear helmets and vests anytime we were outdoors. We were also supposed to pretend our non-sandbagged trailers offered us enough protection to allow us to de-armor once we got home. Colonel Vortex told me I could still swim in Saddam's pool, as long as I did it while wearing Kevlar. I'd have to resume going to the gym, which wasn't any more protected from incoming fire than the pool." Captain Yossarian would have felt right at home in the Green Zone.

At about this same time, I was conducting patrols in Al Anbar Province in a Humvee with canvas doors that would have been even less help in protecting against incoming IEDs than the thin steel walls of Mowle's trailer were against rocket and mortar fire. I was hopeful, as the casualties in our unprepared force mounted, that somebody in Baghdad had a plan, that our troops were not bleeding and dying in vain.

It is infuriating and tragic beyond words that the best strategic thinker we had was an air force major on temporary secondment, trying desperately and in vain to make our actions on the ground coincide with our goals, which Mowle decides include a multiethnic democratic Iraqi government. He states, completely correctly, that "it would be better for our long-term goals if a national unity government were formed after the election. This would become more likely if the Sunni Arabs participated in the election and if the current moderate-led government looked strong, deserving of reelection by the Iraqi people."

Even as Tom was stumbling toward this truth, however, America was planning a second attack on the Sunni city of Fallujah. Some of my troops had supported, with their tanks and fighting vehicles, an immediate response to the killing of four Blackwater contractors there earlier in the year. That first attack succeeded in unifying the country against us. The Iraqis shut down all road transport; we went on short rations before the Bush administration called the attack off. Now, after President Bush's reelection, the United States was hungry for revenge even though, as Mowle notes, attacking the Sunni city was likely to reduce Sunni support for its government and render Sunni participation in the forthcoming Iraqi elections—our principal strategic objective—less likely.

In Fallujah, while making it *less likely* that America will accomplish its objectives in Iraq—creating a country that "would be peaceful, united, stable, and secure, well integrated into the international community, a full partner in the global war on terrorism, democratic, and an engine for regional economic growth"—many good marines will be wounded and dozens will die in some of the fiercest urban fighting since marines cleared Hue after the Tet Offensive in Vietnam. In his book *Places and Names*, former marine lieutenant Elliot Ackerman's Silver Star narrative tells the story of the fighting and the bleeding and the dying that happened in Fallujah the week after Bush was reelected, fighting and bleeding and dying that was not just unnecessary but literally counterproductive to America's strategic goals in Iraq. Mowle had tried to make his superiors see the craziness of an attack on a Sunni city ten weeks before the Iraqi election that would determine how long the fighting continued. This attack, and other American actions, directly contradicted the Sunni Engagement Strategy that Mowle was writing, a strategy endorsed by the American embassy and the commanding general even while they were killing the Sunnis whom they hoped would support the Interim Iraqi Government.

I was back in the States by then, beginning my new job in the E-Ring of the Pentagon, trying to help the secretary of defense understand the war he had initiated with an army that was too small for the tasks it was assigned and improperly trained for the war it was fighting and equipped with Humvees with canvas doors to absorb IEDs. It was at about this time that that secretary of defense said, "You go to war with the army you have," without any recognition of the fact that it was his job to change that army if it was not appropriately manned, trained, and equipped for what the nation needed it to do.

Yossarian had to work overtime to fight the absurdities that marked his service in World War II, as did Mowle in his war half a century later. "Our actions and attitudes were undermining our war aims," he writes. "This was stupid. We are about to lose the fucking war." "If we want to be stupid, we can be stupid without my help." In the climax of the book, Mowle publicly and repeatedly corrects a three-star general, the deputy commander of the Central Command Headquarters that is responsible for overseeing the conduct of the war, on the basics of Iraqi electoral politics. The general knows nothing about the political factors that will determine whether America continues to be mired in sectarian violence—not that Mowle knows much more than he does. As he notes, in the land of the blind, the man with the seeing-eye dog is king.

Mowle is disappointed when his departure gift is a campaign flag embroidered "Operatin Iraqi Freedom"; he'd hoped for one that proclaimed, more accurately, "Operation Iraqi Freedoom."

Yossarian would have loved it.

—John Nagl

Preface

This first-person narrative is told from my perspective as a participant observer. It thus follows the development of my understanding and beliefs over time. No work can include everything that happened; others may interpret events differently than I do. The story intentionally deviates from the facts in only two major ways. The more significant is that dialogue, even when presented as quotations for readability, is offered in the Thucydidean sense of presenting approximately what would have been said at these moments rather than with any claim to exact wording—though some lines were memorable enough for me to jot down in my journal that same evening and are probably fairly accurate. Second, some events have been moved around in time; for example, I did not record on exactly which morning I injured myself while clearing my weapon.

I draw primarily from the journal I kept while deployed, excerpts of which are interspersed in the text to keep time as well as to provide more visceral insight into events. I also draw from unclassified documents, published information, and discussions among people I served with. Throughout, I follow our custom at the time of dropping the prefix from most Arabic names: We always said, for example, "Sadr" rather than "al-Sadr." The contents of this manuscript were cleared for public release by the Department of Defense on May 31, 2022, in letter 21-SB-0187. Per that letter, I note, "The views expressed in this publication are those of the author and do not necessarily reflect the official policy or position of the Department of Defense, the

Defense Intelligence Agency, or the US government." Furthermore, "The public release clearance of this publication by the Department of Defense does not imply Department of Defense or US Government endorsement or factual accuracy of the material."

Acknowledgments

The first people I want to thank are all my peers and colleagues who are named in full or in part in this book. I am grateful that you have allowed me to attach your names to this account of these events. Each of you helped me grow as an officer, a strategist, and a human. Many of you also encouraged me to see this work through to completion, and I thank you for that. I also appreciate the people I have lost track of and thus could not name in the manuscript. I think your contributions and my affection for you are apparent in the text.

This manuscript was more than ten years in the making, and I want to thank the friends and family who kept hearing I was writing a book and supported my goal. I especially want to thank the people who reviewed and commented on various drafts. These beta readers include Joe Barrera, Christina Bergling, Martha Boyd, Sarah Kitonsa, Justin Lincoln, Don McGrath, Clara Anne McKenna, Jeff Nocton, Sandy Reay, Kimberly Reifel, Tom Ruby, Laura Satin, Suzanne Shell, Dennis Showalter, Melina Silverston, Bob Spiller, Marlene Fabian Stiles, Richard Stribling, Rick Weaver, and Hollie Withers. I particularly want to thank Christina and Justin for helping me sort out the comments and suggestions I received. All of you—seriously, all of you—helped this become a better manuscript.

Two writing workshops helped me improve my writing and bring this book to completion. Pikes Peak Writers, particularly Mytchel Chandler and Bowen Gillings, encouraged me to keep going. At their 2023 conference, I learned so much from James Abbate, Fleur Bradley, Deborah Brewer, Rachelle Gardner, LS Hawker, Levi Jacobs, Sam

Knight, Stacey Kondla, Siera London, Pam McCutcheon, Melissa Richter, Marie Whittaker, and Johnny Worthen. The conference focused on writing fiction, and I came away from it believing in my work more than ever before.

The other tremendously valuable workshop was the 2024 Southern California Writers Conference in San Diego, organized by Michael Steven Gregory. This had a greater focus on memoir and nonfiction in general, so it nicely balanced the 2023 PPWC. Thank you to Conor Black, Gayle Carline, Cherie Kephart, Jennifer Silva Redmond, Judy Reeves, Laura Taylor, and Carl Vonderau. All of you gave me insights that improved the final manuscript and, as with so many others, encouraged me to continue.

One lesson from the SCWC was the need to get name, image, and likeness permissions from private individuals named in the book. Thank you Thomas Wing for helping me understand the process and David Inglis and Emma Sky for helping me find people.

No manuscript is published by a press without a query and proposal that intrigue an editor or agent. This may have been the most difficult part of the process for me to get a handle on, so thank you to Savannah Brooks, Alicia Clancy, Samantha Drake, Renee Fountain, Karen Lin, Dale Maharidge, Kat Mowle, and Trish Wilkinson. You helped me hone my pitch until it became successful and, just as importantly, encouraged me to believe that I had a story worth telling.

Thank you to John Nagl for writing the foreword and placing the work in its broader context. I am humbled by the comparisons you make to great works of literature and am glad this book has given me the opportunity to meet you.

Thank you to Ian Keller and Dan Klein at the Department of Defense for facilitating the security review of the manuscript and permitting its release without any changes.

I want to thank my editor at University Press of Kansas, Joyce Harrison; her associate, Alec Loganbill; the marketing team, including Suzanne Galle, Laura Pilcher, and Andrea Laws; the editing team, including Kelly Chrisman Jacques and Lori Rider; and in advance the many other people I will be interacting with in the gap between submission of this manuscript and its actual publication.

Abbreviations

BIAP	Baghdad International Airport
CG	commanding general
CIA	Central Intelligence Agency
CPA	Coalition Provisional Authority
DDR	disarmament, demobilization, and reintegration
DFAC	dining facility
DIA	Defense Intelligence Agency
DIME	diplomatic, informational, military, and economic
EU	European Union
FSO	foreign service officer
HMMWV	high-mobility multipurpose wheeled vehicle
HQ	headquarters
ICG	Iraqi Constitutional Government
IED	improvised explosive device
IIG	Iraqi Interim Government
IRI	International Republican Institute
ISIS	Islamic State in Iraq and Syria
ITG	Iraqi Transitional Government
KBR	Kellogg Brown & Root
MNF-I	Multinational Force-Iraq
MNSTC-I	Multinational Security Transition Command-Iraq
MRE	meal ready to eat
MUC	Muslim Ulema Council
NATO	North Atlantic Treaty Organization

NCO	noncommissioned officer
NSA	National Security Agency
OGA	other government agency
PT	physical training
PX	post exchange
ROTC	Reserve Officer Training Corps
RPG	rocket-propelled grenade
SCIF	sensitive compartmented information facility
SCIRI	Supreme Council for the Islamic Revolution in Iraq
SES	Sunni Engagement Strategy
SPA	Strategy, Plans, and Assessment
SPM	Strategic Political-Military
TRIC	Transition and ReIntegration Committee
UN	United Nations
UNSCR	United Nations Security Council Resolution
USAFA	United States Air Force Academy
VBIED	vehicle-borne improvised explosive device
VRC	voter registration center
WMDs	weapons of mass destruction

Chapter 1
Awareness

There I was: standing on the flight line at Baghdad International Airport, gawking at a pillar of smoke. It towered into the clear August sky beyond a low building and some scraggly trees broiling in the midday heat. The tail of a military aircraft, perhaps the one we flew in on, seemed far too close to whatever was burning.

"Welcome to Iraq, Major!" an airman shouted as he walked by. He added: "If you hear the sound, that means you're not dead!"

No, we were not dead. Neal (the economist), Mike (the historian), and I (the political scientist) were relieved to be alive on the ground after a harrowing flight from Qatar. Neal had been telling us what he'd learned on his call to the Green Zone when the explosion diverted him into a muttered "What the fuck" as he ducked his head and looked to our left.

A soldier who paused to look at the smoke, now billowing into a classic mushroom, told us, "Looks like they got the fuel farm. That's gonna burn for a while."

A few more people stopped, some in uniform and others in civilian clothes, but no one seemed alarmed. Neal preempted my question: "Does . . . does this happen a lot?"

"Pretty often," an airman answered. "One night last month, a rocket hit one of my unit's trailers. Good thing the guy who lived there was in the latrine!"

Aftermath of attack on the fuel farm at BIAP

"Isn't this our main point of entry?" I asked. "Shouldn't it be more secure?" My question evoked laughter as the small crowd started to break up.

A noncommissioned officer (NCO) waved at the highway in the opposite direction. "This had to have been indirect fire, a rocket or a mortar. But right there, along the perimeter, that's the road from Baghdad to Abu Ghraib, Fallujah, and the rest of the upper Euphrates. Closing it would disrupt traffic and the Iraqis wouldn't like it, so we leave it open. That means they can fire small arms and grenades at us as they drive by."

Mike broke his silence: "That's the same road we're taking to town, right?"

"Yes," Neal said. He filled us in about his phone call to headquarters. "They seemed surprised we were here. They said they'd send someone to pick us up when they had some drivers free. Hurry up and wait again, just like at al-Udied."

We dragged our duffels and our luggage over to the curb in front of the arrival trailer and settled in under some palms.

After two days of constantly being together, Neal and Mike and I didn't have much left to say to each other, so I used the time to reflect on the choices that had brought me here. Volunteering for this duty may not have been one of my brightest ideas.

There I was: sitting in my windowless office at the Air Force Academy, rereading the email that would lead me to Baghdad three weeks later. It read something like this:

> HELP WANTED
>
> Strategic thinkers needed for short-term position in fast-paced environment. Ability to multitask and navigate among bureaucracies a must. Duties include mentoring novice leaders in civilian control of the military, sustaining government through transfers in power, and practicing the general art and science of government. Terminal academic degree in social sciences or history required; prior experience or actual knowledge of subject matter desired.

According to the email from the academic dean, the two-star air force general in charge of strategy in Iraq wanted to supplement his team in Baghdad, so he had asked the Academy to loan him three officers. He promised to return us in time to teach in January 2005.

I had been wrapping up a report on the relationship between NATO and the European Union as it stood in that summer of 2004. I enjoyed my research trips to Brussels, though all those late nights with friends and weekend jaunts to Paris and Amsterdam wore me out enough that I was almost happy to be back home in Colorado.

I was uninspired by the prospect of yet another fall semester teaching research methods and international relations theory. It would be comfortable, but I craved something new.

This fit the bill. Granted, it would take me to a war zone, but I figured a headquarters unit should be safe and secure.

I called my wife on my office phone. She supported my desire to take this opportunity to be gone the rest of the year. One matter seemed vital: "You'll get extra pay, right?"

"Yes," I replied. "I'll get hazardous duty pay for being there."

"That's good. And it's tax-free, too, right?"

"Yes. All my pay will be untaxed while I'm there."

Money, or its absence, had become a bit of an obsession in our household. We couldn't afford to live in the ridiculous 4,500 square foot home we had bought two years prior because certain financial assumptions had been wrong. A deployment windfall would be a nice way to avoid having to sell and move for the third time in four years.

"Will this help you get promoted after all?" Ouch. She had a good point, the kind sharp enough to open old wounds. That was the main financial assumption that had been wrong.

When I got to the Academy four years earlier, my career seemed to be going well. I joined my academic department's leadership and helped redesign the core curriculum we taught every cadet so it would place less emphasis on things the air force had decided didn't matter anymore, like international politics. I hoped to be tapped to lead the department when the colonel in charge retired in 2007.

To my surprise, I was not selected for lieutenant colonel the first time I was eligible. People at the personnel center told me I hadn't done anything wrong in my career, but I wasn't a pilot, and I hadn't worked on anything the air force found important. The sting of this failure was not eased by them noting it had been a poor promotion cycle for all Academy officers.

Earlier this year, I had been passed over for promotion a second time. The military has an up-or-out policy, so this signaled a disappointing end to my service and an end to the pay increases that would have covered the mortgage. Unless I somehow earned an unusual late promotion, I would be forced to retire in early 2008. At age thirty-nine, I was in professional limbo. I needed to mark time for three years before starting a civilian career unless I wanted to give up all my retirement pay and future medical coverage.

Going to Baghdad might be important enough to get me promoted, reduce the financial tension that had become acute, and restore the career trajectory I had strategized.

Before I left for Brussels earlier this summer, my failure had become more tangible. I had been in charge of one of the department's academic divisions. There was no reason for me to retain a leadership role that could help someone else's career, so my boss demoted me to managing the department budget. Nothing personal, just business. I no longer had an office with windows opening on a panorama from Cheyenne Mountain to the Rampart Range to distract me from grading and lesson preparation. I no longer had windows at all.

This situation, however, gave me an edge over others who wanted to volunteer to go to Iraq: I wasn't qualified for this duty, but I was easy to replace. I had no special budget skills, and my courses could be taught by someone else. The two other volunteers were less expendable from the perspective of my academic department—the only perspective that mattered.

One of my competitors was a junior intelligence officer with Middle East expertise. She was energetic (like I used to be), smart (like I thought I still was), and poised (in a way I had never been able to master). But she had been chosen for a doctoral program, just as I had eleven years ago. If she went to Baghdad, the department leadership feared she would lose her graduate slot and the opportunity to groom her for future leadership.

My other competitor's background was similar to hers, except Greg—Lieutenant Colonel Rose (he outranked me)—was already part of department leadership. If he went to Baghdad, I would have to be shuffled back into a job I was no longer worthy of having. It was much simpler to send me away, so the Political Science Department nominated me as their volunteer.

Within a week, the Academy leadership ratified their decision. I would be accompanied by an officer from economics and another from history.

Our daughters were spending the end of their summer with my parents. I wasn't sure it was a great idea to wait until they got back to tell them I was going off to war, but maybe that way they could enjoy the rest of their vacation.

I needed a lot of remedial training in the week and a half before I deployed. Between tours of duty at the Academy and in school, I had managed the acquisition of weapons systems (not, as noted by the personnel center, very important ones). People like that don't go to war. We work in offices and visit manufacturing plants. At most, we travel to an engine repair depot or a flight line. I had faced the business end of a firearm only once, on a visit to a missile maintenance facility at K. I. Sawyer AFB in Michigan fifteen years earlier. Entry to where the nuclear weapons were kept involved transiting a long tunnel of wire fencing while security forces held rifles at the ready, awaiting my delivery of clearance documents.

I had rarely used a firearm, either, other than frontier rifles as a Boy Scout at Philmont Ranch in New Mexico. Now I had my own weapon, an M-9 Beretta issued by the air force—two magazines, fifteen rounds each (rounds to be issued after arrival in theater).

My colleague Deron Jackson patiently taught me how to disassemble, clean, and reassemble the pistol. Then he took me to the combat arms training range to qualify me in its use: how to fire, how to clear the chamber, how to load and eject the magazine. I did better than I expected, in that I usually hit the paper and sometimes even the target.

Along with the weapon, the Academy issued me desert gear. Forest green battle-dress uniforms would have been fine if the Russkies were attacking NATO, but they were our friends now. No, I needed desert-colored clothing so I would blend into downtown Baghdad or wherever I was going to be. I appreciated the boots the most—soft tan leather that only needed to be brushed clean rather than polished black. I had never mastered the art of shining shoes. At ROTC summer camp, one of the training officers had called me out of ranks to ask whether I was polishing my shoes with a Hershey bar.

Included with the clothing were sand-toned sweaters and coats. I didn't think these would be needed in August in Baghdad, but the supply clerk said I needed to be prepared for anything. "What if you get sent up to Kurdistan in the winter?"

"Sure, it would be nice to get some time in the mountains, but I will be back by December."

My naivete was reflected in her eyes. "And you know that for sure?"

Could I count on the promise made by this two-star in Iraq?

The cold-weather gear went into giant olive canvas rucksacks, along with the summer gear and the civilian clothes for off-duty hours and the workout clothes and the lockbox for keeping my weapon secure when I wasn't carrying it.

I was also told to pack civilian business attire because I might need to attend an official function where I should not be in uniform. No one knew what I'd be doing or where I'd be doing it. I felt at once overprepared and underprepared. I was prepping for all circumstances someone could imagine, but were we failing to imagine what might happen once I got to Iraq?

The pattern repeated at the base hospital. I had a thorough physical and got mandatory vaccines against anthrax and typhoid. The doc prescribed chloroquine as a malaria prophylaxis (not prophylactic, though that's what it sounded like . . . little condoms for little malaria bugs). I didn't want malaria, which lasts forever, so I asked him, "Do they have malaria in Baghdad?"

He said, "No, probably not, maybe. They might have malaria in Basra, though, and what if you go there?"

I didn't know much about Iraqi geography, but I knew Basra was in a delta by the Persian Gulf. It sounded miserable. I told him I'd rather go to Kurdistan up north.

"Take the pills."

I took the pills.

My final deployment training was learning to wear chemical warfare gear. Glasses don't fit under a mask, so I was issued prescription goggles in case I was able to plan for a gas attack. If I was caught by surprise, I'd just not have the luxury of sight. I joined a group of incoming cadets engaged in basic training. After learning how to get the mask on fast, we filed through a tent full of tear gas to see whether we were wearing it correctly. The sergeant had me take off the mask so I could find out how it would feel if I didn't do it right.

It didn't feel good.

The incoming cadets were joking and laughing through it all. I wasn't surprised at their casual attitude. VIPs I'd escorted around the Academy had said army cadets seemed much more engaged with the war than air force cadets. This made sense to me. Army officers might be deployed as soon as they pinned on their lieutenant bars. Recent West Point grads, friends of current cadets, had already been killed. Most USAFA grads would go on to flight school, and my students assumed the war would be long over before they'd be personally at risk.

I, on the other hand, was beginning to appreciate that I had volunteered for something that wasn't merely different or unknown. Saddam Hussein had used poison gas to massacre Kurds in Halabja during his war with Iran, and there was no reason to believe every bit of his stockpile had been found and destroyed. Even if nothing truly nasty were used against me, I didn't want another tear gas experience. The laws of war would not allow the United States to use tear gas to disperse a hostile crowd trying to storm our headquarters, but Iraq's own domestic security forces could do so lawfully, and the ensuing toxic cloud could drift my way. I might need to use this mask, this gear, so I paid attention to make sure I knew how to do it right.

My academic colleagues didn't take the deployment much more seriously than the cadets. The day before I left, they took me to lunch at a chain restaurant outside the South Gate. They treated it as an adventure, some recalling what it had been like in Saudi Arabia during Desert Shield and Storm in 1990–1991: hot, inconvenient, but not so bad. As going-away presents, they gave me a mix CD with a desert and heat theme, a DVD of *Army of Darkness*, and books on Islam and Arab culture. These reminded me how little I knew.

One of my colleagues had supported peacekeeping missions in Africa. Jim kept his parting gift simple: a plain white T-shirt with a target drawn on it in permanent marker. Later, Jim said he was surprised that I, of all people, had volunteered to do this. "Why?" he asked.

I didn't have a good answer for Jim at the time, and I was still wrestling with his question three days later while trying to stay cool under the trees at the airport with Neal and Mike. The Baghdad afternoon was shimmering toward evening with no sign of our ride. We had no idea what we would do if it didn't arrive. Some war story this was turning out to be. There I was, sitting on the curb waiting for a ride . . .

Jim knew me well. Volunteering was way out of character for me. During my time in uniform, I had taken care to avoid the most difficult or unpleasant duties. Which, come to think of it, might explain why my career had come to a halt. It would have been easy for me to spend the next few years teaching and traveling to Europe. Instead, I had chosen—no, pushed myself into—the unknown. An unknown where people lived or died based on how active their bladder was when a blindly aimed rocket landed.

I had not decided to come to Iraq because I was enthusiastic about the war. No, the Iraq War violated both domestic and international law. A blank check from Congress based on doctored intelligence, vigilante enforcement of United Nations resolutions, pretending a preventive war was as legitimate as preemption—none of these made the war anything other than aggression, the invasion of another country to overthrow its leader.

Beyond being illegal, I considered the war a mistake in its conception and its execution. It had taken the focus off al-Qaeda and undermined the esteem with which the United States was held globally. Furthermore, we had gone in with many fewer troops than what the army's military leaders had advised. This didn't seem to hurt the invasion effort itself—it took only eighteen days to enter Baghdad—but then the trouble started. When Iraqis looted the capital and destroyed infrastructure, we didn't have enough people to keep order. The chaos gave our enemy cover to capture arms and prepare for the next phase of the war.

Early in my career, when it seemed like the US was getting involved in a war every winter—Panama, Kuwait, Somalia, Bosnia, Kosovo—civilian friends would ask if I'd be getting deployed. I'd laugh and say something like, "Don't worry! If I'm shooting or getting shot at, the US is in some serious shit." Was that an accurate description of this war?

Things quieted down by late 2003, but the war never really seemed to be going well. We pulled Saddam out of a hole near Tikrit in December, but that didn't reduce the violence. By spring, rumors that Americans were abusing Iraqi prisoners at Abu Ghraib, just up the highway from where I was sitting, were proven true. This was seen as poor training rather than indicating the US had adopted torture as a matter of policy. In May the new Spanish government, elected after terrorist bombings at Madrid commuter train stations, announced it would pull its forces from the occupation. With wars going on in both Iraq and Afghanistan, American forces seemed stretched to their limits, without obvious progress being made toward victory.

None of this had anything to do with me, other than leading me to offer condolences when I visited with Spaniards at NATO and the EU while I was in Brussels. This was someone else's war, and I could have easily kept it that way. Yet there I was, loitering with my new friends and a pile of olive canvas duffels in the shade of some palms by the side of a road at the Baghdad airport. Why had I chosen to do this?

One reason was that almost nothing I had done during my sixteen years in the air force had required a uniform. At every assignment, I worked with civilians in the same kinds of jobs people did every day outside the military. Almost nothing about my career suggested I was serving in the armed forces. Here, suddenly, was an opportunity to earn the uniform!

A chance for Tom to show his quality after all. I was a big *Lord of the Rings* fan. When each film came out, I scheduled morning dentist appointments for my daughters and then, instead of taking them back to school, took them to an early lunch at Red Robin before waiting in line for the midafternoon premiere.

That might be unduly romantic, but what basis did I have to pass on this? I was unqualified? No, some generals had decided I was good enough. I had other responsibilities at work and at home? No, if I serve, I serve fully. I opposed the war? No, not unless I were willing to resign my commission and give up my retirement.

Perhaps the war was illegal, but international law might be a fiction to disguise the fact that justice is the will of the stronger. Perhaps the war wasn't necessary, but Saddam was indeed a very bad guy. Perhaps it was unlikely democracy could take root in Iraq, but Bush had a point that many good things might follow if it did. Perhaps the invasion distracted us from the people who had attacked us, but we couldn't refocus our attention on al-Qaeda until we had Iraq in better shape. It would be far better for my country if the war went better, and maybe I could contribute. In other words—in words I had included in a quick email to friends the night before I left—military honor demanded I step forward.

I had not admitted to my friends in that email—I barely admitted to myself—that not all my motivations were so noble. Answering the country's call was also a matter of self-respect, of being able to face myself later in life. Dodging this would have required me to admit I was too scared to do this. Too scared to do what somebody else would then have to do.

Going to war might get me promoted after all. Then, after this minor inconvenience, I could continue my career and make enough money to afford my life.

A life I hated. Every morning, I told myself in the bathroom mirror: "You can do this for one more day."

My work life was fine—I was happy if not objectively successful. But at home, I felt as isolated and stretched as our armed forces. My only reservoir of time for my own pursuits was late at night. I compartmentalized the different aspects of my life, but I had been doing this for years and my aquifer was running dry. Travel recharged me, and those glimpses of a possible better life made my real life harder to bear.

This awareness had come into focus a few weeks before. My friend Jorge had spelled it out while walking along the Avenue d'Auderghem in Brussels one evening. "Tom," he said, "you need to stop lying to yourself. You cannot go on like this pretending it will all be OK. You can always make up excuses to not be happy, but this is not good for you, and it is not good for your daughters."

He was right. It wasn't good for them, and I couldn't keep this up much longer. But travel to Iraq offered me a chance to run away and hope things would get better. Maybe trying to change myself and my own life was scarier than going to war.

Deployment day, 11 August, was also the day my daughters started sixth and eighth grade. They had not been amused that we'd kept my deployment plans secret until they got back from visiting their grandparents, nor were they happy to say goodbye at home rather than at the Colorado Springs airport, but I accepted the idea that the first day of school was too important to miss.

What difference did it make, really? Not enough to argue about.

This was my first chance to spend time with the officers deploying to Iraq with me. Both were lieutenant colonels, one rank ahead of me, but we dispensed with formality right away. Historian Mike Davis was about my height, wore glasses like me, but unlike me he still had all his hair. He didn't seem terribly happy about this duty, in part because he didn't think there would be much need for his knowledge of Middle Eastern history and in part because he suspected he wouldn't be getting much sleep for the next four months.

The economist, Neal Rappaport, was quite the opposite. He was shorter than either Mike or I, with hair receded to a widow's peak and a long face that left him looking tired or unhappy despite being the most cheerful and energetic among us. Neal had been eager to volunteer. He had returned only five weeks ago from a year in Macedonia as part of the Kosovo peacekeeping operation. He said it had been tremendous fun to spend so much time in a new culture and work with interesting people from all around the world. Unexpected crises would pop up, but there was plenty of time to enjoy oneself. Possibly, he allowed, Iraq would be a bit more dangerous than the Balkans, and probably there would be fewer chances to fraternize with the locals, but still—this should be a great time.

We flew to O'Hare, where Neal treated us to a business class upgrade for the transatlantic leg from Chicago to Frankfurt. "Might as well use the miles now," he said, "just in case . . ." After sharing stories for our first few hours together, I opened the books I had received the day before at the farewell lunch. It might be useful to learn a little something about Iraq before I got there.

Iraq occupies the lower and middle valleys of the Tigris and Euphrates Rivers, roughly corresponding to ancient Mesopotamia. It was created after World War I by stitching together three provinces of the Ottoman Empire. Each of those provinces had been relatively cohesive on its own, but the country's demographics were a mess after they were combined.

One major divide was ethnic. Most Iraqis were Arabs, but about

20–25 percent were Kurds, a people who had been promised their own country after World War I but found themselves split instead as a minority across Iraq, Iran, Turkey, and Syria. The Kurds lived in the northern mountains, where I might have a chance to use the heavy winter gear in my duffels. The three Kurdish provinces in this area had become essentially autonomous from the rest of Iraq.

The second major divide was religious. Apart from a few Christians, almost everyone in Iraq followed Islam. But Islam had two major branches, Sunni and Shia, stemming from a violent disagreement about the inheritance of political and religious authority after the death of Muhammad. The Shia were a minority in the Islamic world, ruling only in Persian Iran, but they were about half the population in Iraq. Most Shia Arabs lived in southern Iraq, whose major city was the possibly malaria-ridden port of Basra. Central Iraq, around Baghdad and north up the river valleys, was dominated by Sunni Arabs. Most Kurds were Sunni, and their ethnic identity seemed more important than intercommunal religious differences—though they had fought a brief civil war among themselves in the 1990s.

A third divide was economic. Iraq's oil was not distributed evenly. The largest reserves were in the southeast, in an area dominated by Shia Arabs. Most of the rest of Iraq's oil was on the edge of Kurdish territory, around Kirkuk. The Kurds claimed that city as their historic capital, as did a smaller minority, the mostly Shia Turkomen, but Kirkuk now had an Arab majority after decades of ethnic cleansing and population transfers.

The fourth divide was political. Although the Kurds and the Shia Arabs had the numbers and lived near the oil, the Sunni Arab minority had been in power since the British imported a monarchy from the Arabian Peninsula. Those foreign rulers were overthrown in 1958 in a particularly gruesome military coup. Ten years of violent political intrigue ensued before the socialist Ba'ath Party brought itself to power.

Almost as soon as he became the ruling dictator in 1979, Saddam Hussein invaded Iran. He was trying to take advantage of the turmoil of that country's Islamic Revolution to seize oil-producing Arab-populated areas in its southwest. His invasion failed, Iran counterattacked, Iraq pushed them back out: After eight years of war, all that had happened was the restoration of the prior borders. And lots of death and destruction.

Two years later, in 1989, Saddam invaded and occupied Kuwait, which Iraq had long claimed as its nineteenth province—the British had kept it as a colony when it granted independence to the rest of the former Ottoman territories in 1932. President George H. W. Bush assembled a truly international force under a United Nations mandate to first shield Saudi Arabia from possible attack and then expel Iraq from Kuwait.

With those missions accomplished, the United States stopped. It did not move on to Baghdad, try to overthrow Saddam, or destroy the Iraqi military. Instead, the UN imposed sanctions on Iraq until it dismantled its suspected nuclear weapons program. The assertion that Iraq was still hiding a weapons program was one justification for the US-led invasion in 2003.

Some of this I had known, but other parts were new to me. I felt sudden sympathy for cadets cramming for a final exam after half paying attention in class. I'd have to keep all this in the back of my head for context and hope it would make more sense once I got to Baghdad. In the meantime, rather than try to learn more, I decided I'd be better off following Neal and Mike's example and try to get some sleep before we got to Germany.

The Frankfurt airport evoked fond memories. The last time I'd been there was on my way to the Salzburg Seminar in March 2001. That had been such a transformative week for me, living and working in a palace and meeting people who helped me realize how trapped I had let myself become in my life. Hey, this might be similar—after all, I was going to a palace again!

Memories of Salzburg also gave me confidence that I could figure Iraq out. I'd known nothing about Europe three years ago (the friends I made there, including Jorge, dubbed me a Eurovirgin); now I had a book in publication. One constant in my military career was that I often took on new responsibilities (safety engineering, hazardous materials, emissions testing, flight training support, even teaching) without knowing much about them.

This time I did not transfer to a short Air Tyrol flight with real food served on real plates with real silverware. No, we had to drag our gear in the oppressive heat and humidity of a German summer from the civilian terminal to the military one, where we had seats on an ancient L-1011 to Qatar. The food came in a cardboard box. The utensils were plastic.

I was too groggy from intermittent sleep to read anything more, but I had an enlightening conversation with an army captain whose unit escorted convoys between Kuwait and Baghdad, traversing the southern two-thirds of Iraq. Finally, a chance to talk to someone who'd been in the country! I put it to him directly: "How is the war really going? Are casualties common? How dangerous is it?"

He looked at me as if he couldn't think how to answer in a way I'd be able to understand. Then he said, in a tone more nonchalant than the message, "We get attacked about ten times per trip. Usually nothing too bad."

"That sounds like a lot to me," I told him. "I thought the south was OK."

"No," he replied, "not with the Mahdi Army active. From now on we're going to get routed through Amara and Kut to avoid Najaf."

These place-names sounded vaguely familiar to me, but I had no idea where they were and figured I probably didn't need to know. He concluded with this dagger: "None of it is safe, but it's worst around Baghdad. Where you headed?"

We landed at al-Udied Air Base in Qatar at about 2100 local time (that's 9:00 p.m. in civilian usage—just subtract twelve from times above 1200 [noon] to get the afternoon or evening equivalent). A colonel and some first sergeants greeted us with "Congratulations on your pay raise!" During the flight, I had overheard grumbling about people who would fly in to someplace safe like Qatar or Bahrain or Kuwait on the twenty-ninth of a month, fly back to Europe or the States on the second of the next one, and collect the same two full months of tax-exempt hazard pay as someone exposed to daily fire in Iraq.

Everyone from senior officers to junior enlisted formed a line to pass bags from the hold to a central area: hundreds and hundreds of identical duffels mixed with regular luggage. I had tied some ribbons to mine so they'd be easier to find. So had everyone else. We had hundreds of identical duffels with ribbons that would have been distinguishable in daylight but were now slightly different shades of gray. It was almost midnight before we had them all sorted and dragged to staging areas for different destinations. Our pile was marked off with a piece of paper taped to plywood nailed to a short post: "BAGHDAD BAGGAGE."

We had made it to Southwest Asia; now we had to figure out how to get to Baghdad. If our travel to Iraq had been part of a normal deployment, we would have had this connection arranged in advance. But we were part of an off-the-books drug deal between two general officers, so we were scrounging for seats on our own. The whiteboard in the flight shack said showtime for the next C-130 with seats available for passengers was 0510 (5:10 a.m. in civilian terms), so we decided not to bother trying to get a bed for the night. We found a shower and walked to midnight chow. It was cool and quiet in the desert, with a few scattered lights amid festival-size tents and temporary buildings. The mess issued us a ration card for one beer, our last legal alcohol for who knew how long? Clean, fed, and jet-lagged, we took a bus back to the flight line.

Qatar had seemed nice enough at night. Sunrise hit like a squall line as the sun glowered on the barren horizon. We were still at al-Udied. At about 0300, our flight had been canceled. Regretting our decision not to find a bed, we snoozed in the waiting area and hoped for the 0645. That flight was delayed until 0910, and then we got bumped by people with actual travel orders. The air force did not offer us a voucher for a future flight in exchange for our trouble.

At about 1130, we boarded a C-130 Hercules, a versatile propeller-driven small transport that had been in use since the 1950s. The Herc was configured with four columns of side-facing webbed troop seats. I sat in one of the middle columns where the ride would be a bit more stable. Mike sat across from me; Neal joined me in the middle.

We sweated on the apron in the 115-degree humidity for a long time before we took off. We were quiet. Mike said he had a headache, I was tired, and what was left to say after forty-eight hours together? I drifted in and out of sleep, waking up for glimpses of the Arabian Gulf (our allies didn't like it being called the Persian Gulf) and the desert.

A warning from the flight crew snapped us awake. "We are approaching Baghdad; prepare for hard banking." One of the other passengers saw our confusion. "For landings at BIAP, we spiral down directly above the airport to minimize our exposure to ground fire."

Hold it. That level of danger had not been part of the invitation to go to Iraq. I was really entering an active war zone? By choice? Remembering the advice from *Apocalypse Now*, I sat on my helmet so I'd not get my balls blown off. I hoped to use them again someday.

The landing was rough, as might be expected after a steep combat approach, but the Herc is a tough airframe. Neal called into the Green Zone to ask for a ride, we watched the pillar of smoke from the fuel farm, and—after all the hurrying up to get here—we waited on that curb all afternoon and beyond. As people left the flight line for the evening, several warned us we really didn't want to be out after sundown. Would we need to figure out how to bunk down here at BIAP without proper travel orders?

As the sun reached the horizon, two Suburbans pulled up. Some enlisted troops and civilians hopped out. They were all wearing body armor, helmets, and sunglasses; they held their weapons like they knew what they were doing. One of the civilians approached us and asked, "You from the Academy?"

"Yes," Neal said—we had let him assert himself as our leader based on deployment experience. "We're glad to see you, but where have you been?"

The civilian pointed at a shattered windshield. "RPG. Load your gear. Hurry. Getting dark."

We squeezed our gear into the back of the vehicles. Mike asked whether there was anything we should know, and the same civilian—apparently the one in charge, it's hard to tell when people aren't in uniform—replied, "Watch for trouble. Especially at bridges. If we stop, ready your weapons."

"Um, we don't have any rounds," I pointed out.

He was speechless for a moment, which was not enough time for him to stockpile words for long sentences: "They won't know. Ready them anyway."

With bluffing as our rule of engagement, Neal and I got into one Suburban and Mike got into the other. The military drivers accelerated our little convoy east down the highway toward Baghdad, the Green Zone, and the Republican Palace.

Chapter 2

Confusion

There I was: riding in the back seat of a black Suburban with a shattered windshield. Neal was in the middle; a soldier sat behind the military driver so there was an armed presence on both sides. Mike rode in the trailing vehicle.

We drove east at high speed, dodging light traffic on an expressway. Someone had hit the vehicles on the way out to get us; would they attack again on the way in? Deep shadows were everywhere in the twilight. Each overpass offered cover for an enemy atop the bridge or behind its supports. The security detail jabbered with each other in an acronym-filled shorthand that may as well have been Arabic for all the sense it made to me. We passed miles of shops and warehouses and trees and low walls along the parallel frontage road before we at last exited down to the left into a maze of concrete barriers and razor wire leading to a checkpoint.

We'd made it. We were safe in the Green Zone, somewhere in the middle of Baghdad.

We parked in front of what I took for the Republican Palace, and one of the drivers told us to leave our duffels there at the motor pool and follow him inside. While walking the short distance toward an entrance, we flinched at the sound of another explosion. Our escort reassured us that we'd get used to hearing rockets in the distance. He told us we'd soon learn "boomology": the different sounds of small arms, rockets, mortars, and car bombs.

We glimpsed our surroundings as he cleared us through a checkpoint and hurried us up a wide marble-floored staircase to the second floor and through a carved, wooden, cipher-locked door labeled Strategic Political-Military (SPM). Beyond was a corridor crammed with desks and what seemed like an awful lot of people considering it was after 2000 on a Friday night.

We passed several open doors on the right before the driver took us into the two-star's admin section, cordoned from a larger room by cubicle partitions. Soon we heard him call out, "Is that my Academy guys?" and one of the sergeants waved us into his office.

The two-star looked like the fighter pilot he was: compact build, radiating confidence, dark hair uncombed in strands atop tight sides. He had a big grin—he seemed genuinely happy we had arrived. Our hunger and exhaustion must have been visible: The first thing he did after breaking our salutes into handshakes was tell an airman to get us food and Tylenol PM.

We exchanged stiff small talk about our trip. It's awkward to meet a senior officer and not be sure whether it's safe to match their informality. Neal mentioned we'd waited a long time for the ride from the airport, and the two-star smiled like he had a secret joke: "I wondered if you went to the wrong place." This was an odd response—where else would we have gone? Maybe the confusion of the day was catching up to me. So much had happened in the twenty-four hours since we landed in Qatar.

The airman soon returned with some Styrofoam cartons of food that was awful and delicious—our last meal had been at midnight. The two-star waved us out and told us we could "take the rest of the night off" before reporting back first thing in the morning.

After we ate, the airman took us out the other end of the SPM corridor, down some narrow stairs, and then to a small building behind the Palace so we could get some linens for the night. Then he led us back through the Palace and out a different door to grab our bags, which were still sitting, unattended, where we had left them. The building was a maze, but this young man was fully in command of where everything was and the best way to get there.

Finally, he took us to the male transient tent so we could bed down for the night. The tent had five rows of single beds, about twelve to a row with just enough space between them to put your feet down. Despite still hearing mortars in the distance, I slept soundly that first night thanks to jet lag, travel fatigue, and heavy medication.

Soundly, but not long. We were awakened Saturday morning by others starting their day. Individually, they were quiet, but with dozens of men in close quarters, sleeping in was not an option, and we didn't want to be late for our first day in the office. Neal and I reached the same conclusion: Let's follow the people who look like they are headed for a shower.

The outside of the tent was lined with sandbags stacked far over our heads. A winding slot canyon formed by a second wall of sandbags led us behind the tent to a pair of trailers—our latrine, which fortunately we had been dehydrated enough last night not to need to find. The trailers had nowhere near enough stalls and sinks for the number of men trying to wash up and shave this morning, so we all hurried up and waited as best we could.

Back in the tent, we dressed and stashed our bags under our beds. Now we needed food. Still lost and confused, but too proud to ask for help, we again followed people who seemed to know their way around. After stepping around the sandbags, we saw the Palace to the right. Palms large and small dotted the dying lawn we had to cross.

The Palace looked nothing like the one in Salzburg. I suspected not much else about my time here was going to match that trip either. The building had a flat, tan façade, with wings curving out to half embrace a dry fountain in the middle of the grass. The points where those arms joined the central section were marked by white stone towers perched like blockhouses atop narrow two-story arches. These, I recalled from my reading, had once been capped by giant busts of Saddam's helmeted head. Where had they gone?

We stalked our tentmates to the same checkpoint we'd used last night. This opened into a wide, vaulted rotunda under the turquoise

The Republican Palace, as seen from the transient tent

dome at the center of the Palace—the only decorative color we had seen. A corridor to our right led us, after a few jogs, to the dining facility (DFAC).

The Palace was proving to be an odd mixture of ordinary and ornate. The corridor from the rotunda had been all business, but the DFAC looked ceremonial. It was a vast space, maybe fifty or sixty feet square, with chandeliers illuminating intricate geometric designs that climbed two stories of walls and continued into a recessed diamond in the ceiling.

At ground level, this luxury was offset by a cafeteria line of uninspiring but edible hot dishes and a surprisingly bountiful buffet of fruits and yogurt. The room was jammed, so Neal, Mike, and I found a table out in the adjacent marble-lined corridor, near a little snack bar and a barbershop. Neal nudged me and pointed back at the DFAC doors. High on the wall, flanked by pillars and in a recess of a faux archway, some Arabic script was engraved; below it, someone had added a mural of the World Trade Centers. The propaganda that this had something to do with 9/11 and al-Qaeda and Osama bin Laden continued, even here in the war zone.

With basic needs met, we were ready to report for duty. We returned to the rotunda and retraced our route upstairs from last night. We knocked on the cipher-locked door and were escorted back down the hall to the SPM admin section.

When we got there, no one knew what to do with us.

We were here at the personal request of the two-star, rather than on official orders, so we were not assigned to any specific part of the unit. He wasn't around, and he hadn't left any instructions. No one seemed to know where he was or when he would return.

Not for the first time today, we were confused. Hadn't the two-star told us to report first thing this morning? The sergeant on duty shrugged and suggested we wait. Which we did. All day, and most of the next as well.

We spent some of the weekend hanging out at the transient tent, which was not what it was designed for. This was where people visiting the Palace for a day or two or waiting to be assigned quarters could sleep, so it had nothing but beds. I tried to read a bit more about Iraq, but it was too dim with the lights twenty feet above us. The large freestanding cooling units helped in the 115-degree heat, but I found myself drifting off to sleep without retaining much. Mike seemed to welcome the chance to rest, but Neal next to me was fidgety.

From time to time, we returned to the office to see if the two-star was back. Most people there were cordial, but they were busy on projects and didn't have time for random new guys. All we accomplished this weekend, with help from the less diligent, was to get oriented to the Palace area that would be our home for a while: the laundry, the post office, the gym.

The only destination beyond the immediate Palace grounds was a small post exchange (PX), a military store stocked with large quantities of a very limited number of choices: personal care items, protein supplements, over-the-counter medications, soft drinks, and snacks.

Adjacent to the PX was an Iraqi-run shopette. Everyone called it the hajjimart. It carried what the PX didn't: local merchandise, jewelry and curios, and custom-made patches and flags. We were told the cool thing to do had been to get an extra name patch for your uniform in Arabic script—but this had recently been prohibited because too often someone would be walking around with a name tag reading "Infidel" or "Pig-eater."

The route to the PX took us past the ruins of Saddam's command center. The precision of the air strikes the year before astonished me. Part of the complex was nothing but rubble, other buildings were hanging open like an Erector set, and others looked almost intact. No munitions had been wasted on the gate, which was decorated in a series of red, white, and blue archlike designs. Arches and pillars—those were the dominant design elements.

To walk to the PX, the hajjimart, or anywhere else outside the immediate Palace grounds, we had to seat the fifteen-round magazine in our M-9 pistols in case we were attacked by someone who had infiltrated the Green Zone. When we returned to the more secure inner compound, we had to release the magazine and clear the chamber. This presumably had remained empty, but safety first. For now, however, we were doing this for show—we still didn't have any rounds.

That was one of the many things the two-star was angry about when he showed up at his office late Sunday afternoon. He was also angry that no one had added our names to the trailer list, which meant we were about sixtieth in line. That didn't sound good. He was especially angry that no one had given us anything to do and so we had wasted the whole weekend. Somewhere along the way, there had been a failure of leadership. Tomorrow, he swore (literally), we would work, but for now he had too many other things to catch up on.

This last evening of leisure featured an unexpected hazard: The Iraqi Olympic soccer team clinched its group with a win over Costa Rica. This unexpected moment of tremendous national pride inspired celebrations across the city. It sounded like fireworks, and it looked a bit like fireworks, but it wasn't fireworks: The Iraqis were celebrating by firing weapons into the air.

Apparently, most everyone in Iraq was well armed, which seemed sensible of them. Under the laws the United States had imposed, Iraqis had a right to retain one rifle and one pistol for self-defense after registering them with the government. Military-grade weapons, however, were not for private ownership—they were reserved for members of one of the Iraqi security forces. Based on the racket and the tracers in the sky, some ordinary Iraqis had retained a larger arsenal than they were supposed to.

Just as it would if there were incoming hostile fire, the Giant Voice loudspeaker boomed overhead to warn us of the danger of these celebratory rounds as they fell back to earth. This was nuts—two days in country and I was already taking cover! Based on the high approach angle of stray bullets, the sandbags were not going to protect me. I used my body armor as a blanket and put my helmet over my face for the night.

First, however, I added this experience to the journal I had begun.

> Mon 16 Aug: Met an Iraqi exile at the gym who's working here as a translator. She's still in exile—can't even visit her siblings in town for fear of retribution.

The route to the gym from the transient tent took me around the north end of the Palace, where a set of diesel generators kept our power on when it failed in the city. I had to leave the Palace compound through a checkpoint, cross a narrow lane, and go through another checkpoint. The gym featured plenty of exercise machines, weights, and murals of the World Trade Center towers. But it did not have any showers, which complicated getting exercise any time except at the start of the day.

While waiting for a rowing machine, I struck up a conversation with the woman ahead of me. "What do you do?" didn't get us very far: She translated for a civilian agency I'd never heard of, and SPM didn't mean anything to her. "Where are you from?" was more interesting: "Here, technically." She had left Iraq years ago for reasons we didn't have time to explore and had volunteered to help her home country. She had thought she'd be able to reconnect with her family, but it was too dangerous for them if the wrong people found out she was helping the Americans. Her time here wasn't matching what she had expected it to be. We had that in common.

When I got up to the SPM offices, the admin sergeant told me to report to Colonel Haith in the Policy Division. Colonel Haith assigned me to work on how to handle Iraqi militias. I was happy with this duty because it fit with my graduate work in conflict resolution. As I would find out in the evening when we reconnected at the tent, Mike and Neal were much less happy. They were assigned to Assessment, which had little to do with their skills and knowledge.

I spent my first day drafting a six-page summary of our militias policy. It wasn't clear to me whether this was something the boss didn't know or just a way to get me up to speed.

One of Coalition Provisional Authority (CPA) Administrator Paul Bremer's last acts in office before restoring Iraqi sovereignty exactly seven weeks earlier had been to issue Order 91, which stated that armed groups and militias were illegal unless they agreed to participate as "residual elements" in a "transition and reintegration process." Only militias that had fought Saddam's Ba'athist regime were eligible for this process. Almost all these groups were comprised of either Kurds or Shia Arabs.

By far the largest of these militias were two groups of Kurdish *peshmerga*, seventy thousand strong. They had been fighting Saddam for decades and were generally pro-American because the United States had helped create a nearly independent Kurdistan over the past decade. Their priority was protecting their own region.

The next-largest militia was the sixteen thousand Shia Arabs in the Badr Corps, the Iranian-backed military arm of the Supreme Council for the Islamic Revolution in Iraq (SCIRI). It had fought for Iran against Iraq during the 1980s and then backed the doomed Shia Arab rebellions after Desert Storm. Iran seemed grateful we had destroyed its enemy Iraq, but we remained the Great Satan. The Badr Corps was waiting to see what would happen.

Another ten thousand Iraqis belonged to three smaller militias attached to political parties: Iraqi Hezbollah and the Iraqi Communist Party, both mostly comprised of Shia Arabs, and the Iraqi Islamic Party, a Sunni Arab group linked to the Muslim Brotherhood.

Three other Shia Arab groups were eligible for transition and reintegration but claimed to no longer have active militias: Ahmed

Chalabi's Iraqi National Congress, Ayad Allawi's Iraqi National Accord, and Ibrahim Ja'afari's Da'wa Party. All of these had engaged in some sort of plotting or armed resistance against Saddam's regime, mostly bombings and assassinations. No doubt Saddam had called them terrorists, but we considered them good guys as long as they weren't attacking our forces.

Separatists, Iranian Islamists, Hezbollah, Communists, and the Muslim Brotherhood—these were the good guys? Anywhere else in the world, we would have tried to keep all of them far away from power.

Instead, we had given them power. As part of the restoration of Iraqi sovereignty at the end of June, Bremer had created an Iraqi Interim Government (IIG) to govern the country until elections could be held. The IIG included the political arm of each of these militias; the interim prime minister was Allawi, a former Ba'athist who had broken with Saddam in the 1970s. In other words, the militias were part of the very body responsible for their disarmament.

Bremer had selected the IIG's leadership; today it was holding a national conference at the Convention Center a short distance away within the Green Zone. I spent a few hours with some of my new colleagues in Policy trying to learn something about the one hundred delegates. All we had received were names, many with alternate guesses at their spelling, and sometimes a home city or province. We went about this hopeless task while listening to indirect fire—mortars and rockets—aimed at the Convention Center.

These attackers may have belonged to one of the armed groups that had not been invited to this national conference. Prime among these was Moqtada al-Sadr's Mahdi Army, a Shia Arab group that, as I had been told on the flight from Germany, was occupying the Imam Ali Shrine in Najaf, holding off coalition and Iraqi forces amid the world's largest cemetery. Along with organizing the new sovereign Iraqi government, one of the prime agenda items for the national conference was deciding what to do about Sadr.

> Tue 17 Aug: Feels as though I've been here for weeks already. . . . My work on militias is expanding into a no-kidding look at which armed groups we even care about.

With a day's work under my belt, Colonel Haith assigned me another duty: attending the daily senior consultants meetings.

CPA Administrator Bremer's very first order last year had been to ban all members of Saddam's ruling Ba'ath Party from public office. Thus, no one in the new Iraqi government had any meaningful administrative experience. To remedy this, the US had named a senior consultant (more often called a senior advisor) to each of the IIG's ministries. They mentored and advised their Iraqi counterparts and reported back to the Embassy at this daily meeting.

Attending these meetings made sense for my job because the militias policy required cooperation from several Iraqi ministries. It also seemed like a great chance for me to learn more about what was going on.

But there was another aspect to this assignment. Colonel Haith told me to take notes and report back on what the Embassy and the Iraqis were up to. In other words, I was a spy for the Multi-National Force-Iraq (MNF-I), led by four-star General George W. Casey, against the US Embassy, led by Ambassador John Negroponte. Each of them had an office along the rotunda, but it seemed the Departments of State and Defense had not patched things up much since the invasion.

The walk to the senior consultants' meeting drew me deep into the south wing of the Palace. The building seemed bigger inside than outside, continuing for room after room beyond the DFAC, with new construction tacked on beyond the end. The major attraction in this part of the Palace was known as the Michelangelo Room. One of its many murals depicted very erect Scud missiles thrusting heavenward. On the opposite wall was a lovely pastoral scene of hills and a mosque: Jerusalem, with all signs of Jews removed.

In contrast to the haphazard arrangement of the SPM offices and other parts of the Palace, the conference room was very tidy, very put together. It felt like a place I'd attended meetings before, with a long wood table dominating the center and extra chairs along the wall for people like me. A couple dozen people were in attendance this morning, some of them military officers as junior as myself and others civilians whose rank was less apparent. I didn't understand much of

A mural of Scud missiles being launched

what people were talking about, but I figured I'd start piecing things together over time. Colonel Haith seemed happy with the notes I wrote up, at least.

Wed 18 Aug: Today truly sucked.

For starters, the two-star told my Academy colleagues and me that he wanted to keep us in Baghdad for a full six months, rather than four as he'd promised. I was too shocked to think of a way to object in the moment. A longer tour might bolster my case for a late promotion, but going home in mid-February would cancel that out by leaving me with no teaching assignments for the spring semester. It would be easy for someone to conclude I might as well stay till next summer.

That was not the deal. The importance of getting back on time had already been emphasized in the long emails from home I was getting every day, as well as in my first "morale call" yesterday—we were allowed two per week. Things seemed to be going about as well as I could hope after less than a week away from Colorado Springs.

Then we learned we should expect to spend a month living in the transient tent. This was not an ideal arrangement. We were in the office until 2130, so there was not much time to get home and wind down before lights out at 2200. All night, our sleep was disrupted by men stumbling around in the dark to get to the latrine. If we wanted a morning workout—there wasn't time at night—we had to get up early enough for the round trip past the north wing, wait for a shower, and get dressed and fed before reporting to work by 0700.

Sleeplessness and stress do not mix well with heat, humidity, and shitty coffee. I felt awful most of the day, with diarrhea and dehydration distracting me from my duties.

Physical and emotional distress aside, my workspace made it difficult for me to focus on either my primary tasks or pop-up assignments. The SPM offices included a suite of three large rooms (one of which was used as a conference room) and two small rooms (one of which was the two-star's office). These rooms were along the outer wall of the front side of the Palace, opening onto a main corridor on the inner side of the Palace, above a courtyard.

The Policy Division didn't have its own room. Most of its officers were strung out at desks in the hallway, vulnerable to everyone's idle interruptions and without room for two people to talk without blocking the path.

My own desk was outside the northern secure door, at the top of the wide stairwell from the rotunda area.

Thu 19 Aug: This was exciting.

The next day I still felt ill. The coffee seemed to make certain things worse, so I tried to do without caffeine despite the lack of quality sleep. That didn't work well either, so I slipped back to the transient tent for an afternoon nap.

Sleep came quickly with the heat.

Sleep ended just as quickly with an explosion, followed by a much louder, much closer one. Giant Voice pointed out the obvious: we were under fire and should take cover immediately. I and a few others in the tent bolted to the nearest shelter, a set of concrete slabs arranged like a cave or tunnel. As we ran, I could see smoke coming from the Palace.

If I hadn't been overdosing on anti-diarrheals, I might have made a mess.

Once the all clear was announced (how would they know?), I went back to the office and learned that a rocket had struck the Palace near the dome. Two people from the State Department had been hurt in this attack, only a hundred or so feet away from my desk.

Following the lead of those around me, I had been treating the Green Zone and the Palace compound as if they were safe places. Earlier today we had finally been able to get cartridges for our pistols, and we'd walked to the armory without bothering to wear our body armor or our helmets. It was too hot to put all that heavy gear on!

I had maintained this casual attitude, as if the war were somewhere else, even though in six days I'd already seen the fuel farm hit at BIAP, ridden in vehicles that had been hit minutes before, hidden from celebratory fire, and heard more or less distant explosions all the time.

It was time to stop pretending—though pretending did make it easier to cope.

The Republican Palace after a rocket hit near the dome

> Fri 20 Aug: In Early Bird [a daily email aggregating published news and opinion from the United States] you can read columnists saying the situation in Iraq is better than the media say. They're wrong. Whole sections of the country are basically off-limits to the coalition, so they don't even make the news. There are good things happening, but they so easily are destroyed or disrupted. There are rumors too of impending food shortages. That's just what we need.

We were allowed to come in late today because Friday was the Islamic Sabbath. This was a sensible policy for those who worked with Iraqis, and it had been extended so everyone would get a half day off every week, unless there was work to do. A more relaxed pace to and from the gym gave me a much better attitude on life, as did a dreamy night of sleep.

Very vivid dreams were a side effect of the chloroquine I was taking to prevent malaria, dreams so realistic one would remember them all day as if they were real. Both Neal and I at different times had passionately insisted to our colleagues that something had happened that had not, or that we'd been given some project that didn't exist.

The militias project, however, did exist, and it was a high priority for the two-star. His boss, General Casey, seemed to be pushing for rapid progress so the overall security situation would look better. One of our metrics for assessing progress was "control," as in "coalition control," "local control," or "mixed control" of provinces. The goal was to turn much of Iraq over to its own security forces before the upcoming elections. As local control was achieved in one place, coalition forces could either focus on other areas or be drawn down. This would look like progress toward winning the war.

Militias were at least a philosophical obstacle to local control. Our policy asserted that "no state can exist and prosper with the presence of armed groups outside legitimate government control." How could the current or future Iraqi government be considered sovereign over its own territory if it were sharing that space with organized armed groups? How could it build legitimacy among the population if it did not have a monopoly on the use of force? Thus, we needed to get rid of these militias.

This was a nice principle for an ideal world, but I pointed out that many countries exist, even prosper, despite armed groups in opposition. The United Kingdom did so despite the Irish Republican Army, as did Italy despite the mafia. The United States had armed groups like the Republic of Texas militia that had once asked my commander in San Antonio to please vacate our air base by month's end.

The question shouldn't be whether these groups existed but rather how much they challenged the government. The groups we were trying to demobilize through the formal process were not impeding the government at all—in fact, they were all part of the IIG.

Beyond the good militias, every other armed group was labeled an "enemy of the new Iraq." Some were comprised of leftovers from Saddam's secular Ba'athist regime, mostly Sunni Arabs who had been members of his security services. CPA Administrator Bremer's second order last year had been to dissolve the Iraqi Army. Whether or not they were true believers in Ba'athism, regardless of their degree of personal complicity in Saddam's crimes, Bremer's first two orders left them jobless and unlikely to become friends of the new Iraq.

Other Sunni Arab fighters were radical Islamists under the banner of Abu Musab al-Zarqawi's al-Qaeda–inspired Monotheism and Jihad. There had been few terrorists in Iraq when we invaded. Sure, Saddam had sheltered some nasty people like Abu Nidal, but he had died in 2002 after repeatedly shooting himself—at least, that was the official story. The Mujahedin-e Khalq had also been in Iraq before the war, but they were Shia Persians whose terrorism was aimed at overthrowing the Iranian regime. Zarqawi was himself a Jordanian, the most prominent of the Arabs who had come to Iraq to fight off the American crusaders.

It seemed unlikely that either of these groups could be brought into a political process.

The other major opposition militia was Sadr's Mahdi Army, which was comprised of Shia Arabs. We, and now the IIG, had tried to suppress his popular movement. Although we had always been able to concentrate enough force to counter his actions, we had also always been too afraid of the reaction among his supporters to try to arrest him or knock him out completely.

It seemed a bit more likely that the Mahdi Army could be brought into a political process, but it was unclear whether Sadr wanted his group recognized as legitimate. Perhaps he preferred the flexibility to support or oppose the Iraqi government as he wished.

Between these extremes, an unknown number of smaller, local armed groups had sprung up. They couldn't be considered good militias because they were formed after Saddam's ouster, but they also weren't actively enemies of the new Iraq. One, the First Fallujah Brigade, had been created after our abortive operation in that city in April. It was supposed to keep the peace there in exchange for being left alone. Were they "good" or "bad"? How could I tell?

> Sat 21 Aug: Talked to a soldier here in the tent about how safe Tikrit is. Maybe there are success stories, if we can only learn from them.

There were an astonishing number of colonels (the rank below general) in SPM. Today, one of them, Colonel William Wenger, invited me to visit the Political-Military section of the Embassy. This was located a fair distance away, in the north wing of the Palace, along a mezzanine above the vast open space of the North Ballroom. Most of the State Department people—foreign service officers or FSOs—looked ready for a day in the office in any capital city. They weren't spending much time in the city, but this was their uniform as much as camo was ours.

One man stood out, however. He looked like he'd be more comfortable out in the streets or villages, and he offered the first good idea I'd heard in the week since I'd arrived. He suggested that when we measured economic improvement, we ought to count money paid to Iraqis rather than money paid to Halliburton and other contractors. Even though it may be more efficient to hire an American contractor to bring in heavy equipment to dredge an irrigation canal, it would be better to hire a few hundred local men with shovels. Sure, fewer profits would go to the corporations that were profiting from the war—here in the Green Zone, the laundry was operated by Kellogg Brown & Root (a division of Halliburton)—but the money would stay in the Iraqi economy, local people would feel more ownership of the canal, and they might begin to prefer our constructive help over the resistance's destructive actions. This, he thought, could help turn the Iraqi people against the insurgents, even if they never really came around to liking us.

This seemed like a good idea to me on its face . . . so good that it seemed surprising this needed to be said after eighteen months of occupation. It drove home a comment Neal had made the other day: "We aren't exactly dealing with the best and brightest here." Although that somewhat misrepresented David Halberstam's classic critique of Vietnam policy (the best and brightest were JFK's people in DC who got us into that war), he had a point. There was a lot of activity in the SPM office, but there didn't seem to be much creativity or reflection.

Was that why the two-star had brought in a bunch of academics from the Air Force Academy? The man did seem to understand there was a problem—in Iraq and in his unit—but I was still too confused about what was going on to be part of any solution.

Iraq had another Olympic soccer match tonight, playing Australia for a chance to advance to the medal round. I stayed in the Palace to watch the game. It was nice to hang out with a bunch of strangers. I found some people who liked to play cards, so I hoped I might soon develop some life to balance my work. After Iraq won, I stood on a balcony to watch the tracers lighting the sky over the city. It was kind of pretty. It didn't seem as scary as it had a week ago.

When I returned to the tent, Neal and Mike were crawling on the floor. They had heard a bullet ping off one of the support bars and roll along the cement foundation, but they couldn't find it in the dim light. When we got to the office Sunday morning, we learned two rounds had punched through the top of the two-star's trailer. He wasn't hurt.

The gunfire reminded me I was supposed to be in Detroit today. It was still Saturday back home, and I was missing my brother Mike's wedding.

Instead, I was off to my first meeting of the TRIC, the committee for militia transition and reintegration. Those of us going, mostly senior advisors to different Iraqi ministries, got ourselves fully armored up for the trip. The security team briefed us on the hazards we might encounter during the drive. We turned left on the main street in front of the Palace and took the first exit from the traffic circle. After a few blocks we pulled into a parking lot next to a very ugly gray concrete-block office tower, disembarked from our vehicles, and hurried to the building so we wouldn't be exposed in the open parking lot for very long.

Then we hurried right back—this was the wrong building. We needed to go a bit farther up the street to another ugly gray concrete-block office tower: the Council of Ministers building.

Total travel time: less than five minutes, all within the Green Zone.

We tromped up a stairwell reminiscent of a parking garage and through dim corridors to a very nice conference room. No one we glimpsed along the way looked happy. What an impression we made! We were openly carrying weapons, still armored up for the tremendous danger we perceived from the people we had put in power!

Like the senior advisors' meeting, the TRIC meeting seemed familiar. There I was, a week into a new job, meeting with the other principal players on a major project. And, as usual, the project is pretty fucked up and everyone is pointing blame at someone else. Ten Iraqi organizations were supposed to be represented, but not all had bothered to show up.

While waiting for the meeting to begin, I was struck by the astonishing physical variety of Iraqi men—and they were all men. Complexions, facial features, height, and build all differed more than what one would see in a European country or in an American executive meeting. Perhaps one legacy of Mesopotamia being a crossroads of civilizations and invasions for millennia was that there was no "Iraqi look."

The meeting was chaired by Dr. Saad al-Obaidy of the Ministry of Interior, which handled internal security functions like the national police. Only one of our group was conversationally fluent in Arabic, so we had to rely on translators. Dr. Saad spent a lot of time complaining about his budget and how he was not being shown enough respect by the other ministries. The rep from the Ministry of Education said he didn't know why he had to attend a meeting called by someone as junior as Dr. Saad (the Education Ministry's senior advisor, Jim Mollen, rolled his eyes a bit at this). The rep from the Ministry of Defense went on a very long tirade, which was translated as "he doesn't trust them." Another translation was interrupted by the Iraqi speaker; in perfect British English he chastised the translator for his failures and addressed his concerns directly to us Americans. I wondered whether he thought he gained anything by reminding us that he (and probably others) had a language advantage over us.

Very little about the TRIC's plan, adopted from Administrator Bremer's order, seemed workable in the real world. The first step in the process would be to purge from the "good militias" all their personnel who were criminals, terrorists, or foreign agents. Each militia was supposed to certify its own personnel. They were refusing, or rather they were gravely offended by the insinuation that such people were in their group. Next, each militia was supposed to turn all its weapons over to the Iraqi Ministry of Interior. Finally, the individual members of these militias were to be mustered into one of the new Iraqi security forces (army, police, border patrol), receive a pension as a veteran, or enroll in a vocational training program. Widows and orphans of "those martyred in the fight against Saddam" would get the same benefits as the survivors of Iraqi servicemen.

However . . . the Ministry of Defense didn't want any "Islamists" signing up, and the peshmerga didn't want to join any security force except Kurdistan's. Furthermore, many militia members did not aspire to a military life now that Saddam was gone.

. . . And getting a pension as a veteran required proof of continuous service in the militia, and the militias hadn't kept such records. Furthermore, the militia leaders were claiming ranks higher than seemed warranted for their low level of experience and accomplishments.

. . . And all the vocational training centers outside Kurdistan had been looted after the invasion. There was very little money to restore and staff them so that the promised programs could be offered. As Martha Boyd, an army major who was senior advisor to the Ministry of Labor and Social Affairs, noted in an aside to me, there were no jobs in Iraq to be trained for anyway.

In summary, not only was the TRIC process engaging the wrong militias, it had proposed solutions that could not be implemented even if the committee weren't dysfunctional.

The only good thing about the meeting was the tea. Oh my, I had never tasted anything so good as properly prepared, sweet, minty Middle Eastern tea.

After I returned to the Palace, Neal pulled me over to his work area—he had space in an actual room—to discuss a question from his assessment work: How could we measure the legitimacy of the Iraqi government, and what could we do to build legitimacy?

I challenged his premise: Could an imposed government ever be seen as legitimate? Neal said sure, look at Japan and Germany. But, I countered, we left the Japanese emperor in place to provide continuity with the old system. We had broken links with the old Iraq by disbanding the military and banning Ba'ath Party members from power—not that anything tainted by the old regime would have been accepted by the Kurds or Shia Arabs. And though Germany had a liberal heritage before Hitler, Iraq had none as far back as history might take us.

If legitimacy somehow appeared, how could we measure it other than by an absence of violence (which would mean we'd won and didn't need to be measuring it)? Opinion polls asking "Do you support the government?" were unlikely to be accurate in a country where saying no could get you killed by the government and saying yes could get you killed by someone else. An indirect measure of legitimacy would be voluntary tax payments, but in Iraq there were no taxes to be collected or evaded.

We were stumped about measurement and had no idea how to convince Iraqis that their government was legitimate. Yet this question seemed very important to the success of our mission. Were we not creative or knowledgeable enough to find an answer, or was there no answer to be found?

After dinner, Neal and Mike and I met up with Colonel Neal Barlow, who was the head of the Aeronautical Engineering Department back at the Academy. Colonel Barlow blended a commanding presence with a friendly nature—he seemed so much more confident and relaxed than the army colonels back in the two-star's SPM.

Colonel Barlow was here in Baghdad on a very special mission: repairing the relationship between the Pentagon and the Academy. The air force leadership felt the Academy's leadership was out of touch with the realities of the military. They weren't wrong. Each academic department was headed by a "permanent professor," a full colonel who could serve in that position as long as they wished, never leaving Colorado Springs, before retiring as a one-star general. A sweet deal, really. This had been my own goal if only I had been promoted to lieutenant colonel. Maybe that could still happen.

A few years ago, the Air Staff in the Pentagon had suggested department heads should take short tours in operational units to get reacquainted with those missions. Some permanent professors had replied that their academic role was far too important for them to comply. This had not gone over very well. Part of the Air Staff response, Colonel Barlow said, was to crush the Academy's promotion rate for people with doctorates.

People like me.

After two cycles like this, the permanent professors had caved. Periodic yearlong operational assignments would become mandatory for permanent professors. Colonel Barlow volunteered to be the first to go, and he chose to set a strong example by going to Baghdad.

His initial duty had been as the Commander's liaison to the United Nations mission, setting the UN up in a new compound within the Green Zone after their facility at the Canal Hotel had been destroyed almost exactly a year before by a vehicle bomb that killed many, including the UN's special representative.

He relayed this background while taking us on a tour of the Green Zone. Just the four of us, no extra security, no threat briefings, no super-armored vehicle.

We first drove to the banks of the Tigris, one of the great rivers of the world. Its muddy water was the only thing separating us from the city and whoever might be watching us and wanting to kill us. Our side of the river had a big lagoon rimmed by assorted "palaces" that had been used by different members of the Hussein family. Next was the parade grounds, famous for the crossed swords at either end. Then he took us through the Baby Assassin's Gate and up the start of Haifa Street until it dead-ended at the al-Rashid Hotel and the Convention Center that had hosted the National Assembly.

This was so much fun, my first experience since arriving that felt normal. I used up almost all the film on the single-use camera I'd purchased at the PX last weekend—I had not wanted to bring my bulky, expensive digital camera.

The only downside was that I lost my hat somewhere. But this gave me an excuse to buy the slightly different but somehow much cooler army hat! With luck, my lost hat wouldn't end up as part of some infiltrator's disguise.

> Mon 23 Aug: I told COL Wenger that I'd help him with his project to rejuvenate the Iraqi Boy Scout program. Keep busy, be useful, & don't count the days.

When I left the gym this morning, the Palace was on fire!

No, not because an enemy had used my hat. The fire was sparked by overloaded wiring in the communications and computer center. It burned for a long time because the lanes between the concrete barriers were too narrow for a real fire truck to be brought alongside.

Colonel Haith told all of us in his Policy Division to go home until

The author, Neal Rappaport, Neal Barlow, and Mike Davis at the Parade Grounds

1000. Home was where? A hot tent? Instead, I walked over to the PX to get my new hat, a mirror so I could shave without having to wait for a sink, and another disposable camera. The PX did not develop film, so I took my camera to the hajjimart next door. There did not seem to be any concerns about what Ghazi, the proprietor, might learn from the photos being taken without much restriction throughout the Palace and Green Zone.

The lawyer assigned to Policy joined me on this errand. He was a joy to be around, perhaps the happiest person I'd run across despite being a vegan in a decidedly carnivorous habitat and having a wife back home who was pregnant with their fourth child. Even worse, he had to spend a lot of time directly advising the two-star because his primary job was to identify the impact of Bremer's CPA orders on what we were trying to do, look at legal issues relating to the campaign plan, and bring his legal training to bear on policy questions.

The lawyer may have been the very first person to arrive in our unit through one of the boss's drug deals. He had been deputy staff judge advocate at Kirtland Air Force Base, New Mexico, when the call came for special help. He got to Baghdad in late June, right before Bremer transferred sovereignty back to Iraq, but (like Neal and Mike and me) he had no idea where he was supposed to report for duty. He ended up working at Abu Ghraib prison on legal issues surrounding the treatment of detainees for about a month before the two-star figured out where he was and brought him to the Palace. He was already due to go home soon. Maybe that was why he was so happy.

When we got back at 1000, the midsection of the Palace was still full of fumes, so I wandered over to Pol-Mil in the north wing and traded PX snacks for fragments of homemade cookies received in care packages.

Lunch was different today, thanks to the fire. On normal days, the DFAC served all you could eat, four times a day if you wished, at no cost. These meals were a grand communal experience: People of all ranks and nationalities waited in cafeteria lines to see what the mostly South Asian kitchen staff had put together. Groups of friends, colleagues, and strangers occupied tables that overflowed into the surrounding hallways.

Today, however, the DFAC was only serving meals ready to eat (MREs), self-cooking high-calorie packages guaranteed to resolve any problems with loose digestion. To balance that, the two-star joined our table. He suggested we grab some extra MRE packages for future emergencies or if we "want to have a party." I found it difficult to have a normal conversation with him; fortunately, he was just making the rounds of "his" people and left soon enough.

The lawyer laughed at my discomfort and related how much the colonels disliked the boss and were terrified of his erratic behavior. It seemed the two-star tolerated no disagreement from them and always had to get the last word even though they were all experienced ground combat leaders and he was a fighter jock in a war where air power no longer seemed relevant.

After lunch, we were still locked out of work, so the lawyer and I went to the trailer of one of our Policy colleagues to watch *Spider-man 2.* The movie had only been released to theaters last month, but we had bought the DVD earlier that day from the very thin young man who sold copies of all the latest films on the sidewalk in front of the hajjimart.

If the lawyer was among the happiest men in the Green Zone, our colleague was among the gloomiest. He seemed unable to break focus from the brutal fact that this all sucked, so he wasn't great company. The poorly written English subtitles combined with the Arabic dubbing made the movie hard to watch, not that I much liked Spiderman anyway.

It was the best social experience I'd had since I arrived!

After the movie, we reported to work even though the air was still pretty nasty. By 2030, the colonels rebelled against the two-star and shut down the office. It was still full of fumes, and who knew what kind of chemicals were in this place?

> Wed 25 Aug: Had to skip a night [of journaling] since I didn't get to the tent until after 10 [lights out]—not working, but at WC Milne's having a civilized evening.

This unexpected social break on Monday—and then another the next evening with the fifth member of the Policy team, recently arrived Brit wing commander Jez Milne—energized my work on militias and armed groups. I was starting to feel I was getting a grasp on my little corner of the war! On Tuesday, I completed a summary of twenty different groups across the country and distributed it to others engaged with the TRIC process.

My next step was to address what should happen next. Some lessons learned from analogous situations might help, so I asked Deron Jackson, my marksmanship mentor from the Academy, to search academic databases I could not access from Iraq. The best studies looked to be some UN publications describing how the disarmament, demobilization, and reintegration (DDR) process had worked in different countries, but these were not available online. I could order them, but shipment would be slow, costly, and out of my own pocket. So late on my Wednesday, I called the UN library in New York (our phones were routed as if they were in a Long Island area code), described the situation, and someone there agreed to scan the reports and email them to me within a few days at no cost.

I found this level of support astonishing. The United Nations was a notoriously complex bureaucracy and institutionally opposed to our invasion of Iraq, yet when a junior officer called from Baghdad asking for help, it responded.

The UN's support was in sharp contrast to what I had within my own unit. I didn't have any clear direction about how to proceed. I was acting like an entrepreneurial action officer, working on issues of my choice in the way I thought best. There seemed to be a lot of this going on, as people picked up and advanced projects of personal interest—for example, Colonel Wenger and the Iraqi Boy Scouts—in the absence of any comprehensive plan to guide us toward what was important. While I was gaining knowledge about militias and sharing it with others, I wasn't sure how much this mattered.

For one thing, these issues should have been resolved a year earlier, or before we invaded. How to handle militia DDR was an interesting question, but at this point the IIG would decide what it would do. It was their country now. The same applied to handling Sadr's occupation of the Imam Ali Shrine in Najaf or the drafting of the Iraqi constitution.

Furthermore, if I came up with any good ideas regarding militias, I was not advising the TRIC or the IIG directly. I sent things to Colonel Haith, who could go to the two-star, who could go to the Commander, who could go to the Ambassador, who could go to the Iraqis. When I faced a similar bottleneck of decision-making while I was working on the T-6 trainer program in San Antonio, I took a chance and bypassed the formal chain of command. Going directly to Dr. Saad did not seem like an option, let alone a good option.

Early the next day, even using the chain of command seemed risky. The week before, the two-star had received a letter from a tribal sheikh who was alleging bad behavior by others in his area. He wanted to help us or maybe undermine his rivals. The two-star had told me to draft a forwarding summary for him to send to the Commander; amid everything else, I had forgotten about having turned it in for approval until he called me in to talk about it. I knew this was not going to go well when he opened with: "I don't like this font. Use a different one."

"Yes, General," I said, taking care to only roll my eyes inwardly.

He turned to the substance of the letter: "We're not supposed to identify the sheikh. Take his name and location out."

Without stopping to think, I replied, "No, General, that doesn't make any sense. We can't send a letter to the Commander telling him there's some guy up north who wants to help us, but we won't tell you who or where."

The two-star now looked at me for the first time and I thought to myself while looking back at him: *Fuck, the lawyer's advice was to never, ever directly contradict the two-star.* As the staring contest dragged on, I reflected that the worst he could do was send me home.

At last he turned back to my letter. "OK. Where's the letter from the Commander to the sheikh accepting his offer?"

This had not been part of my assignment, so I told him, "I can have that ready in an hour, General."

He decided something else was missing: "And what about the letter telling our force commander about the allegations made?"

"Right after the other letter, General."

I survived this encounter with minimal harm, but I was steaming within. What exactly was I doing here? I was writing routine correspondence. I was taking on self-initiated projects about disarmament. And I was sitting out in the hallway at the top of the stairs, detached from everyone else in the unit. I had spent too much time in my air force career working on projects no one cared about. This looked like more of the same: An FSO in Pol-Mil had told me when I dropped by on the day of the fire that the Embassy didn't really care about the TRIC process itself. It was kept going for confidence-building purposes.

After drafting the additional letters for the two-star, I wanted to sit down with my actual boss, Colonel Haith, and demand to know what my duties really were and how they matched up with anybody's idea of our mission.

I liked Colonel Haith. He was a good guy—courteous, supportive, engaged, and serious about building the Policy group into a team. For example, though we ate breakfast and lunch on our own, he tried to always have the Policy team eat dinner together, talking business as well as getting to know each other. He certainly knew how to lead, but this paperwork and intangible multitasking wasn't his thing. As he'd say when things got too bureaucratic, he'd much rather have been out in the field, commanding troops in pursuit of a concrete objective.

Colonel Haith wasn't at his desk, which saved me from making a fool of myself. While I was waiting, a runner summoned me to Pol-Mil (electronic communication between the Embassy and the military within the Palace was difficult). Whatever their opinion about the TRIC process itself, they thought my armed groups paper would help reframe what we needed to do, and they wanted to pass my ideas up to the Ambassador. Maybe I was contributing to the mission after all.

On my way back across the North Ballroom, which over the past few days had become filled with cubicles and temporary walls, I ran into the two-star again. My heart started racing when he said, "Tom, what are you doing way over here?" I told him I was sharing my work with the Embassy and waited for him to tell me I was violating the chain of command. Instead, he responded, "Good job! This is exactly why I brought you here!"

When Colonel Haith was free to talk later, I told him I was enjoying my work and all was fine. The Policy Division took our dinner outside, where we ate under the trees by the pool and listened to the muffled beat of mortars in the distance.

After work, I went to the Thursday night Embassy party at the same location. I didn't know very many people yet, so I stood around making small talk and watching other people drink, dance, and after a while pair up and slip off together. It was a sober party for me. The US military were forbidden from drinking in Iraq, a policy the Aussies and Poles also followed (in public). US civilians, the Brits, the Dutch, and pretty much everyone else in Baghdad (including most of the Iraqis) were OK with alcohol.

> Fri 27 Aug: This is my morning off. It was nice to finally get to swim in the pool. . . . I was surprised I could do 12 lengths after all this time not swimming. I wish I could go more often, but it's just not practical. Maybe once I get into a trailer and the distances for changing aren't so far.

Today my time hanging out at the Embassy paid off! A delegation from the European Union was visiting Baghdad; Tammy Fitzgerald, an FSO in Pol-Mil, was looking for ideas about what we could ask the EU to do for us. I suggested the EU could help us with militias.

First, it could provide money for the underfunded incentive programs so people who signed up for veterans' and educational benefits don't become disillusioned when promises are not kept. Second, it could provide technical assistance during the disarmament process, the collection and destruction of small arms and light weapons. The EU had a lot of experience with similar programs in Africa and the Balkans, and armed groups might be more willing to turn weapons in to a neutral party like them than to the Iraqi government or the coalition. The EU could credibly promise the weapons the militias turned in would not be used against them.

These anti-Saddam militias did not trust their new government, even as they comprised it. Interim Prime Minister Allawi had been a Ba'athist before having a falling out with Saddam some thirty years ago. Although Allawi had survived an assassination attempt while exiled to London, he was still viewed with suspicion. According to the *Baghdad Mosquito*, a collection of local media reports, some Iraqis were saying Allawi had been in deep cover all this time, a sleeper agent who would bring back Saddam's regime. After all, no one survived one of Saddam's assassination attempts, and who sends a guy with an ax if they're serious about the job? Other than Stalin going after Trotsky, that is.

The Kurdish and Shia Arab militias didn't really trust us Americans either. After Desert Storm, the US had urged them to rise up and overthrow Saddam on their own. They answered that call, and they were slaughtered. The United States stood by as Saddam's surviving military forces, aided by helicopters that were not covered by the no-fly zone, brutally put down the Shia Arab rebellion in the cities and marshes of the south—draining the latter to destroy the ecosystem that provided the livelihood of the so-called Marsh Arabs.

The Kurds fared better than the Shia Arabs only because they could take midwinter refuge across the mountains in Turkey—not a friendly country for Kurds, but a NATO ally and one accessible to the media.

Another UN-sponsored mission followed, during which the US protected some of the Kurdish areas from the air while their peshmerga fought on the ground.

Redeeming this legacy of betrayal was one of the reasons CPA Administrator Bremer had felt he needed to ban Ba'athists from public office and disband the Iraqi Army right after he took over last year.

Tammy and her colleagues liked my idea well enough to ask me to put together a proposal grounded in the EU's own priorities and present it to their delegation that very afternoon.

While I was working on this at the Embassy, the Pol-Mil section got a call alerting them that a chemical laboratory had been discovered in Sadr City, the northeastern section of Baghdad. Could this at last be some trace of the long-lost WMDs? It was exciting to think about, even if that wasn't exactly the district where you'd think Saddam would have hidden a facility.

Sadr City was a vast impoverished Shia Arab neighborhood, named after the line of clerics of which Moqtada, the leader of the Mahdi Army, was the most recent and least distinguished. The district had been called Thawra before the Sadrs became illustrious, then Thawra again after Saddam started murdering the family. After the invasion, the locals went back to their preferred name, but we in the military were supposed to stick with Thawra to avoid giving any more credibility to Moqtada.

Speaking of Sadr: I had not been spending much of my time worrying about the course of the war or events in Iraq in general, but we did now have a success of sorts in Najaf. The day before, Grand Ayatollah Ali al-Sistani, a Shia Arab leader who had been in the United Kingdom getting medical treatment since before the Mahdi Army took over the Imam Ali Shrine, had returned home. He had flown to Kufa and led a bunch of people the short distance to Najaf, more or less saying he was making a pilgrimage and Moqtada better not be there when he arrived. This was probably neither the full story nor an accurate story, but there definitely was a truce and the Mahdi Army evacuated the city. The battle was over, though the combatants remained at large.

In the evening, Colonel Haith took the Policy team out to a special dinner. He had finally gotten permission from the two-star to let us eat at a Chinese restaurant up Haifa Street, toward the market and the Convention Center. Apparently, a couple of Chinese entrepreneurs had decided after the invasion that there was a business opportunity in catering to servicepeople in Baghdad, so they came over and opened a restaurant. It had enough white plastic lawn tables and chairs to seat dozens, but the place was nearly vacant. The food was awful, and it was wonderful to get outside the compound.

Even better: Iraq lost its medal-round Olympic soccer match to Italy. There would be no more celebratory gunfire to dodge.

> Sat 28 Aug: It's like an Air Force career in miniature. People come and go every week, so I guess if you don't like the mix, just wait a bit.

This evening, on the terrace above the courtyard, we had a hail and farewell ceremony for the arrivals and departures from our unit. The mix of people here changed so quickly. Already I had tried to follow up with someone I'd talked with often and discovered they'd gone home. This and the pace of work made it difficult to develop and maintain after-hours friendships, but I wanted to try to find some balance. Today, for example, I reached out to a bridge group I'd heard about. I'd wanted to learn how to play beyond the basics, and they might be more serious about getting together than others seemed to be.

Today's arrivals included a new executive officer who would be overseeing the two-star's daily business and correspondence. As long as he was competent, this would allow things like the sheikh's letter to go more smoothly. Also arriving was a reservist from Kentucky who would be the only female officer in SPM—until now, I had not quite realized we were all men, except for one sergeant in the two-star's admin section.

Today's departures included the head of the two-star's security detail, who was going back home to Texas to retire. His crew often drove people between the two halves of the military headquarters, which was split between the Republican Palace and Camp Victory, adjacent to the airport. This meant lots of drives back and forth on the expressway I'd rode in on only two weeks earlier, a route code named "Irish." This route took its name from my alma mater, Notre Dame, presumably because the final words of its fight song were "onward to victory."

Today's departures also included everyone I had been working with in the Policy Division, including my boss, Colonel Haith. Colonel Haith was leaving to fulfill his wish of having a field command rather than sitting in the Palace all day. Rumor was he'd had a screaming match with the two-star, telling him he thought—maybe that others also thought—he was a crazy idiot flyboy who was incompetent at actual leadership. Maybe this didn't really happen, but a lot of people shared that opinion quietly.

Everyone else in Policy, everyone I'd been spending time with these past two weeks, was leaving because we were taking this quiet moment in the war to reorganize the command staff.

Military reorganizations were easy to be cynical about. They were a great way for a commander to have a tangible accomplishment: "Colonel X wisely identified inefficiencies in the unit structure and corrected them by [pick one] (a) bringing the organization into better compliance with doctrine and best practices, (b) justifiably deviating from the previous commander's slavish devotion to doctrine, or (c) rearranging the desk chairs on the *Titanic* to mask their complete failure to accomplish the actual mission."

Reorganizations were also a great way to get rid of problem people by eliminating the positions they filled: "We have five branch chiefs, but after this reorganization we only have three branches. You and you: Go find a new job."

Reorganizations could also, sometimes (it was said), make a unit work more effectively. Although I had come to feel competent and confident about my own work, I was still completely confused about the bigger picture. About all I knew after being here for two weeks was that I worked on militias and other stuff for Colonel Haith in a division called Policy, and Colonel Haith reported to the two-star, who was in charge of something called Strategic Political-Military. The two-star had been there for quite a long time, starting out under Lieutenant General (three-star) Ricardo Sanchez when he commanded

Combined Joint Task Force 7; now the boss reported to the Commander of MNF-I, General (four-star) George W. Casey.

I knew my chain of command, but I had hardly any idea what else happened in SPM. I didn't work much with anyone else in my own unit; rather, I worked with the senior advisors to the Iraqi ministries, who were a mix of military civil affairs officers, Embassy foreign service officers, and CPA holdovers. The militia TRIC committee was similarly interagency. All I knew about the rest of the SPM directorate was that it included Assessment, and I only knew that because Neal and Mike would tell me how awful it was to work there.

I was thus a bit excited to get a four-color org chart handout describing how things would fit together after the reorganization. The two-star's new organization would be the SPA: Strategy, Plans, and Assessment. The SPA would have four divisions in addition to its administrative staff. Appropriately enough, these were Strategy, Plans, and Assessment. And Campaign Plans.

Although it was great to discover something about the larger organization in which I had been working, I didn't know what this would mean for me. I had been working on militias, and militias had been in Policy, and Policy was going downstairs to Major General Stratman's directorate. It would be logical for me to follow my job, but I was not officially assigned to the command. Rather, I belonged to my two-star.

Sun 29 Aug: All that had happened in the prior week was that the sun had risen and set 7 times.

Until the reorg took effect at the end of the month, I was still working on militias, so Sunday meant my second weekly TRIC meeting. It was about as enjoyable as stabbing myself repeatedly in the eye with a fork. Nothing useful had happened on the Iraqi side.

And Dr. Saad was pretty pissed about it.

Tomorrow was the deadline for each militia to turn in its roster of members, and none of them had done so. Dr. Saad and his colleagues in government suspected the militias were signing up new members, beefing up their forces now in peacetime using the promise of future benefits as a lure. This (if true) would increase the cost of providing those benefits, increase the number of people who would feel betrayed if the government didn't live up to its promises, and leave the militias larger if they did not disband.

In addition, the militias were refusing to sign the transition agreements the Iraqi TRIC had drafted. These one-page agreements would commit each militia to completely dissolve, surrendering all its weapons—including those legal under Administrator Bremer's CPA Order 3—to the Iraqi government by the end of November. Members who were recruited into Iraqi security forces would have to agree not to engage in any political activity.

In exchange, the Iraqi government promised to provide opportunities and benefits to members, with the details to be determined later. For some reason, the militias did not appreciate what a great deal this was.

At least the tea was still marvelous!

The next day, I received the eight reports on DDR lessons learned I had requested from the United Nations. Most of these were from Africa, with others from Cambodia and Central America. I had also picked up separate reports on Bosnia and South Africa online.

After reviewing these, certain lessons became clear. The militias in these countries had protected the interests of a group of people, usually based on ethnicity or religion but sometimes or also based on class or region or ideology, against a government they perceived as hostile or oppressive. Such militias would not willingly disband until they believed their group no longer needed to be protected from the central government. This trust building generally took about three years; pressure placed on militias tended to reinforce their suspicions. Once trust was built, however, militia members usually demobilized on their own as the lifestyle of an idle warrior became more boring than heroic. The government could then aid their reintegration into civilian life or move people into state security forces. A final lesson was that militia members must be brought into the army or police only as individuals, not as part of a whole unit. If a militia were simply given an official name and role while left intact, it would become a nexus for dissent and future rebellion.

Based on these lessons, I concluded that most of the TRIC process was poorly conceived. The pressure the TRIC was placing on the "bad" militias to disarm would backfire or at best fail. None of the militias were going to agree to disband and disarm, turning their weapons over to the government they were hedging against, before the political process even began. If Iraq were able to hold free elections, and if the security and economic situation were good by 2006 or 2007, then the armed groups problem would start to resolve itself. Lieutenant General David Petraeus, who was standing up a new unit, the Multi-National Security Transition Command-Iraq (MNSTC-I, pronounced "Men-Sticky" out of earshot of its leadership), reportedly was perfectly happy to leave the pace and extent of transitioning militia members into Iraqi security forces as something to be determined later. If so, he was right.

The biggest red flag I saw was the reluctance of the biggest militias to be broken up. The peshmerga would only transfer into the service of the Kurdistan Regional Government. This would make it easier for the Kurds to assert autonomy from Baghdad if they wished. The Iranian-backed Shia Arab Badr Corps was willing to consider being brought into Iraqi security forces, but only as intact units, where they might defy a future secular government. Meanwhile, the Sunni Arabs would have no countervailing force except in the extremely unlikely scenario that whole units of the neo-Ba'athist resistance would be granted amnesty.

> Tue Aug 31: Over the last 2 nights, watched the awful *Day After Tomorrow* with WC Milne. The best part was the refreshments—fudge he'd gotten from his fiancée, and some nuts I'd received from home. He had a bottle of wine left by his predecessor, but no corkscrew. We were fortunately able to use the butt end of my flashlight to get it open.

Militias became an orphan project once my colleagues in Policy left to join their new unit. Lacking guidance or oversight, I tried to help Mike and Neal a bit with their assessment work.

I ended the day even more glad I did not have their jobs. They were traveling often back and forth on Route Irish to Camp Victory to meet with other units, and then staying up late into the night working on hundreds of PowerPoint slides. In place of worrying about the lack of meaningful data, generals were weighing in on the color scale to be used! Should it be red/yellow/green? Was there room for orange—excuse me, amber—if something was not completely a crisis? Should there be a blue rating for "better than our wildest dreams"?

The pressure and futility I picked up from dabbling in Assessment mirrored what I was feeling from home. It seemed like every email or phone call brought a new crisis I was not around to fix. The phones were out. A toilet was clogged. The children were mouthing off. I couldn't help with any of this, and I didn't need new things to worry about. The only morale I was getting from these calls was low morale.

Wed 1 Sep: This was a good day, if it can continue.

My morale improved today, even beyond clocking in for another month of hazard pay. This evening, I would get to move to Colonel Haith's temporary trailer. He had already shipped out to his combat assignment, but the SPA decided to keep his key rather than turn it in so we could get people out of the transient tent. I could stay in his old trailer until either my name got to the top of the permanent trailer list or I was evicted when someone realized I was squatting in a trailer that probably ought to go to someone else. This system of hoarding of course contributed to the housing shortage.

I wasn't worried, however, about the unknown person whose home I was appropriating. I would have privacy, peace and quiet, and uninterrupted sleep. I would have furniture, so I could stop living out of rucksacks stuffed under the bed frame. Even working out would be easier: I was closer to the gym and living on the same side of the Palace as the pool if I preferred to swim laps.

My morale also improved at work. The Embassy staff decided the whole militia approach ought to be revised along the lines I was recommending. The initiative had to come from the military side because it related to security and control, so I put together some talking points for the four-star so he could engage with the Ambassador and Interim Prime Minster Allawi.

We wanted the Commander to emphasize to the Iraqi prime minister that we still wanted all illegal armed groups in Iraq to disband and accept the transition process, but we didn't want to make promises that couldn't be kept, nor did we want to provoke needless conflict with groups that were quiet and represented in the National Assembly. Both of those dangers were present in Dr. Saad's current approach, although the four-star was not to say so directly to Prime Minister Allawi. The most important goal was that the militias did not disrupt the upcoming elections or prevent areas from being fully under the control of the official Iraqi security forces.

The Commander was to repeat many of those same points to the Ambassador and expand on them. Rather than following Dr. Saad's agenda, we on the coalition side needed to figure out exactly what combination of actions and timetable was realistic and then work to get the Iraqis to follow a process we thought made sense. To achieve this, the Commander would set up an interagency working group to mirror the Iraqi TRIC. Embassy participation in this would be welcome but not required.

The general consensus was that I should be appointed as senior advisor to the TRIC. I had mastered the issues involved, I knew all the other participants, and my doctorate would signal respect for Dr. Saad's credentials. Indeed, there was no one else to put in the job.

This was quite a shift from the confusion and angst of only a few days prior. In less than three weeks, I had taken ownership of an important piece of the coalition mission in Iraq, become recognized by my colleagues and superiors as an authority on the topic, and now would have a clear and challenging set of duties for the rest of my time in Iraq.

This was important enough to get me promoted and put my career back on the track I had wanted for myself.

I would also have lots of chances to drink more of that amazing tea!

Chapter 3
Resentment

There I was: sitting at my new desk in my new office trying to decide how to reply to the greeting from my new boss. "You're from the Academy. You must think you're pretty fucking smart."

The two-star had vetoed me becoming the senior advisor to the TRIC the day after it was proposed. The militias issue would follow the Policy Division to the Political-Military-Economic Integration office. But I was in Baghdad as a result of his personal drug deal with the Academy, so he was keeping me in his unit. He told me I had two weeks to train my replacement, a very young civilian who had barely participated in the militia process so far, after which I was supposed to forget everything I had learned over the past three weeks.

The two-star kept me in his unit, but he didn't seem to know what to do with me. That night, before the unit screened *Master and Commander* for the Thursday movie, he had told me I'd be working in Strategy and also in Assessment. The next morning, he had said I should work on "international stuff" involving NATO and the UN, not much of which was going on.

By then, I'd gotten over being disappointed about not getting a cool-sounding title and remembered I'd not much enjoyed militia policy anyway. The role would have been a dead end, with little ability to influence what the Iraqis would do and no one much caring about the outcome. I'd had that kind of job before. They hadn't gotten me promoted.

In contrast, either strategy (how should we go about accomplishing our goals) or assessment (how well are we accomplishing our goals) seemed far more interesting and central to the war effort. I hoped he would settle on the Strategy Division. From what Neal and Mike had said, Assessment was a dreadful place to work.

Late on Friday afternoon, I landed the job I wanted and met my new boss. It didn't start well, as I could find no response to his greeting. Behind the Colonel, I could see the posters above and around his desk. One depicted John Wayne saying, "Life is tough. It's tougher if you're stupid." Another featured a smiling infantryman holding out some coffee while suggesting, "How about a nice cup of Shut the Fuck Up?" After working for Colonel Haith, this was going to be an adjustment.

The Colonel didn't assign me any specific work that evening, so I slipped off to play poker with some people from the Embassy's Economics Section. We met in an alcove off the South Lobby, around the corner from a very loud Blackwater game: supposedly $100 ante, no limit. For contractors earning a rumored $1,000 a day, tax free, that seemed reasonable.

Our stakes were lower, which was fortunate because one of the players was a shark who ended up with everyone's money. Most fun I'd ever had losing five dollars.

When I got home to my trailer, I was further entertained, whether I wanted to be or not. My new solo quarters were carved out of a row of shipping containers set end to end. It had enough room for a bed, a locker, and a small table with a lamp. Just like after the Embassy pool party the night before, my lusty Brit and Aussie neighbors were taking full advantage of the privacy offered by the walls between our units. Those walls were thin. I might need to wait until I had a permanent trailer to get some peace and quiet at night, at least on weekends.

Still, this was a clear upgrade from the transient tent. Outside my door, a palm tree grew in the three-foot gap between the rows of trailers. Rather than being dim and filthy, the latrine was bright and clean, with a row of sinks at one end, then toilets, and finally ranks of shower stalls with benches running between. My personal life had taken a turn for the better.

> Sat 4 Sep: Late in the day, had a strategy team meeting. My first task is to look at possible outcomes to the Iraqi elections, with an eye toward different strategic responses. The better news is that [the two-star] made an explicit reference to 4 months [as the length of my tour] today.

Other than perhaps the two-star himself, the Colonel in charge of Strategy was the most intimidating of the senior officers: big, bald, bad-tempered. Blessed as I was to be assigned the desk closest to his, I noticed he almost never smiled, never greeted anyone, never left his desk in the corner except to criticize. He dropped F-bombs like Curtis LeMay over Tokyo.

The work was also a bit intimidating, but it seemed more interesting and relevant than militias had been. First, the Colonel told me to look at how the upcoming Iraqi election might go so we could prepare for different outcomes. But the next day, he told me he had a "PhD Challenge" for me. He said I had twenty-four hours to answer three questions and thus, I guess, establish once and for all whether I was pretty fucking smart.

The first question was a ridiculous example of bureaucracy. Our victory conditions, our "desired end state" were: "Iraq would be peaceful, united, stable, and secure, well integrated into the international community, a full partner in the global war on terrorism, democratic, and an engine for regional economic growth." This was classified, perhaps to leave us room to alter the goals and declare victory without anyone knowing about it.

Recently, however, someone in Washington had substituted "ally" for "partner." The Colonel's first question was: What (if anything) did this mean for our strategy in Iraq? I was supposed to answer without asking someone in the Bush administration what it meant.

Why not ask them?

Asking for clarification might suggest we were too stupid to understand. Asking for clarification might lead the administration to think we were criticizing their communication skills. Asking for clarification might result in an answer we might not want to hear: "Yes, our new goal is a formal treaty negotiated with Iraq and confirmed by the Senate."

Not asking for clarification—giving the question to the guy who'd been in the office for two days—meant we could develop an interpretation we could live with.

How was an ally different from a mere partner? Formal allies, such as Japan, Australia, South Korea, and the members of NATO, were ones with which we had a mutual defense agreement. There was also a category in US law called "major non-NATO allies," which included friendly countries like Israel and some less consistently friendly ones, such as Egypt, Jordan, and Argentina. Bush had recently declared Pakistan to be such an ally, though it wasn't cooperating much in the Global War on Terror—some wondered if Pakistan might be sheltering Osama bin Laden. The primary effect of being an ally rather than a mere partner was to allow some of Congress's rules on arms transfers to be waived.

A treaty would require Senate approval, but the lesser designation could be announced at the president's discretion. Neither required Iraq to adopt any particular policies. Most importantly, they did not require us in Headquarters MNF-I to do anything at all.

The Colonel told me this was a pretty fucking good answer, but half the day was gone and I had only answered one of the questions in his challenge.

The second question was: What would happen if Grand Ayatollah Ali al-Sistani died? This was far more challenging. For starters, I knew next to nothing about Shia Islam or its leaders, other than that people called ayatollahs were behind the Iranian Revolution, embassy takeovers, and chants of "Death to America." They usually had long white beards, turbans, and glowering expressions. Sistani seemed a bit different. He had the beard and the black hat and the stern mug, but he primarily used his power in ways that supported, or at least didn't impede, our desired outcomes.

Unlike anyone else in Iraq, his power came from morals rather than mortars. Sistani had demonstrated his power ten days earlier when he ended the standoff with Moqtada al-Sadr at the Imam Ali Shrine in

Najaf simply by showing up. He was the "object of emulation" for most Shia Arabs in Iraq—the senior religious figure whose guidance they would try to follow. Sistani advocated for patience among the Shia Arabs, telling them to stand down in their resistance and trust the process he had engineered. It was difficult to imagine how we could manage the war without his calming influence on about half the population. If he called for solidarity with other Iraqis, the people would act accordingly. If he called for mass protests against an American proposal, the streets would fill with demonstrators—who would then go home when he said his point had been made.

What would happen if Sistani died? This wasn't a random concern, after all: No one knew why he had needed medical treatment in London. Furthermore, though he may have talked Sadr out of Najaf, Moqtada probably wasn't very happy about it. The young radical was generally believed to have been responsible for the murder of Grand Ayatollah Abdul Majid al-Khoei in the immediate aftermath of the invasion. Khoei would have been a strong advocate for a democratic Iraq, one more assertive than Sistani. I could hardly imagine how things might have been different if he had lived. If one grand ayatollah could be killed in Najaf, so could another old man who lived off an alley in the same city. In whatever manner Sistani might die, what would happen next? How would a new spiritual leader be selected? Who would it be? What impact would this have on our campaign?

I had concluded that though the State Department might have answers to questions about the future, they seemed reluctant to share such answers with me. I decided to talk to the guy in the Political-Military Section who had shared ideas about funneling development money directly to Iraqis rather than American corporations. He wasn't an FSO; rather, he worked for one of the OGA, the "other government agencies." These might be CIA, DIA, NSA, who knew? If anyone could help, he could.

To get to the OGA suite I walked north from the rotunda, past the chapel, along a cluttered but otherwise vacant corridor, and finally up the stairs to a dim landing with a well-locked door. Stepping into the OGA lobby was like stepping into another building in another place. There was real furniture, along with tasteful art on the walls and carpet on the floor. There were plants, probably fake, but maybe not.

The OGA man gave me enough information to put together a report for the boss.

Before turning in my answer, I had to take another step. This man had a reputation for speaking his mind at meetings. I didn't know the details firsthand, but apparently he would embarrass people by pointing out something everyone was trying to ignore or by correcting their facts. The two-star had had enough of this and warned his people against communicating with this loose cannon. He would press about whether information was from him.

This approach did not encourage truth telling, especially among those who had a career they were looking forward to.

To evade this restriction, I took my report over to the Embassy and laundered it through one of the senior foreign service officers. State Department people wouldn't volunteer any ideas about what might happen, but they were willing to review finished products and confirm their reasonableness. Then I could say one of them was my source.

My conclusion: Sistani's view of mosque and state was not exactly Jeffersonian, but he sharply disagreed with the Iranian model of "rule of the jurisprudent." He believed clerical rule would lead people away from their faith. Politics corrupts, so people inevitably become cynical about politicians. If the politicians are clerics, people will transfer that contempt to religious leaders in general, and ultimately to Islam itself. Rather than risk this, lay leaders should rule in accordance with Islamic principles. If they rule badly, the clerical leadership could remove their blessing from them without Islam itself being tainted by association.

Sistani's successor would be chosen after a period of mostly intellectual rivalry among the other grand ayatollahs, only some of whom agreed with him. Sistani's particular moral authority was not transferable. Shia Arabs could choose their own spiritual model, so his followers would most likely split their emulation among several options. We had no idea how this would develop, but no one would have Sistani's influence, so a greater proportion of Shia Arabs would likely be drawn toward grand ayatollahs who more strongly opposed the American occupation and its democratic goals. Or toward people like Sadr.

> Tue 7 Sep: So scary that my input on something like Sistani—or even more importantly Fallujah—may be taken seriously. I knew nothing about the Najaf clerics 36 hours ago, now I have an official assessment. I know almost nothing about Fallujah now; will have an assessment seriously under consideration this time tomorrow.

Tuesday morning, the Colonel told me I had failed his challenge: "Good work on Sistani, Tom, but your time is up. What fucking happened? Why didn't you get it done?"

I replied, "Sir, this shit takes time if you want it done right."

He smiled and gave me a two-day extension.

The third element of the Colonel's PhD Challenge was much more difficult and serious than the other two. Command wanted to know: Where would it be most useful for us to seize the initiative and launch a major kinetic operation (military jargon for shoot, bomb, and kill) to improve the security situation before the Iraqi election, which was expected to occur around the end of the year?

The options under consideration were the northern cities of Baqubah, Samarra, Mosul, Tikrit, Ramadi, and Fallujah, as well as Baghdad itself. Cities were the focus because small-scale efforts like those ongoing in towns and rural areas of northern Babil Province and in parts of Nineveh near the Syrian border would not have a dramatic effect either way.

This question had already been addressed by two others in Strategy: one of the regular US army officers and a British army officer. I was to take a third crack at it without knowing their conclusions. My first step was to get a map and find these cities. I had not been much concerned with Iraqi geography during my first three weeks in Baghdad.

To answer this question, I inverted my training in risk analysis as a safety engineer. Rather than calculating the chance of failure in an aircraft part and the severity of the damage that would result, I focused on the probability of success of a kinetic operation in each city and on how much security would be improved if the mission were successful.

I based the expected gain in security on how much violence could be reduced and how many people would benefit as a result. In places that were relatively quiet, like Tikrit and Mosul, the capitals of Salah ad-Din and Nineveh Provinces on the upper Tigris, a kinetic action could not gain us much. These cities hosted much of the secular armed opposition—the former Ba'athists loyal to the old regime—but they rather sensibly kept their own backyards peaceful.

Among more violent places, the gains from a successful operation would be greater if they were achieved in a larger city. This argued against Fallujah and Samarra, which were much smaller than the other options, and even Baqubah, despite being the capital of Diyala Province.

To estimate the probability of success, I looked at the size of a city and the depth of hostility within it. A kinetic action in a large city like Baghdad or Mosul would be more difficult, more time-consuming, more costly in lives and matériel, and at greater risk of going wrong than one in a small city. Moderating this, some cities, like Ramadi, the capital of al-Anbar Province, were nearly universally hostile to the occupation; more diverse cities like Baqubah and Baghdad were less so.

None of the options were very good. We could either execute a relatively low-risk operation that would produce little gain (in Samarra, for example) or a high-risk operation that might produce a bit more gain. I suggested the best answer was: "Don't attack any of these cities," but I acknowledged the Commander had asked "where" to take action, not "whether."

The best bet, in my opinion, was to focus on Baghdad itself: Security would be improved for the greatest number, we knew the city well, forces were already nearby, and we believed a decent proportion of its people were not yet in violent opposition to our presence.

I argued the worst choice for military action was Fallujah, along the Euphrates in al-Anbar Province. It had a lot of violence, but it was the smallest of these cities, so success there would not improve security for very many people. Furthermore, the operation would be very difficult. Even under Saddam, as I understood it, the city had not been fully under government control.

Although I hadn't been asked, I added that if we were going to do this, we should do it soon so it would be over before the start of Ramadan on 15 October. Starting an operation during the Islamic holy month would probably go over poorly among the Iraqi people. Waiting until after Ramadan ended, after the feast of Eid al-Fitr in mid-November, would push us close to the Iraqi elections, which might happen as early as December. There was no concrete policy against starting a major kinetic action just before the election, but it seemed best to leave time for some reconstruction and pacification.

When I delivered this answer, I learned I had reached the same conclusion as my colleagues. This, the Colonel told me, was the wrong fucking answer. Fallujah would be the target, and it would happen soon. I pushed back on this, but that only evoked more vulgar sarcasm from the Colonel about how useless education and academics and social scientists were. Air force pukes like me were especially useless. We had no understanding of what war was all about or how to win.

I resented being treated like this. After all, I had reached the same conclusion as the regular army officer. *Why,* I seethed to myself, *did you ask me if you think I'm so fucking ignorant? Would you have valued my opinion if I'd given you the answer you wanted, you big jackass?*

I saw a bit of sympathy from my colleagues as I got back to my desk—there was no privacy, everyone heard everything—but I had to admit it hadn't helped my credibility as a legitimate military officer when I had managed to take a bite out of the base of my thumb a few days before while I was racking the slide on my weapon. Painful, bloody, and a good lesson in taking care to do things the right way. The Colonel never said anything, but I'm sure he saw Mike Lewis, an attorney who had recently arrived from the Academy, trying to help me stop the bleeding during one of his team meetings.

In any case, this wasn't about me. The decision to take kinetic action in Fallujah had been preordained. I—and the others—had been supposed to find a better reason to do it than the lingering resentment about what had happened there earlier in the year.

At the end of March, the enemy had ambushed four Blackwater

contractors, killed them, mutilated their bodies, and strung them up on a bridge over the Euphrates. We responded by assaulting the city five days later.

Invading a city as retribution for killing four of our guys, stretching the meaning of "our" guys to include hired guns? This was like a rash, disproportionate action out of a different era, one undertaken to teach the whole city a lesson for atrocities committed by a few.

That April offensive did not go smoothly. Civilian deaths created a backlash throughout Iraq, as Shia Arab leaders like Sadr and Sistani stood in solidarity with the Sunni Arabs in Fallujah.

Then something truly remarkable happened. CPA Commissioner Bremer's handpicked Governing Council asked us to stop. And we did. This showed the Iraqis they had influence and perhaps planted in them a seed of hope that they really would be able to regain sovereignty. It also reinforced hope among other Iraqis that resistance might not be futile.

US forces withdrew, and security in Fallujah was turned over to a local Iraqi force, one of the militias whose status had been uncertain in the TRIC process. This First Fallujah Brigade failed to keep the peace, the city continued to be a stronghold of opposition, and American military leaders yearned to redeem this defeat at the hands of weak, back-stabbing civilians.

Thus passed my first five days in Strategy. I was exhausted, I was scared of my own conclusions, and I was thrilled. This was the kind of thing I had only imagined working on: real-time, real-world contingent assessments. I may not have known what I was doing, but as I looked around, it didn't seem like anyone else did either.

The Strategy Division had about a dozen officers in two rooms. Most were regular army on a headquarters rotation, and others were called-up reservists. None had any expertise at this kind of war. How could they? The US military had little recent experience with whatever we were doing in Iraq. Desert Storm, Grenada, Panama—they were all quick in and quick out. Kosovo, Bosnia—they were peacekeeping operations in low-risk environments. Lebanon, Somalia—not so quick, not so safe, so we got out at the first sign of trouble.

Now we were trying to figure out Afghanistan and Iraq, which were neither quick nor benign, and we couldn't cut and run this time. We hadn't done a protracted occupation of a large territory with a hostile population since Vietnam—and that hadn't turned out so great. We had no idea what might work here. Promising examples had been demonstrated by people like Lieutenant General Petraeus in Mosul, but there was no consensus about how much of his success was due to strategy and tactics versus fortunate circumstance. Nothing was "doctrine"; nothing was the received and validated wisdom of experience.

We didn't even have a real plan. Apparently going two out of three on his challenge was good enough, because the Colonel told me to organize an interagency team to review the entire campaign plan with a focus on the next six to nine months, through the election and its immediate aftermath.

This seemed like a more sensible task than those in the challenge. After all, we'd been in Iraq for almost a year and a half so it was time to take fresh look at . . . a campaign plan that had been finalized just before I arrived. Not only had it been developed long after the invasion, but it also came into being after all the major decisions had been made about disbanding the Iraqi Army, barring Ba'ath Party members from public life, and designing the guidelines for the upcoming elections. Furthermore, the plan amounted to little more than a list of different agencies' goals, assembled under one cover with equal priority.

For reasons of bureaucratic expediency, we would not go to the trouble of formally replacing or revising the official campaign plan. That would take a long time to approve and would allow awkward questions to be raised about why the prior effort was being tossed aside so soon. Instead, I was leading a "strategy review," a parallel determination of the real decision/decisive points in the campaign plan and the real critical paths toward desired, acceptable, and unacceptable end states. Our strategy could then focus on the results of this review, and we could unofficially ignore the official plan.

This sounded meaningful, important, and right in my skill set. I wasn't expected to have these answers myself; rather, I was to synthesize information from people who knew a lot more than I did. I'd done this often; it was like figuring out how to help Strategic Air

Command resume missile maintenance after they shut it down over isocyanate concerns in 1990 or working across bases and services to figure out where and how to install the T-6A Training Information Management System while I was in San Antonio. Thanks to hanging out at the Embassy and attending the senior advisors' meetings when I had been in Policy, I had plenty of contacts to draw on.

One group of people I still needed to meet was Red Team. That group tried to replicate the mindset and priorities of our adversaries and develop ideas for actions they might take to oppose us. This concept is at the core of strategy, properly speaking. "Strategy" is often understood to mean nothing more than a very complicated and thorough set of plans, but the term actually reflects accounting for an adversary's own goals, priorities, and possible actions. A goal of ours might be to increase electrical distribution; a plan would be how to do so. A strategy must recognize that goals and plans may be opposed by our enemy, who would try to shut power back down.

Red Team was located at the al-Faw Palace on Camp Victory, an eleven-mile drive back toward the airport on Route Irish. The trip required obtaining vehicles, drivers, and security. Others made this trip often, but this would be my first trip outside the Green Zone since my arrival.

I was going with Colonel Sandy Storrie, the division chief for Campaign Plans, so we followed British procedures. The American mode of transit was to go hard and heavy: travel fast to minimize the time exposed to the enemy and use armored SUVs that could survive minor attacks. This was how we had driven in from the airport last month. The downside to this technique was that it attracted attention, so you were more likely to be attacked—as our arrival convoy had been.

Speed plus top-heaviness also increased the risk of an accident. My new friend Mike Lewis had experienced this during a recent trip to the Justice Ministry. He had to help cover an accident scene while the drivers worked to get the vehicles back in operation. Unlike medics and chaplains, lawyers are considered combatants, but they don't train in weapons any more than acquisition officers like me do.

The British model for convoys was different. They viewed attention as a bad thing and immobile time after an accident as too dangerous. Instead, they tried to blend in with the traffic by driving at normal speeds in a normal SUV: hiding in plain sight, so to speak. If we were attacked, this was a problem, but at least we would not be drawing fire like the Americans.

Colonel Storrie and I armored up and walked down to the motor pool in front of the South Lobby. I got in behind the driver, a Nepalese Gurkha, and the colonel sat behind the vehicle commander. She briefed us on the mission goals, procedures, and hazards, and then turned to me and said, "Major, you have the left."

I stared at her, trying to process how this was significant. *Yes, I'm on the left side of the back seat.*

She elaborated, "Major, you secure the left side of the vehicle."

Colonel Storrie tried and failed to conceal his glee as I processed this to myself: *Ah, right, that made sense. The driver can't do that—hold it, what?*

The vehicle commander decided she needed to spell this out in full detail: "Lower the window, ready your weapon, and fire at your discretion."

I managed some words: "Got it."

This trip was more terrifying than riding in from the airport or taking cover after the rocket hit the Palace—more terrifying, in fact, than challenging the two-star in his office or presuming to pick a target city for attack. My rules of engagement were to watch out the window, scan the far side of the highway for anything threatening, and, if I judge it necessary, shoot at it without asking questions.

The drive was once again a relentless series of houses, trees, walls, garages, shrubs, walls, trash, people, walls, other cars. Nothing looked any more or less threatening than anything else. I knew I would not be able to hit a target while moving down the highway, but I might hit a bystander while hoping my target ducks long enough for us to drive by. Not that my target would probably be a real threat.

But I was certain I would fire if I saw something dangerous. This was my assigned job, however far it might be from my training and expectations. There was an enemy out there, and he had no qualms about shooting at me (poorly and impersonally to be sure). Only fair for me to return the favor.

The author at al-Faw Palace

I didn't need to test this resolve: I saw nothing. After a very long fifteen minutes or so, we turned off the airport expressway into a comforting maze of Jersey barriers. We were in another somewhat secure zone.

Al-Faw emerged from an island in a reservoir, and as Colonel Storrie and I walked across the pedestrian causeway we paused to get pictures of the first attractive building I'd seen in Iraq. The Republican Palace was fine, but except for a few elements its façade was mostly tan and flat. Al-Faw was built in what I took to be a more classic Arabic style: white stone, vaults, arches, pillars, script.

While wandering around the building, which had helpful plaques in English, I was struck by the luxury of its bathrooms. They had marble-esque basins and goldish mirrors—I had no idea what was real and what was fake. The oddest aspect of these was the very low density of fixtures. Several feet separated urinals. Al-Faw was more for show than for use. The more ceremonial parts of the Republican Palace matched it, but closer to my office upstairs, some restrooms were cramped little closets, and others had full bathtubs. I didn't know whether anyone ever lived in the Republican Palace; the king who had commissioned it was assassinated before it was finished.

Today, al-Faw's grand rooms were empty. I spent a good part of the day in one of them, waiting for our short meeting with Red Team, catching up on thinking and reading, and napping on a shelf. This downtime gave me a chance to get to know Colonel Storrie, who admitted he knew what he was doing when he maneuvered me to sit behind the driver on the way out.

As a British infantry officer, Colonel Storrie had experience in a wide variety of wars: counterinsurgency in Northern Ireland, garrison duty in the Falklands, and peacekeeping in Congo with the UN. He had arrived here at about the same time as I had and expected to leave in mid-December, like I did. He had volunteered to come to Baghdad after being promoted to colonel because he had a few months to wait before starting a professional military education course in January.

This was my best day in Iraq so far. Any day away from my Colonel would have been nice, but the chance to talk with someone friendly and just think and reflect was a rare luxury. The daily pace in Strategy was so frantic with overlapping assignments from early morning until late at night, I had no time to reflect on the bigger picture.

My thoughts returned to the cities question that had been resolved in favor of attacking Fallujah. My analysis had omitted whether this kinetic action would help us achieve the desired end state (united/democratic/secure/etc. Ally!). Why? Because we didn't have a plan or strategy worthy of the name. That was the purpose of this strategic review the Colonel had tasked me with organizing: to figure out what was most important so Colonel Storrie could integrate them into a more refined campaign plan, so others could develop more detailed operational plans for achieving those strategic goals, and so Assessment could know what was worth measuring. Until I finished this up, there was no basis for saying whether a military success in Fallujah would move us closer to our goals.

The meeting with Red Team went fine in terms of getting to understand their viewpoint. Unfortunately, they were fully and unreflectively on board with the notion that our enemy was exactly as it was described by the Bush administration: evildoers who hated freedom and could not be reasoned with. They saw the enemy as simply anti-Iraq forces whose goal was to destroy Iraq.

Red Team did not seem to consider that the enemy might in part be an insurgency, an indigenous Iraqi force motivated by its exclusion from the new order we had created there. Nor did they seem to consider that the enemy might in part be a resistance, an indigenous Iraqi force aimed at expelling the occupying Western forces.

Red Team's prism refracted most of our enemy into its foreign elements, especially those associated with the Jordanian Abu Musab al-Zarqawi's Monotheism and Jihad. This Sunni Arab group could quite rightly be described as terrorists—al-Qaeda was said to regard them as a bit extreme—and its exclusion from Iraq's future was appropriate. Lumping all our opponents into that one category did not, however, help us understand their motivations.

Those motivations mattered if we were trying to predict what the enemy might do in different scenarios. A resistance would take actions designed to get the United States to leave but might not attack a new Iraqi government. An insurgency would want to control the new Iraqi government, attacking us as a means to that end. Sunni jihadis would be attacking all who did not follow their doctrine: Westerners, Shia Arabs, moderate Sunni Arabs, and Kurds.

Granted, all three types of enemy would be trying to kill us, but Red Team would have been more helpful if they had been more sophisticated about this.

After the meeting, we had to wait for the return trip. Once it started cooling off toward evening, Colonel Storrie and I walked in the shade of the tall palms along the lake to shop at a PX, one larger and better stocked than the one near the Palace. We were getting a bit anxious about the passing time. Although driving at night might conceal our identity as coalition members, it would also expose us to random crime. We had not come prepared to check into temporary quarters at Camp Victory, which would be a sensible way to prevent us from getting killed.

Our ride returned just before sunset. I insisted that Colonel Storrie take the honor of sitting behind the driver and secure our left. This allowed me to pay more attention to the drive while the vehicle commander watched the right side by herself. She also, however, had to keep an eye on the driver, as he seemed to have no idea where he was going. To his credit, he would ask for directions, but the vehicle commander became increasingly annoyed by the distractions. We almost missed the left-side exit toward downtown and the Green Zone, in which case we would have headed south in the twilight and gotten lost in a bad part of town.

> Sat 11 Sep: Came home to a series of big explosions—just like I woke up to: Happy Anniversary, eh? These were close. And it was home—I was able to move into a permanent trailer with the perfect roommate—one who isn't here. He's sharing a house with a bunch of other guys, but he says that the "fucking State Dept" (a phrase you hear far too often here) is throwing them out soon.

The next day brought fantastic news: After ten nights in my own little slice of Babylon, I could move to a permanent trailer in the Palms! Even better, I would continue to live alone for a while. I encountered my roommate-to-be Hank, an army major, while moving in. He told me he was going to continue occupying a villa in a different compound as long as he could.

The Palms was one of several clusters of trailers (another was Poolside Estates; they sounded like Florida subdivisions) that seemed to go on forever behind the Palace. Somewhere along the Tigris, according to rumor, was a gap in the Texas barriers (bigger than Jersey barriers) wide enough for people to slip through if they were able to get across the river. My trailer was a long way from the water; in fact, it was very close to the Palace, north of the laundry and post office, at the intersection of two wide routes between the communities.

The trailers were intermodal freight containers suitable for seamless transfer from boat to truck to train. They were about twenty feet long and eight feet wide. Trailers were shared by two people (in most cases) and paired up to form a four-person unit with a sink/toilet/shower module in between. This would be much more convenient than the communal latrine. I expected much quieter nightlife: a chaplain lived in the adjoining unit.

The interior of the author's trailer in the Palms

Each end of the trailer had a wardrobe, a small set of drawers, and a bed with lovely donated linens. I would have preferred one of the blankets with the blue evil-eye motif but instead got a gold floral pattern. We also had a microwave and a mini fridge for storing non-alcoholic drinks and kiwi yogurt swiped from the DFAC. The combo TV/DVD player was useless. There were no English-language TV stations to receive, and the DVD player was Euro-standard.

> Sun 12 Sep: That was one hell of a night & wake up call. Various mortars during the night, and a steady barrage starting around 0630. The ground was shaking around this utterly unprotected trailer. You always think the last one was the last one, but they just kept coming in. New guy in our office got cut up by shrapnel leaving the tent for shelter. Col T & I looked at the damage later to the vehicle it hit. Press said no injuries. They lie.

Unlike the tent and the temporary trailer, however, my part of the Palms was not protected by sandbags. This was a problem because shipping containers are designed to be as light as possible. The walls would not stop shrapnel from a near miss. In fact, the walls would become shrapnel.

This had been salient on my first night, and more so as the next night turned to 11 September in the United States. To commemorate the third anniversary of the al-Qaeda attacks that had become a false pretext for the invasion, someone was shooting at us. Giant Voice told us to run to one of the concrete revetments and hide there.

Perhaps because of the scale, perhaps because of the date, the American press reported this attack for a change but reassured the home front there had been no injuries. This wasn't true, though I imagined they were reporting what they were told. An officer who was a recent arrival to the SPA, and thus staying in the transient tent, was injured while trying to find shelter. He was told he wouldn't qualify for a Purple Heart because he wasn't in a combat unit. It did not improve morale in the Palace to realize any injuries we suffered wouldn't count, just like we were hearing was the case for John Kerry's Swift boat medals.

US election news was hard to follow from Baghdad, and politics is an awkward topic among officers of different ranks. Most of us seemed to think the war was going poorly—it was hard to look at the war from the inside and think W's team had its shit together—yet most officers seemed to refuse to consider any change. I had heard one senior officer ranting about how awful and incompetent and dishonest Rumsfeld and Wolfowitz were. I asked him if he would thus vote for Kerry to get rid of them. He looked at me as if I'd suggested going for a stroll in Sadr City.

This dilemma among many officers stemmed from how a war they supported was being conducted. One reason for this was the age-old resistance to political interference—the 6,000-mile-long screwdriver wielded by Washington (length of screwdriver varying by theater of operations). In this case, a more specific reason was that we had gone into Iraq very light, against the army's best advice. General Eric Shinseki, chair of the Joint Chiefs of Staff, had told Congress in February 2003 (a month before the invasion began) that "several hundred thousand soldiers" would be needed to win the war and its aftermath. His reward was humiliation: His successor as army chief was announced fourteen months early, Secretary of Defense Donald

Rumsfeld said Shinseki's argument was "not logical," and Deputy Secretary of Defense Paul Wolfowitz said it was "outlandish" and "wildly off the mark."

The dispute with Shinseki over force levels was very troubling to the military. Going to war or not was a political decision, one for civilian leadership. But if you are doing it, then most of us thought you should listen to the people who know what they are talking about. Publicly humiliating those who say what you don't want to hear does not usually lead to smart decisions. It had been disturbing to realize our elected and appointed leaders were not interested in inconvenient truths that clashed with their preferences.

Some of us were less conflicted about the election, as we did not support the war's concept or its execution. Several of us who supported John Kerry for president would meet at lunch or dinner in a quieter corner of the DFAC as what we called the "Kerry cell." We were so sure he'd win that we talked about trying to trademark "Kerry On" as a slogan for his 2008 reelection campaign.

> Mon 13 Sep: Talked to Martha Boyd as a fellow member of the Kerry cell about the "Ramadan offensive" Red Team package. . . . I didn't come here to die for the election of George W Bush. I guess I'm naïve to think anything else, but it's gotten to the point where our concerns seem to be as much about the US election as the Iraqi.

These consecutive nights of indirect fire attacks on the Green Zone fit into a narrative Red Team had been promoting. They thought our enemy regarded Western public opinion as a critical factor. Thus, they expected the enemy to launch what they called a Ramadan Offensive in October: a series of attacks, similar to the 1968 Tet Offensive in Vietnam, to try to undermine the American war effort. In the standard military myth, Tet's urban assaults were tactical failures but strategic successes because they turned Walter Cronkite against the war, followed by the public at large, and led to our failure to keep the war going. We would have won, too, in this version, if it hadn't been for those meddling hippies. As late as the mid-1990s, I would see "Jane Fonda urinal targets" in latrines.

Red Team's guess about enemy strategy was reasonable. Insurgencies or resistances win by either attracting meaningful outside help (not a realistic option for them, other than individual Sunni volunteers from elsewhere in the Middle East and beyond) or by sapping the willingness or ability of the government (and its allies) to fight. Precipitous and unilateral withdrawal of coalition forces would hurt our ability to achieve our goals in Iraq; if not, why were we there? Concern about American public opinion thus seemed appropriate; perhaps this motivated the reluctance to admit people were getting hurt inside the Green Zone.

Red Team, however, drew a starker conclusion: a Ramadan Offensive might lead to Kerry's election, which they thought would hurt the war effort. This was wrong in many ways: A dramatic attack on American forces might rally people to support the president and the troops, Kerry wasn't running on a platform of withdrawal, and the close enemy here in Iraq and its more distant foreign supporters may have wanted Bush to be reelected because he was a great recruiter for them. This was also wrong in another sense: The outcome of the US election was not an appropriate concern of the US military.

I found this kind of debate much more interesting than working on militias in Policy had been. On the other hand, the Strategy office was a much less happy place to work. I would generally be at my desk by 0700 to see if anything of interest had happened overnight. Then I would grab some breakfast and be back by 0900 for what the Colonel called Morning Prayers, a stand-up meeting of the whole Strategy division at which we would learn about wild rumors masquerading as intelligence, report on our own projects, and get tasks requiring immediate action because they were more urgent than what we had already been assigned.

Some of my colleagues called the Colonel "the Vortex" for his habit of whirling out of his office demanding immediate answers; after he sucked in the response, it would vanish for days before it suddenly reappeared, attached to a demand for further quick action. We had little idea what happened on the other side of the Vortex. For example, had our views on the wisdom and timing of Fallujah been brought forward fairly and in their entirety, or had they been sanitized by the Colonel or the two-star before getting to the Commander? I had to give him credit for working hard, however. Almost always, he was the first one in the office and the last to leave; he carried meals back to his desk rather than spend time in the DFAC associating with the troops.

Close of business was generally 2200 or later. Thank goodness I had my own trailer now and didn't have to manage the transient tent in the dark! Those of us unlucky enough to be in the same room as the Colonel found it hard to slip out without being called back to sit and wait for a later discussion and rehash of the day's work. His attitude was the day was over when it rolled over into the next one.

Even a PT break wasn't sacred on this Monday morning. I ran into the Colonel as I was taking my laundry to the KBR contract cleaners on my way to the pool to swim laps. He told me he was headed to Qatar overnight and needed the latest version of the strategy review. Now.

I turned back toward my trailer to get back in uniform, but he interrupted: "I need it now."

So I went back to the office with my bundle of laundry wearing my swimsuit and flip-flops and a towel over my shoulder (it was already 110 degrees) to copy the files from my Secret computer system onto a flash drive, email the files to him, and print a hard copy. I brought them to his cubicle and said, "Colonel, here's the copies you needed for your trip."

He didn't turn to look at me. "Put them down."

I glanced around his work area, which was a mess of papers and old dishes and shit all over the place. He repeated himself: "Just put them fucking down."

When I got to the pool, I swam twenty-four laps to celebrate his departure and work out my resentments.

Given the hours, the heat, the mostly crummy food, the horrid coffee, and the possibility of enemy action, personalities grated on each other. I was often pigeonholed by someone who wanted to complain about another officer, then later by the other party complaining about the first. I did my best to bury any feelings and drown everything out with my iPod.

I also tried to get away from whining by seeking out other people, even strangers, at meals. This led to a baffling encounter after dinner with the two-star's sense of humor. He dropped by my desk and said: "Tom, are you looking for another job?"

I considered for a moment: *Not a bad idea, I kind of hate working for you.* Instead, I replied, "Um, no, General, I'm not. Why do you ask?"

"Any time I'm in the DFAC, if I want to find you I just say, 'Where's State sitting?'"

"Yes, General, I was talking to Jim in Econ about supporting the campaign plan review."

The two-star said, "I don't know Jim, but I know Tammy!"

I imagined he did, as she worked in Pol-Mil on a lot of our issues. I started to tell him she had been introducing me to Jim when he interrupted with, "And watch out for General Stratman!"

Feeling off-balance in this conversation, I offered, "OK, General, but he just joined us at dinner after we sat down. Why?"

"He's a fisher!" he proclaimed.

All I could do was stare at him and think, *What!?*

The two-star elaborated: "He'll just sit there, but if he sees any signs of intelligent activity, he'll try to reel it in."

I wondered whether this was meant as some sort of compliment and thought, *Then I could be working militias again and away from the Vortex!!* Instead, I said, "OK, General, I'll be careful about that. I'm not trying to get another job."

He said without a trace of humor: "That's right you're not."

I took this as a warning the two-star had nothing better to do than surveillance. And possibly was unstable.

Other than that, this was a nice, early evening. When the Colonel called at 2030 wanting an update for his morning meeting in Qatar, one of the other colonels told him the two-star had told everyone to go home by 2100. That pissed him off.

It probably would have pissed him off even more if he'd known I snuck out for a big chunk of the next day.

Most of the time, there were few ways to slip away for very long other than meals and the gym. It was OK to join others on a trip to the PX because it was so very dangerous to leave the Palace compound. Someone would announce a need to go there, and one or two of us could get away with forming a pedestrian convoy for safety. Given the heat and humidity, however, it wasn't much fun to put all your gear on and go watch someone buy toothpaste.

My strategy review project gave me an excuse to leave the office to visit another one, but without transportation I still had to stay in the Palace. Today, however, I ventured out with Martha Boyd, the senior advisor for the Ministry of Labor and Social Affairs and fellow Kerry cell member. She had been part of the TRIC process and was now one of my points of contact for the strategy review. She had access to a vehicle, so we drove over to meet with an operational unit, the Steel Dragons, who were using the building from which Baghdad Bob had broadcast that Iraq was winning up to the bitter end. Their mess hall was better than ours.

After the meeting, we diverted to the villas where my invisible roommate Hank was still living—Martha and he were in the same civil affairs unit. That neighborhood was nicknamed Docs and Cops: Before the invasion, it had been home to senior security officials and Saddam's personal medical team. After they fled, some of the buildings became home to squatters, both US troops looking for better quarters and Iraqi civilians who moved in ahead of them. We didn't think it would be good public relations to evict them, but Iraqis living in the niches between compounds were a source of some nervousness. We had no idea how many of them lived in the Green Zone or what danger they might pose.

We climbed to the roof of Hank's villa and for the first time I saw Baghdad. The top of a four-story building is a high point in a flat city! The Tigris oozed below us in the 120-degree heat. Across the river were the Palestine and Sheraton hotels, protected fortresses for journalists and others who were visiting the war without holing up inside the Green Zone. Upstream, beyond the villas, beyond the al-Rasheed hotel, beyond the Convention Center where the IIG met, were the high-rises of downtown Baghdad.

We lingered rather than going back to the Palace. I walked around the tree-shaded streets amid real houses with no vest and no helmet, even though two Iraqis had been killed when a rocket hit the home next to Hank's a few days prior. They had been hired to renovate the property before it was handed over to officials of the new Iraqi

Downtown Baghdad up the Tigris from the roof of Hank's villa

government. They had stayed overnight rather than take the risk of traveling back to their home neighborhoods.

> Wed 15 Sep: [The Vortex] has been strangely civil since his trip. The project is moving along well. . . . His advice from Qatar was actually useful.

The villas adventure aside, I was working late and hard on this strategic review of the campaign plan. Those conditions gave rise to what people called Baghdad time. This was a curious warp in the space-time continuum when people might say, "Do you remember when . . ." and the answer was, "Yes, that happened this morning." Seriously. Things that happened the day before, or longer ago, would vanish from short-term memory. All you had was what was in front of you now, with little time to reflect on things from the distant past (in other words, last week) unless you were reminded of them.

My spirits were lifted by a reminder of the outside world: an email from my friend Jorge in Belgium. He had been taking the standard monthlong European holiday and doing so without checking his work email. It was so nice to see this in my inbox:

A rocket hit this villa, killing two Iraqi workers

My dear American, Umberto Eco quoting, friend,

I do hope that you don't get your soul too scorched down there and that you do get your military-academic, Nixonian-realist arse back intact so that I can go on kicking it for a long while.

I am keeping a bottle of Glenfiddich tied with a ribbon until you're back (should you get "neutralised" I would just have to drink your half of it on your behalf, which would be a bloody pity).

I have asked one of my believer girl-friends to put up a prayer for you.

Cheers, Jorge

PS: I hope your daughters are doing OK.

They weren't OK. Adding to the stress I felt here in Iraq, things weren't going well at home. The so-called morale calls kept getting worse. The incoming barrage of bad news mirrored the incoming fire most nights: One daughter didn't turn in homework. Other daughter is exchanging instant messages with strangers. Money problems, house problems, parenting problems—I didn't want to be trying to deal with any of these. All I wanted from these calls was to hear my girls' voices, not lecture or discipline them from halfway around the world.

This wasn't how it was supposed to go. The deployed spouse is supposed to minimize any sense of risk, in fact not even talk about any dangers other than those in the news, such as the salvos we took on September 11. And the spouse at home is supposed to keep things going without adding to the deployed person's worries.

Whatever faint hopes I'd had that time apart might improve the family situation were not being fulfilled.

The most disturbing news was that my older daughter had been cutting herself. We had seen some scars on her arms earlier in the summer, but she had claimed they were from one of the cats scratching her.

I could not comprehend this; my only resource for help was the internet, which tried to reassure me this was more a sign of anxiety—a cry for help—than a suicidal disposition. But this was limited reassurance at best. My wife had taken steps to address the situation with her school and removed sharp objects around the home, as impractical as that was.

I decided to send a picture of ducks to my daughter. When Martha and I were walking around the villa neighborhood a few days before, we had come across a large pond, and the pond had ducks, or geese, or some kind of swimming bird—they were all ducks to me. This had reminded me of home, and not just because ducks were a lot more normal than date palms. My daughter liked ducks. During our tour of Europe the summer before, we had taken many breaks to watch ducks (and other swimming birds), in Cambridge, in Bruges, in Maastricht, at Mad King Ludwig's Linderhof.

It was inspiring that one of the villa ducks was swimming with the others despite having very little of its left wing, just bones sticking out of its flank. It was a sign of resilience in the face of violence and trauma, as well as another innocent victim of the war.

I'd have to wait until the mail got through to find out whether this had been a good idea.

> Sun 19 Sep: The Strategy review is starting to degenerate into a bit of a pissing match w/State. [They have] a point—the whole end state discussion

The author in front of a large duck pond

> is ridiculous, but [they don't] seem to be able to see past the past & that I want to use the leeway Col [Vortex] is giving me to adjust it.

Working with the State Department could be incredibly frustrating. They didn't want to think about hypothetical futures, which is a core part of strategic analysis. One of my colleagues said it was as if they were following *Star Trek*'s Prime Directive: observe, but do not interfere.

Part of their standoffishness may have been lingering resentment about how State had been treated in the run-up to the war. They felt Secretary of State Colin Powell had been set up with biased intelligence to try to persuade the UN that Iraq had an active WMD program.

State then developed a plan for postinvasion Iraq. That study, "The Future of Iraq," was drawn up by seventeen working groups during a day and a half of brainstorming about what the new Iraq might look like. It was far from perfect—it had missed some issues entirely, like militia disarmament, and it had the same hard-line policy on the

Ba'ath Party that Bremer had implemented. Nevertheless, it proved that some people in the State Department were willing to think about the future rather than just sit back taking notes.

The Defense Department ignored the study as it prepared for war. When Wolfowitz said, "Fundamentally, we have no idea what is needed unless and until we get there on the ground," that was another lie.

Now, as part of my group that was trying to review the campaign plan that hadn't been written until a year after the invasion, State had developed a bit of an attitude: Now you want to figure out our goals? Now you want to figure out how to achieve them? Now you want us to help clean up your mess?

State was particularly hostile to the part of the strategy review that looked at options short of full success, what we called alternative end states. We could fall short of our goals in many different ways. State flat-out refused to weigh in on whether some of these outcomes were more acceptable than others. As far as they were concerned, all outcomes short of our full desired goal were equally failures.

At least State knew how to throw a party! We may have had professional tension, but interpersonal relations were fine. For example, the Embassy invited me to a going-away dinner for Tammy Fitzgerald from the Political-Military section. The event was at the al-Rasheed Hotel, famous not only as the place where Bernard Shaw and CNN covered the start of Desert Storm in 1991 and Wolfowitz was almost killed by rockets in 2003 but also for the (now covered) mosaic of George H. W. Bush that filled the lobby—to be walked on, disrespectfully.

I'd been working with a lot of these people, but Colonel Vortex didn't want to let me out for the evening. The two-star overruled him, however. He knew Tammy, after all, and he was in a good mood because a touring singer was arriving in Baghdad to perform for the troops and he had somehow managed to get himself associated with the show. He said I could go to the Embassy's party if I promised to learn something useful.

I kept that promise.

I loved this entire evening. About twenty of us enjoyed dinner around a single table, decorated for the occasion with a rose runner and an orange and yellow floral centerpiece. The room was more intimate than the DFAC, with the light absorbed by dark tiles where it was not reflected in mirrors or geometric mosaics. I was the only military officer there as far as I could tell—I did not break out the now-crushed jacket and tie I'd lugged from place to place, but perhaps others had. I knew many of the civilians from the strategic review and recognized others in passing.

I had the good fortune to sit next to Safa Rasul al-Sheikh, the chief of staff of the Iraqi National Security Council. Safa was a tall man, with his hairline receding more quickly than he was graying (not that I was one to talk). His angular features were set off by a thin mustache and deep eyes that seemed designed not to disclose too much. It was my first opportunity to have a one-on-one conversation with an Iraq official.

We had a great conversation about Iraqi politics while eating real food—savory meat, olives, bread, wine for those able to imbibe—that we didn't have to stand in line and get for ourselves. Safa was very interested in learning what election outcomes would be acceptable to the United States. I told him I didn't know and hadn't given it much thought. Which at this point was technically true.

After dinner, I went to a much less formal and much better attended party at a contractor's rented flat. In addition to office buildings, squatters, and the villas, the Green Zone included some low-rise apartments to the west. These were being rented by private security firms and others for outrageous sums. I wasn't authorized to ride over and back in an unsecured vehicle at night, but it wasn't likely the Vortex was going to come looking for me in my bed (though such things had been known to happen).

After the after-party, while walking back to my trailer in the early morning, I saw a silvery fox trotting along. No doubt it was hunting the stray kittens some among us illicitly fed. Ducks, foxes, kittens, parties: despite the Vortex, things were getting more enjoyable.

Tue 21 Sep: [Hank] is slowly moving his stuff in, but still is staying at the house. I think we'll get along fine once he moves in, but it will be another adjustment to give up my privacy again after 3 weeks of being my own master once off work. May sleep better tonight—had a big explosion around 5:30 this morning. The bastards should let us sleep longer.

The State Department's casual approach to security contrasted with our own, illustrated tonight when most of the SPA attended a very different going-away reception, this one for Brigadier Newton, the two-star's British deputy. Our general was very worried about ambushes within the Green Zone. Although we all thought this was ridiculously overwrought, we convoyed the short distance in our armored SUVs. Somehow, I ended up manning the 50-caliber machine gun, spending the whole drive pointing it out the back window at Mike Lewis, one of my best friends in the unit, who was sitting in the front of the trailing vehicle. My training for this mission involved an NCO telling me "Squeeze this to fire." Roger that.

The reception was at the Maude House, the British military HQ. The Maude House was optimistically or insensitively or ironically named for the general who had taken command of British forces in Mesopotamia during World War I after their defeat at Kut in 1916. General Maude went on to capture Baghdad and proclaimed in victory: "Our armies do not come into your cities and lands as conquerors or enemies, but as liberators." Contrary to his promise, the British would remain in control of Iraq until 1932; after that, they maintained bases they used to reassert control during World War II to make sure Iraq didn't side with Nazi Germany. British forces would not leave Iraq for good until 1954. They came back in 1991, and now here we were again. This party was rather more sedate than State's unofficial one. We Americans and the Aussies stood around drinking fake beer (which after a while you imagine tastes OK) while the Brits flaunted their different interpretation of culturally appropriate libations.

Wed 22 Sep: Had a bit of disagreement w/Red Team over their slides—they want to put the impact on Bush's election as an effect of a loss of public support. I told [them] that they needed to change it for their revisions, or I would. [They] said that that is a big focus for Gen Casey. I said that's a real shame and I wasn't going to brief it that way. And that's a fact. If asked, I will decline comment; if pushed, I'll fall on my sword. I am not going to imply that 4 more years for George W is a desired end state—even if I supported his re-election.

It took less than two weeks for the interagency team I organized to finish the strategic review of the still-warm campaign plan. All that was left was to massage the presentations for the Commander.

The goal of the review had been to determine the "decisive points" for the next year, through August 2005, which was the (extendable) deadline for the soon-to-be-elected Iraqi Transitional Government to write a constitution that would be submitted for popular ratification. Army doctrine tended to view such decisive points from a geographic or physical perspective, a bias that was more useful for conventional maneuver warfare than for counterinsurgency. Although we retained the physical security of Baghdad in our review—it included about a quarter of the Iraqi population, after all—we mostly used the joint doctrine definition that extended the meaning of decisive point to include "key events, critical systems, or functions" that would create an advantage in the war.

When we began the review, each agency—parts of the military, parts of State, the Brits, the OGAs—had submitted its ideas regarding the decisive points within its area of interest, describing them in enough detail to be understood by others. I had assembled these into a single set, and then I distributed the full list of candidate decisive points back to everyone with instructions to annotate the points with antecedents and predicates:

What other points' success will become more likely if this point is achieved?
What other points' success will become less likely if this point is not achieved?
What other points' success will make this point easier to achieve?
What other points' failure will make this point harder to achieve?

If a candidate decisive point had no meaningful impact on other candidate decisive points, it was eliminated from the analysis.

Once we had agreed upon the full list of decisive points (with Bush's reelection not included among them despite Red Team's advocacy) we arranged them according to the "DIME," the four instruments of power, each of which had its own "line of operation" that guided agency responsibilities.

"D" stood for the diplomatic instrument of power, which became the political line of operations. This included the process of setting up and conducting elections, forming a new government, and writing the constitution. This line of operations was beyond direct MNF-I or even Embassy control: The Iraqis would conduct their elections with expert advice from the United Nations.

"I" stood for the informational instrument of power, which became the communicating line of operations. This focused on Iraqi opinion and attitudes, particularly the perceived legitimacy of the political process.

"M" stood for the military instrument of power, which became the security line of operations. In addition to any kinetic action taken by MNF-I, this included the development of Iraqi security forces and the overall level of violence.

"E" stood for the economic instrument of power, which became its own line of operations. This included the state of Iraq's economy and its reconstruction. This was pretty much beyond hope in the short term: The UN and World Bank had estimated $56 billion was needed for reconstruction, but the US had allocated only $18.5 billion for fiscal year 2004 and by July (the tenth month of the fiscal year) had only spent $458 million. We'd done less than 1 percent of what was needed, even without accounting for the fact that what we built was often quickly destroyed by the enemy.

All these different lines of operations were aimed at what we understood to be the enemy's "center of gravity": the support among the general population for the resistance (insurgency/terrorists/enemy) relative to the support the general population gave to the Iraqi government. Anything that increased support for the Iraqi political process and government or reduced support for the enemy would contribute to our goals. The converse would hurt our goals.

We also reviewed those goals. The desired end state was for Iraq to be peaceful, united, stable, secure, democratic, an ally, prosperous, globally connected, and a regional role model. This was rather a lot of conditions to achieve all at once. We did not share State's apparent view that all failures were equal, so we created categories of "acceptable" and "unacceptable" end states by relaxing each of the victory conditions. We decided it would be OK if Iraq was not fully an ally, or if it didn't "prove the fruits of democratic governance to the region." Internal peace, on the other hand, was a prerequisite to most of the other end states, so Iraq being indefinitely at war was not acceptable. We also couldn't see any route to breaking up Iraq that would not result in more conflict, so only a united Iraq would be acceptable. To the credit of US leadership, a nondemocratic Iraq was never considered acceptable.

Although we never wrote it down in so many words, we more or less edited the end state goal into "Iraq must be a united, stable, peaceful democracy; ideally, it will also be secure against its enemies, prosperous, integrated into global institutions, and a model to its neighbors."

The final step in the strategy review was to connect the decisive points with their antecedents and predicates across the different lines of operation. The initial spiderweb of events and outcomes was rearranged and simplified until it became clear that all paths to the desired or acceptable end states passed through one set of decisive points: an election for the Iraqi Transitional Government by the end of January (political line) that was perceived as free and fair by the Iraqi people (communicating line).

The Iraqi center of gravity could only be turned against the enemy if the Iraqi people generally accepted the political order in Iraq, which could only happen after the Iraqis wrote and ratified a new constitution via popular referendum, which in turn could only happen after the government that would initiate that process was elected and accepted.

Any delay in the election would undermine whatever credibility we and the Iraqi Interim Government retained, causing popular support to move toward our current enemies. New enemies might arise if the Shia Arabs and Kurds recalled how they were betrayed by US actions at the end of Desert Storm. The Shia Arabs and their militias could make southern Iraq as unsafe for the coalition as the northern Sunni Arab areas were, especially if Grand Ayatollah Sistani turned against the process. Although the Kurds would probably not fight us directly, an impatient declaration of independence would trigger a whole new round of fighting over their state's boundaries, especially around the city of Kirkuk.

Therefore, we needed to aim all our economic and military efforts at increasing the likelihood that the election would happen on schedule and be accepted as legitimate. There was no likely solution on either of those lines of operation without first achieving success on the political and communicating lines of operation.

Unfortunately, we reached this realization toward the end of September, and it still needed to be accepted higher up the chain of command. If the election had been the focus of the campaign plan a month before, then the cities question Colonel Vortex had included in the PhD Challenge might have been addressed differently. Rather than a vague sense that we don't want to launch kinetic actions too close to the elections, I could have emphasized that doing so would jeopardize the key decisive point of the campaign. More importantly, the question would have been filtered in terms of political and informational gains instead of security gains. Rather than asking how much we might reduce violence and at what cost to ourselves, we might have been wondering how the action would be perceived by the Iraqi public.

Of course, as Colonel Vortex would remind us, you cannot develop a strategy by imagining a different past.

My thoughts drifted to wondering why the Fallujah operation had not happened yet. We were already only a couple of weeks away from the start of Ramadan. It had only taken five days after the Blackwater contractors were killed and mutilated before we attacked the city in April. It seemed like there had been plenty of time to do it again, especially since Colonel Vortex had assured us it was imminent.

Maybe the Fallujah attack wouldn't happen after all. Maybe our obvious preparations for the attack were some elaborate feint to distract the enemy into devoting his own time and resources toward defense rather than offense.

Hoping isn't much of a plan. One of my friends had taken to calling the impending action "The Big Phallujah," because it would fuck everything up.

Chapter 4
Frustration

There I was: standing under the palms by Saddam's pool on a breezy Thursday night with a bottle of water. Music, dancing, laughter, conversation: so nice! When I had last dropped by, back on Labor Day weekend, I'd felt lost and a bit alone. After working with so many people over the past three weeks, I no longer felt like a stranger. I could get used to this.

> Fri 24 Sep: Still trying to work the alternative end states w/State. . . . The whole relationship is messed up. State doesn't seem to want to be constructive sometimes—just complain about what we're doing.

With the campaign plan review drafted and swirling in the Vortex, I returned to my original task of anticipating outcomes to the upcoming Iraqi election and evaluating their consequences. This assignment had seemed like busywork, something to do as I had time amid other projects. Now everything had changed. Our review had concluded that the only route to the desired end state was through the election, so it was more urgent to learn what might happen at that decisive point.

My attention was on the first of the three elections scheduled to take place between late 2004 and late 2005. Its winners would replace

The pool behind the palace

the incumbent Iraqi Interim Government, an expanded successor to the Governing Council created by CPA Administrator Paul Bremer. The IIG had held its first meetings here in the Green Zone around the time of my arrival—my first days had involved puzzling over the names of the delegates to see what we knew about them. The IIG had no legitimacy because it had been created by the United States. It was a caretaker government, ruling under Bremer's Transitional Administrative Law until elections were held for the National Assembly (parliament). This first election had to be held no later than the end of January 2005—four months from now.

The winners of this election would form the Iraqi Transitional Government (ITG). The ITG would have limited legitimacy: It would have been elected by the Iraqi people, but under rules set by the Americans. The ITG would select a committee of its members to write a new Iraqi constitution by August 2005. The resulting document would need to be approved by the National Assembly and then submitted to the Iraqi people for ratification in a general referendum. That would be the second Iraqi election of 2005.

If the new Iraqi constitution was ratified, then a third election would be held by the end of 2005 to elect the first democratic Iraqi Constitutional Government (ICG). This ICG might have legitimacy because it would have been chosen by the Iraqi people according to rules drafted by their elected representatives. This clever if complex scheme was a way to bootstrap legitimacy where none had existed—the very question Neal Rappaport and I had debated a long month ago, before either of us knew anything about the process already in place.

Our strategy review had concluded that the only route to victory was through the Iraqi people giving their allegiance to this ICG rather than to those who fought against it. A successful first election was a necessary step to that end state, but it would not be sufficient: How Iraq entered this political tunnel could influence what came out the other side at the end of next year.

Indeed, I could see many ways the final result could be a problem. Knowable problems included the election in late 2005 of an ICG hostile to our goals, rejection of the new Iraqi constitution in the fall 2005 referendum, inability of the ITG to draft a constitution on schedule (if at all), and the first election being seen as illegitimate by too many of the Iraqi people.

My focus was more immediate: the outcome of that first election. Might the ITG itself be hostile to our goals? What if the winners of the election could not form a government?

This last problem would sound odd to Americans—how could a legislature not be able to select its own leaders? Mike Lewis, the military lawyer assigned to Strategy, helped me understand the complicated rules Bremer had laid out for the election after Grand Ayatollah Sistani had mobilized the crowds against Bremer's original plan.

The next prime minister of Iraq would not be chosen by a mere majority of the new National Assembly, as would be typical in a parliament. Rather, members of the new parliament would elect a three-member Presidency Council by a two-thirds majority vote. This Presidency Council would then unanimously select a prime minister, subject to approval by a legislative majority. Finally, the prime minister would select a cabinet that would need to be confirmed by both the Presidency Council (unanimously) and the National Assembly (by majority).

I told Mike it was interesting that when the United States had the chance to design another country's government—now, and in Japan and Germany after World War II—it never created anything that looked very much like our own. It was almost as if America's senior leadership didn't regard its own Constitution as a perfect, divinely inspired document.

Indeed, as I recalled from my time in militias and hiding from illegal celebratory fire, Bush's people did not view the right to bear arms as an essential Iraqi freedom.

Mike pointed out that such musings were distracting us from our work.

The goal of requiring supermajority support for both the prime minister and the Presidency Council was to make it difficult for a simple majority of Iraqis to oppress a minority. Another provision to protect minorities was that the new Iraqi constitution would be subject to more than mere majority ratification in a nationwide vote. It would be vetoed if two-thirds of the voters in three of the eighteen provinces voted against it. People called this provision the Kurdish veto because the Kurds dominated the three provinces of Irbil, Sulaimaniya, and Dohuk. Only a constitution that respected Kurdish interests could be ratified. If the constitution were rejected, then the December 2005 election would be for a new National Assembly that would restart the process.

Those were the rules of the game. To predict how it might turn out, I needed to understand something about the players. Which parties and candidates would run in the election, what would be the likely distribution of votes, and how might those parties align to form a governing coalition?

To get answers, I took the familiar walk to the Embassy: downstairs, under the rotunda, then up to the second floor of the north wing. This time I was visiting the Political section rather than the Political-Military shop I had worked with on militia policy and the strategy review. Given how poor my relationship with Pol-Mil had become after Tammy Fitzgerald had left, this was fortunate. Maybe I would get a fresh start with the people down the hall from them.

The Political suite was quite a contrast from the light and activity and noise that filled Pol-Mil. The room was so dark and quiet that I paused a moment, wondering whether they had moved and left their nameplate on the door by mistake (this happened from time to time, as I'd found while rounding up members of my strategic review team). But no, there were people there, all doing something in isolation under dim bulbs.

Once I got their attention, the people in the Political suite were cordial, but they met my questions with bafflement. After staring at me for a while, one of the senior foreign service officers asked me why I wanted to look ahead like this—in a few months, after all, we would know what had happened without putting so much work into hypotheticals.

Hypotheticals? The war seemed real to me.

I suggested he humor me and my assigned project. It wasn't up to either of us to decide whether it was worthwhile: I was just doing what my boss wanted me to do. He thought this over for a bit longer than seemed reasonable before referring me to a very junior FSO he said was gathering information about Iraqi politics. Why was that not the job of everyone who was working in the Political section of the Embassy? What was everyone else in this section doing?

My new contact had approached her work with the energy of someone who had not yet burned out. She had developed a chart identifying possible ties among twenty-two Iraqi political parties, which she had classified as "Sunni," "Moderate, secular," or "Religious Shia." For example, she asserted that one of the Kurdish parties, the Patriotic Union of Kurdistan, was funding the main parties representing the Turkomen and the Assyrian Christians. This suggested an alliance that might continue after the election.

I had not known this, so it seemed useful, but I was skeptical about other parts of her chart. She had a drawn a solid line between the former Ba'athists and the Iraqi Islamic Party, a branch of the Muslim Brotherhood that had been the only Sunni Arab resistance to Saddam's regime. She had also drawn a line from the Ba'athists to Interim Prime Minister Allawi. He was indeed a former Ba'athist, but we assumed he had renounced those ties. She had grouped the Communists with the Sunni Arabs rather than with the secular parties—and I recalled from my militias project that they were mostly Shia Arabs by heritage if not by devotion.

Her chart indicated Iran was providing money to several religious Shia parties—the Supreme Council for the Islamic Revolution in Iraq, the Office of Moqtada al-Sadr, and a branch of the Da'wa Party—and these were expected to form an electoral coalition and seek the blessing of Grand Ayatollah Sistani. I had to wonder about her information. Could an electoral coalition include both Sadr and the Shia parties his Mahdi Army was fighting right now? Was Iran funding both sides of that war?

If this was anything more than speculation, why was it unclassified?

Some of this sketchiness was understandable. In a normal country, State Department personnel mix with the local movers and shakers and develop an independent assessment of the state of national politics, an assessment based also on past trends.

Iraq was not a normal country.

FSOs could not move as they might wish within Iraqi society and learn from anyone who was not already part of the government. Furthermore, Saddam had not permitted even a pro forma opposition party, so there was little foundation other than demographics on which to build an electoral model.

Beyond this taxonomy of parties, she told me to my surprise that there had been a bit of opinion polling conducted over the summer. I wondered how valid the responses could be—How could the pollsters find willing and honest participants? How representative would they be of the voting population?—but bad information seemed better than no information at all.

A June poll of Iraqi voting intentions taken by Oxford Research International had the Islamic al-Da'wa Party in the lead . . . with 9 percent. There were three Da'wa parties and the survey blurred them together, so this was even less impressive than it seemed. The two major Kurdish parties split 12 percent of the vote in the poll; no one else exceeded 3 percent. The most common answer, given by 67 percent, was "Difficult to say." This was an odd response, not quite the same as "I don't know whom I'm voting for."

A July survey conducted by the International Republican Institute had similar results. An astounding 82 percent of its respondents said there was no political party they supported. Half of the 15 percent who expressed a preference supported one of the two major Kurdish parties. The leading Arab party was again the Da'wa, though it won support from less than a fifth of the 15 percent who stated a preference—in other words, from less than 3 percent of the voters surveyed. Deeper in the results of this survey, Saddam's Ba'ath Party had almost the same level of support as Interim Prime Minister Allawi's Iraqi National Alliance. If Saddam was still as popular as the prime minister we had picked, the struggle for popular loyalty was not going well.

> Sat 25 Sep: Finally got caught up on a lot of personal email . . . and just talking to people. Saw *Mummy 2* w/Jez . . . last night—better than *Spiderman II* or *Day after Tomorrow* because it didn't take itself seriously.

Emails and movies offered me the briefest respite. This renewed focus on my primary duty of examining possible election outcomes lasted one day before Colonel Vortex assigned me a side project drawn from an idea proposed by Simon Tustin, the only non-American assigned to the Strategy Division. He was one of the officers who had reached the same conclusion as I had about the wisdom of attacking Fallujah.

Simon was a terrific guy, quiet, very smart. The other British officers in the two-star's SPA would tease him about how his doctorate was from Cambridge rather than Oxford, which he seemed to take with good spirits. Simon was also religious, which was unusual for a Brit. One evening he invited me to a Bible study meeting. I was desperate enough for some downtime activity that I said I'd think about it. His list of study questions was a bit deeper into scripture than I could handle, so I decided to stick with losing money playing poker.

Simon was among the more pessimistic officers in Strategy. He believed the war was going more poorly than we wanted to admit—in fact, he thought we were losing. His go-to analogy was from soccer, so it was lost on most Americans: "We are a goal down in injury time." In other words, we needed to start taking some big risks even if they offered a low chance of success. Playing it safe would lead to defeat.

This sense of desperation led Simon to pitch an idea within his chain of command just as he was about to leave for a posting in Kuwait: What if we announced a planned end date to the occupation, perhaps sometime late in 2006, two years out? The Vortex gave me two days to develop Simon's idea into a proposal I could present to the "Smart Guys."

It said something about the quality of US personnel that the leadership could identify all the Smart Guys and get them together in one room on short notice.

Simon's idea addressed a couple of problems the coalition was about to face. Three months ago, in June, UN Security Council Resolution (UNSCR) 1546 had legalized our continued occupation. The international community could occupy Iraq until after the third 2005 election. Once that sovereign democratic government took office, UN authority over Iraq would end. Iraq could then tell us to leave, regardless of whether our own goals had been met.

Another problem: Bush's "coalition of the willing" was getting reluctant. Many countries had joined the United States for what was supposed to be a quick operation to depose Saddam Hussein; uncover the weapons of mass destruction; and usher peace, prosperity, and democracy into the Middle East. A year and a half later, Saddam was gone and WMDs had not been found, but the other goals were in short supply. Allied leaders were facing their own elections, and they attributed the fall of the Spanish government that past spring as much to war-weariness as to the subway bombings. American diplomats were begging coalition members to not leave yet, but they had little to offer in exchange.

Simon thought announcing a plan to withdraw in 2006 could help with these issues. A coalition member considering leaving might be willing to stick it out until then. It would also avoid the humiliation of being forced out by a hostile Iraqi government. The announcement could be worded to allow a future friendly (or desperate) Iraqi government to ask foreign troops to stay after all.

I had a more positive argument: It might shape Iraqi public opinion, which, after all, was the center of gravity of the whole operation. We described our enemy as insurgents, terrorists, enemies of the New Iraq, anti-Iraq forces, or evildoers; we rarely described them as a resistance. From the standpoint of the actual enemy fighters, this didn't matter: They wanted to kill us until we left.

If our goal, however, was to reduce how much the Iraqi public supported our enemy, then it might be worth understanding why they supported them. Did Iraqis support our enemy as insurgents, favoring one of their competing goals of a restored Ba'athist regime, a Salafi Sunni state, or Iranian-style rule of the jurisprudent? Or did they support them as a resistance who were fighting us as occupiers?

It seemed unlikely that our occupation would ever be accepted. The best thinking on successful occupations was that they required three things: a population that felt defeated, a population that felt it had started the war and therefore deserved the occupation after losing, and a common external enemy for the occupied and occupier to focus on. This had applied in Germany and Japan after World War II. Both countries' people had been bombed and starved into a feeling of defeat, they could more or less accept that they had supported the leaders who had started the war, and they perceived an aggressive threat from the Soviet Union.

Allied occupation of Germany's Rhineland after World War I was a counterexample: The German population did not accept it had been defeated, they did not accept the Allied narrative that they were responsible for the war, and there was no common military enemy.

These same unfavorable conditions applied to our occupation of Iraq. The 2003 air strikes and invasion had been swift and surgical enough that most Iraqis did not feel utterly defeated, they were not convinced they had started this war—maybe Saddam had, but they had nothing to do with it—and there was no external enemy they feared. True, some Iraqis, especially Sunni Arabs, were suspicious of

Iran, but many Kurds and Shia Arabs saw Iran as a friend that had sustained the opposition to Saddam and given shelter and sanctuary to much of the IIG's leadership.

The new International Republican Institute poll suggested the Iraqi people supported resistance much more than insurgency. It said 40 percent of Iraqis thought it was OK to kill Americans, but a mere 2 percent thought it was OK to attack Iraqi police or destroy infrastructure. In other words, they wanted us out (or dead) but supported the new government.

Colonel Storrie, lively as always where his countryman Simon was quiet, pointed out to me that in this poll, only 38 percent favored killing Brits. Thus, he would be safer than I if we were to go for a walk in the Red Zone or make a stop on our next trip to Camp Victory. Who came up with these questions, and who were the 2 percent of Iraqis who distinguished Yanks and Brits?

A more detailed poll of Baghdadis had been conducted by the First Cavalry Division, with similar results. Residents of the capital had confidence in the police (69 percent), army (60 percent), national guard (59 percent), and IIG (53 percent). They had little confidence in the coalition (11 percent) or the United States (9 percent—damn it, there's Colonel Storrie's 2 percent who like the Brits again). Of those who opposed the coalition, 59 percent said it was because we were "occupiers."

On the other hand, Baghdadis seemed to support our most basic goal. A full 87 percent said Iraq needed democracy, and 86 percent thought other Iraqis wanted democracy too. Only 27 percent had confidence in the "armed national opposition."

These poll results bolstered the idea that we were creating our own problem. Iraqis supported the institutions we had created and the political goals we espoused, but they opposed our presence.

Furthermore, if we believed rumors picked up in the *Baghdad Mosquito*, a daily compilation of open-source intelligence, Iraqis assumed we intended to occupy Iraq forever. If we said we were not that kind of country, Iraqis would ask when we were going to remove our occupying forces from Germany and Italy and Japan. Wasn't sixty years after World War II long enough? They were not reassured by our conditions-based exit criteria, the idea that we would draw down our forces in Iraq once the country was stable and secure.

Simon's plan, which was becoming my plan, offered a solution. If we announced we would leave soon after the seating of the ICG in early 2006, we might undermine the rationale behind the resistance to the occupation and contain the insurgency to the tiny minority who preferred an extreme Shia, Sunni, or secular socialist dictatorship over democracy.

Furthermore, though we did not yet know whether we preferred any outcome to the upcoming elections—I was having trouble staying focused on that task—it seemed it might be useful to remove "Vote for me, I'll expel the Americans!" as a campaign point for radical candidates or parties. If Interim Prime Minister Allawi could announce he had negotiated an American departure, that might strengthen the appeal of moderate or secular parties like his own in the upcoming election and increase the chance the future Iraqi government would include all segments of Iraqi society and align itself with American goals.

One drawback to this argument was that though Iraqis opposed the coalition presence, the occupation was not their major concern. A tiny 2 percent in the Baghdad poll listed the coalition presence as their number one concern, and only 10 percent had it among their top three concerns. Their number-one priority, given by 43 percent, was security and crime. Concerns about schools and economic issues were their next two priorities. Although Iraqis would be happy to see us leave, they weren't thinking about us as much as we were thinking about them.

The most obvious objection to announcing a withdrawal plan, however, was that it might embolden the enemy and undermine our efforts. I tried to find historical examples of countries that invaded another, overthrew its government, installed a new one, helped it against domestic enemies, and then announced a withdrawal date prior to having achieved victory or suffering defeat. The closest comparison to our situation was the one the Soviet Union faced in mid-1987. The Soviets announced they would withdraw from Afghanistan in eighteen months even though the various *mujahedin* factions were still fighting against the government the Soviets had installed in Kabul.

This analogy was of course too outrageous to advance other than in quiet comments to Simon or to Neal, who seemed happy to have moved out of Assessment to join me in Strategy.

The Soviet analogy also had flaws. The Soviets did not install a democratic government, its resistance was well funded and armed by its global enemies, and Soviet losses after seven years were far heavier than ours had been so far. On a more hopeful note, withdrawal from Afghanistan did not precipitate a collapse: The government the Soviets left behind in 1989 managed to hang on for three more years.

Vietnam was a poor comparison, partly because its lessons were contested. The United States had not invaded to install a democratic government; rather, we were supporting South Vietnamese forces at the request of the nondemocratic government we pretended not to have installed by coup. Furthermore, though the early stage of Nixon's Vietnamization program was unilateral, the final withdrawal of American ground troops in 1971 was part of a peace agreement with North Vietnam, whose conventional forces had become the primary threat to Saigon. The South Vietnamese government would remain in power for another four years before falling to a conventional invasion that was essentially unopposed by the United States.

I settled on examining three British withdrawals: from India in the 1940s, Malaya in the 1950s, and Aden in the 1960s. In each case, an occupying (colonial) power facing an insurgency granted full sovereignty to a local government that was not in immediate danger of losing.

Of these, India was the least useful. Muslims, Sikhs, and Hindus had already begun fighting over the future unity of the subcontinent before Britain announced in June 1947 that it would pull its forces back to their bases pending granting independence to a divided India in August. Millions died in escalating violence during the ensuing partition, but it was hard to blame that on the announcement itself. The violence seemed more tied to the partition than to the withdrawal, which suggested any ideas about partitioning Iraq were not very clever.

Aden fit the analogy better, and it had been a disaster. In 1966 Britain announced it would not leave any military force behind after it granted independence in 1968, despite having promised to do so two years prior. This seemed to encourage the insurgency, which was supported by neighboring Yemen; the two countries would merge in 1990. This suggested that announcing a departure plan would not bring peace.

Malaya offered more optimism, though there was no single announcement of impending withdrawal. Its independence was negotiated in the context of a communist insurgency and granted in 1957, with Britain agreeing to support Malaya through military victory a few years later. People seemed to think this campaign was the ideal case for counterinsurgency. Its lessons were the basis of John Nagl's *Learning to Eat Soup with a Knife*, which was widely recommended if not actually read or applied very consistently in Iraq. A key step in this process was a national election in 1955. This concrete step toward Malayan self-government helped convince Malayans the British would in fact leave. It also created an alternative to the insurgency for patriotic Malayans.

Lacking any truly comparable case, the proposal would have to be debated by the Smart Guys on its own merits.

> Mon 27 Sep: Reaction was mixed . . . COL [Vortex] wants me to revise & sharpen to continue the analysis forward.

The debate among the Smart Guys—and they were all guys—elicited a wide range of opinions. I was surprised the military officers supported a withdrawal announcement more than the civilians. For quite some time, the US military had wanted any operation to have three things: a clear and achievable goal, public support, and an exit strategy. Our war seemed to have none of these. A deadline would create its own exit strategy, a milestone to reach before public support was lost.

The first risk raised by this ad hoc group, by the Embassy representatives in particular, was that the withdrawal announcement might be irreversible. If a future Iraqi government wanted the United States to stay beyond 2006 after all, would we? The counterargument was it was not unprecedented to reverse a planned removal of forces. Being asked to stay would place our presence in Iraq on sounder footing, as allies rather than occupiers.

The second risk was that the announcement might look like we were admitting defeat. This was met with the suggestion that the announcement be held off until after something that looked like a victory, much as Lincoln held off on the Emancipation Proclamation until after Antietam. Pessimists pointed out it might be a good idea to do this soon, in case the war deteriorated until we could no longer find anything we could declare to be a victory.

The third risk was that the announcement would encourage the enemy to keep fighting. The counterargument was they did not seem to need any encouragement, and this would support our goal of reducing the enemy's popular support.

The fourth, and opposite, risk was that the announcement would lead the enemy to stand down and preserve its strength so it could be used against the Iraqi government after American troops left. The counterargument was that those eighteen to twenty-four months of relative peace could be used by the Iraqi government to build up its own legitimacy and strength.

The most vocal opponent of the withdrawal announcement was one of the civilian senior advisors. He dismissed the premise that a constitutional government could tell us to leave in 2006—it was inconceivable a future elected Iraqi government would do that; if it did, we could disregard the demand and remain. I found this troubling: If US forces declined to leave at the request of this now sovereign and legitimate government, wouldn't we be declaring war on the very government we had spilled so much blood to put in place?

Today's debate pretty much ignored whether doing this would help moderates in Iraq. There was no reason to assume we wanted to do that, and we were nervous about appearing to favor one election outcome over another. Our guidance was to ensure a level playing field for Iraqi politics, not to sway the election one way or the other.

Wed 29 Sep: More late days but at least I have an end date now: 13 Dec. [The two-star] wanted me to stay until 30 Dec, but I begged off, saying that under the circumstances, I needed the 2 weeks with family. He understood, even to the point of emphasizing that if things got worse the mission could be terminated w/o prejudice.

As September ended, I sent yet another revision of the campaign plan strategy review to the Vortex—I had thought I was done with it, but I was wrong—and the revised withdrawal announcement proposal went to Washington for more senior review. Just like at the end of August, the turn of the calendar was matched by turnover of personnel. Simon was leaving, of course, a respected colleague as much as a friend. I'd miss Jez Milne the most of all—who would I find to enjoy movies with after hours?

Quite a few of the people I'd worked with on the strategy review team were also leaving. Some I'd gotten to know well at meetings and meals, others were faces and names attached to a task, but all of this was going to wreck operational continuity. Some of their unfinished work would need to be picked up by their replacements or others in their units. The newbies would not understand the issues as well as the members of my team had.

I'd been in Baghdad for all of six weeks and I was feeling like an old-timer.

The departing friends might be replaced with new ones or with people I didn't much like. Since his arrival a month ago, the new executive officer had fallen into the latter category.

The Exec was held in high esteem by the two-star, less so by others. He acted as if he wore the stars himself, picking up all the boss's bad habits without having the rank to get away with disrespecting his seniors. Today, for example, he interrupted the Vortex's daily stand-up Morning Prayers by walking in, pointing at me, and saying "You. The General. Now."

Colonel Vortex rose to the occasion with his profanity. He told the Exec to go back to the two-star and explain to him that I was fucking busy in a meeting and that I fucking wasn't going anywhere unless the two-star came down the fucking hall to get me himself.

Which he did.

The Vortex had done me no favors in this, which no doubt amused him. However angry the two-star had already been, now he had afterburners on as he escorted me to his office.

Why the fucking motherfucking fuck, he wanted to know, had the militia policy handoff package, including the talking points offered to Ambassador Negroponte and Prime Minister Allawi, not been coordinated with other offices yet?

I had no idea. I had turned it in to the Exec a couple of weeks ago. I reminded the two-star he had told me not to even think about militias anymore. So I hadn't.

Lots more profanity ensued, and he called the Exec in. No, the Exec hadn't sent it to other offices for their review and approval because . . . I guess he had some fucking reason, but somehow this remained partially my fucking fault for not having made sure the fucking Exec had done his fucking job.

I hated these run-ins with the two-star. Colonel Vortex was harsh and demanding, but the work he gave me was interesting and important. He seemed to be trying to drive me to be better, which suggested he thought there might be some hope for me. He was frustrating to work for but consistent. The Vortex also wasn't writing my performance report and didn't control when I would go home.

The two-star, on the other hand, was scary because he was so unpredictable and controlled my future. He could in a moment flip from funny to angry to weird and seemed to jump to conclusions about which members of his unit were responsible for things going wrong. Yet, as had happened in August after our little exchange over the letter to the mystery sheikh up north, the aftermath of this conflict was unexpected support later in the day.

After weeks of back-and-forth about my redeployment, I had told the two-star and the Vortex about the problems my daughter was having at home—the cutting, in particular. People back in Colorado had helped me believe it would be OK if I kept my commitment, but I feared news of an extended deployment might push everything over the edge. An officer is supposed to leave personal issues at home and not get distracted from the mission. I apologized for not showing more dedication to the mission and begged that the promise be kept.

The two-star told me he would honor the original deployment end date of 13 December rather than keeping me in Iraq until February. He suggested if things got any worse, I might get sent home early.

This decision allowed me to define my "Baghdad Doughnut." Most of us had this on our computers, set to pop up as soon as we logged in each day. It detailed how many days, minutes, and seconds were left until departure. I edited the official version to replace the pictures of 9/11 with ones I found more appropriate to the actual situation.

That actual situation in Iraq was nasty and vicious, which came into greater clarity for me the next day. Now that I was concerned with Iraqi politics, I took more interest in the news than when I'd been looking at long-term militia policy or an abstract strategic review. For political information beyond what was reported in the international media, the only option was the *Mosquito.* Our own special version of the Pentagon's *Early Bird*, it had articles and transcripts from the newspapers and radio stations that had proliferated since Saddam's defeat. Taken together, one could get a hazy idea of what the average Baghdadi might be thinking and feeling.

Which today was horror. A big crowd had gathered for the opening of a new sewage treatment center. American public affairs officers were handing out goodies to the children. A success story, on both the economic and informational lines of operation! It was interrupted by a car bomb sent by Zarqawi's Monotheism and Jihad, followed by two more car bombs targeting the rescue and recovery workers. Dozens were killed, most of them children.

Later in the day, the coalition launched a kinetic operation against an Iraqi urban area—in Samarra, not Fallujah.

Samarra seemed a bit more appropriate as a target than Fallujah: It should be an easier campaign, and it was home to the al-Askari shrine. Also called the Golden Mosque, the shrine was third on our list of places that better not get blown up. It was critical to the Shia Arabs, as it was associated with the occultation of the Twelfth Imam, the Mahdi who would return at the end times and was the namesake of Moqtada al-Sadr's militia. We were all vague about the theological details, but we knew this: If something happened to the shrine, all hell would break loose among the Shia Arabs.

I and others had argued against the Samarra campaign unless it was going to replace the one planned for Fallujah. Doing this now meant delaying the other, which we'd argued needed to be completed as soon as possible and above all before Ramadan began in mid-October. Energy expended in Samarra also detracted from our ability to improve security in larger cities like Mosul or Baghdad. Most of all, attacking Samarra didn't seem to serve any clear strategic purpose. There were bad guys there, but there were bad guys everywhere. We could go kill a hundred of the enemy, but there was no plan for keeping them away or changing the economic conditions that led to them being welcome there in the first place.

At this point, I didn't see much point in another fruitless argument with the Vortex, but from my desk around the corner from the Colonel's I could hear Tom Ruby challenging him: Now what? What's the goal? How will this help us reach the end state? Rubes was new to the SPA and perhaps didn't know how this would go. Soon enough, Colonel Vortex told him he was a fucking ivory-tower pointy-headed academic who knew nothing about war and needed to get the fuck out of his fucking office and get back to his job in Campaign Plans.

On another front of the war, Sadr's militia had moved to northeastern Baghdad, across the river from us, after leaving Najaf a few weeks before. Shelling of the Green Zone was becoming more frequent, and the coalition was responding in kind. For the first time, we could see the war as it happened. It was awesome, in the original meaning of the word, to see an AC-130 gunship laying down fire while in orbit around a target in the evening. We also were more often seeing two-ship medevacs, as casualties were getting closer to home.

The atmosphere at the Thursday party tonight was more anxious than chatty. It was also starting to seem a little risky to be outside. We were all starting to wonder how safe the Green Zone was. In addition to the Iraqis of questionable loyalty living among us, the Iraqis of questionable loyalty brought in to work in the Palace, and the rumored gaps in the wall, we had noted the Gurkhas manning the security gates didn't seem to be very careful about matching IDs to faces. We hoped none of this would lead to any problems. Somebody might have found the hat I had lost on my tour with Colonel Barlow, after all.

> Fri 1 Oct: Finished the Sistani paper that the [commanding general] suddenly wanted; made more progress on the strategy review; the announcement brief is still holding.

I watched the first presidential debate between George W. Bush and John Kerry this morning in the small movie theater in the Palace basement. It focused almost entirely on Iraq and the Global War on Terror.

Kerry presented a crisp critique of the wisdom of invading Iraq at all, a solid summary of how the invasion was conducted without planning for the aftermath, and a good overview of how the invasion had affected international order. But he didn't have any ideas about how to win the war. Kerry said he'd "do a better job of preparing for elections"; since the critical first election would need to be held within ten days of his inauguration, that seemed tough to believe. If he was ignorant about that, what else didn't he know?

W repeated the same old lies about 9/11, weapons of mass destruction, and the presence of terrorists who hadn't been there until after we invaded. He said the war would be good for Israel, which would not be a plus within Iraq, and that Kerry's negativity would discourage our allies.

The president did not leave me optimistic about the withdrawal announcement proposal. He said timetables were "artificial" and "it's essential we not leave." Pressed, he said he wanted to "see the Iraqis perform and to see the Iraqis step up and take responsibility." He defined "as soon as the mission's done" as "When our generals on the ground and Ambassador Negroponte tell me that Iraq is ready to defend herself from these terrorists, that elections will have been held by then, that they're stable and that they're on their way to a nation that's free, that's when."

This language seemed likely to feed Iraqi resistance to our occupation. It would be a long time before anyone would decide Iraq was "stable," especially if our presence in Iraq was helping trigger and sustain some of the violence.

Kerry seemed to recognize this. He asserted, "A critical component of success in Iraq is being able to convince the Iraqis and the Arab world that the United States doesn't have long-term designs on it"; he then affirmed this was not the case. But Kerry's implicit if inadvertent support for an early withdrawal plan would further poison it among Bush's people.

I stayed up late discussing the debate with some senior officials (including the Vortex). One of them thought Bush must have had very poor debate preparation. I supposed one could call it "poor debate prep," but Bush didn't seem to understand what was going on in Iraq. Shouldn't Iraq be important enough for him to understand it without a whole lot of extra preparation?

> Sat 2 Oct: A frustrating day. [The Vortex] still needs to look at the strategy review, now he also has the announcement brief. Until he gets to this stuff, I don't have much to do . . . They were going to shut down the power—maybe—so we got sent home; lacking anything else to do I'm a bit bored. Plus we're a bit under attack.

It was draining to be busy until late at night coordinating complex projects, but it was almost as bad when I got a break. Work kept my mind off the reality of the situation, which was being halfway around the world from my distressed family in a place with a miserable climate, failing sewage systems, fewer friends than a few days ago, and daily indirect fire attacks. We were in easy range of the Mahdi Army across the river and of the Sunni neighborhoods on our side of the Tigris.

> Sun 3 Oct: I guess this is the mid-tour blues. . . . Or so it seemed around dinner time at least. Thankfully [the Kentuckian] and Lt Col Tom Ruby were able to talk me down a bit.

It's difficult when your teenager says she wants to tell you something on condition that you don't share it with the other parent. I tended to think the right answer was not "No, anything you tell me I will share with her," because that would shut down the communicating line of operation on this issue and others in the future. Nor was the right answer "Sure, I will keep any secret you want" because some truths need to be relayed. I tried to go with "I can't promise that up front. If it endangers your health or welfare, or affects her, I'd need to be able to talk about it."

My daughter's Big Secret earlier in the summer had been that she no longer wanted to follow Christianity but instead wanted to adopt

Wiccan spirituality. She felt I would accept this but Mom wouldn't. I didn't know whether that would have been true or not, but I said she should not keep this a secret and agreed this wasn't "dangerous" enough to compel me to share the information. As far as I was concerned, if she wanted to explore some other form of spirituality, however strange it might seem to me, that was up to her. Five years at Notre Dame had pretty much turned me off to Catholicism, so I had no room to object. In any case, objecting would not have changed what was in her heart and would more likely have made her resolute in the pursuit.

I had forgotten about this—there had been a lot on my mind of late—but a few days ago the teenager had decided to tell Mom, which was good. She also told Mom I already knew about this, which was not so good. My wife seemed to handle the news from the daughter about as supportively as one might expect but was telling me on the phone and over email how upset she was with me about having kept this secret. Her suggestion was I should have told her in private and then she would not have revealed to the teenager that she already knew about it. Yeah, I guess. This gave me something to ponder while I was crowded into the basement with everyone else in the Palace, hiding from rockets.

After a few days of not being busy enough to block out the reality of life in Baghdad, waiting for something to emerge from the Vortex, and getting shelled on the home front, I got myself pretty spun up about how much this sucked and was pointless and stupid and how we were going to lose the fucking war. At times like this, it was good to realize I had some friends in the SPA, people who could hear me out and calm me with reason or perspective or humor.

The Kentuckian had become one of those people during the past month. During mealtime gripe sessions, she could counter any complaints I had about what it was like to work for Colonel Vortex in Strategy with stories about what it was like preparing daily briefings for senior leadership with Mike Davis in Assessment. She thought my fundamental problem was I didn't understand the Army Way of Doing Things. Unlike anyone else, she tried to help me figure things out.

One of my main frustrations was that in the army, or at least at this headquarters, everything had to be distilled onto a single bulleted page. Second pages would not be read; often, nothing beyond the first line (the "bottom line up front") would be read. I found it difficult to write concisely.

The Kentuckian showed me tricks like shrinking the line spacing so more could fit on a page and helped me learn to use shorter words and punchier phrasing. Over time, I became satisfied that I was not just providing useless bullshit up the chain of command, but I wondered whether better decisions might be made if I could provide more complete information.

Another great friend was Lieutenant Colonel Tomislav Z. Ruby. He had arrived from Air Command and Staff College, so he was quite comfortable with joint doctrine and with challenging senior leaders on their thinking, no matter how many times they shot him down. In Rubes I had someone who was eager and able to talk over the more abstract issues of strategy and the nature of the enemy. Considering how quickly he concluded we were losing and how often he found himself on the wrong side of Colonel Vortex, he was also remarkably cheerful.

Rubes had brought music. I had by now pretty much exhausted the novelty of my iPod playlist. He had CDs of great old stuff—the Call, the Alarm, Midnight Oil, Roxy Music, Queen. The song I would most often crank up in my ears and repeat was the Ramones' "I Wanna Be Sedated."

My feelings of being stuck and useless ended abruptly after dinner. I heard Brigadier Nick Smith, the two-star's new British deputy, arguing with Colonel Vortex in his office near my desk. The withdrawal announcement proposal had gone up to Whitehall, the British foreign ministry, and they rather liked it. Here in Baghdad, however, the Vortex had told me to smoosh the whole idea down to eight slides, and then he had cut it further. By the time he was done, the briefing could have been summarized as "Here's an idea that maybe looks OK at first but is way too risky and shouldn't be adopted." The Brigadier was critical of this editing and wanted ideas and arguments reinserted and elaborated.

I invited myself to this discussion and implied to the Brigadier that I was responsible for the weaknesses in the PowerPoint. I agreed he had some good ideas I should have included from the start. Before long the Colonel was just watching as the Brigadier and I engaged directly in reediting the presentation so it was less biased against itself. This boosted me with the Brigadier and deflected heat away from the Vortex.

This was one of those days when more happened after dinner than before. I later met with Tom Ruby and Colonel Storrie to talk about how to work the strategy review into the full campaign plan. The process was stuck because the review was not yet officially approved. Yet the war went on. Their two-man Campaign Plans shop would proceed as if the review were final, which would mean any tweaks introduced later would not be reflected in the plan. With my help, they would focus first on reengaging with a higher level of the Embassy about alternative end states, trying yet again to figure out what lesser accomplishments would be acceptable if we could not achieve all our goals.

Rubes told Colonel Storrie about our music exchange—theirs was the only shop in the SPA where people seemed to get along—and Colonel Storrie passed me a CD called *Chilled: The After-Hours Sessions*. Punk had its time and place, but sometimes chillin' is needed too. Otherwise, you're liable to lapse into angry profanity.

> Mon 4 Oct: Day 4 of COL [Vortex] sitting on the 2005 review. At some point, of course, it will blow up and become urgent. . . . We are losing due to half-measures—too few troops, not hitting hard enough, not being fucking decisive. We're so fucking afraid of making a mistake that we do nothing until we are forced to, and then we lose all freedom of action. We could use real no-shit leadership somewhere here. Winning requires decisions.

Despite the changes to the briefing, word came down from Washington that the withdrawal announcement idea had been rejected. We had neglected to consider an overriding concern: Such an announcement would contradict Bush's campaign themes (we do not negotiate

Colonel Sandy Storrie at the British Embassy

with terrorists and we do not cut and run) and undermine his reelection chances.

This was pretty fucking ridiculous. Kerry had exactly one argument regarding the war he had supported from the start: If you elect me the war won't go on forever. If Bush announced a plan for declaring victory in Iraq, what would Kerry have to say about it anymore? Fuck. Maybe we could announce it after Bush gets reelected? No? Fuck.

A few days ago, *Early Bird* had included a *New York Times* op-ed by Daniel Ellsberg titled "Truths Worth Telling." Its distribution shocked me, as Ellsberg was essentially suborning betrayal. He reflected on how he had held back the information that would become the Pentagon Papers for a long time, during which another fifty thousand Americans had died in Indochina. He regretted this and wrote, "Don't repeat my mistakes. Don't wait until more troops are sent, and thousands more have died, telling truths that could end a war and save lives. Do what I wish I had done in 1964: go to the press, to Congress, and document your claims." He then called out "the planned offensive against resistant cities in Iraq that appears scheduled for November. If military or intelligence experts within the government predict disastrous political consequences in Iraq from such urban attacks, these judgments should not remain secret."

Was he writing to me? I knew about such a planned offensive. Now that the strategic review had been completed, I understood its drawbacks for our desired end state better than when I had merely said the potential gains in security from success in Fallujah were not worth the risk. I knew partisan considerations were influencing our decision-making. But leaking that information? Loyalty and duty are important, and I did not need Ellsberg to tell me that "the personal risks of making disclosures . . . are real. If you are identified as the source, your career will be over; friendships will be lost; you may even be prosecuted." If in fact "our nation is in urgent need of comparable moral courage from its public officials," it wasn't going to get that moral courage from me.

I also couldn't think of a way to get credible information out of Baghdad in time to do any good.

The op-ed reminded me, however, of Ellsberg's essay on foreign policy decision-making, "The Quagmire Myth and the Stalemate Machine," published in the journal *Public Policy* a year before the Pentagon Papers. This article had disturbed me so very much while I was in my doctoral program at Ohio State. Using the rich data he had access to, Ellsberg dispelled the notion that Vietnam was a "quagmire," that the United States kept getting sucked into greater levels of involvement in Vietnam because gosh darn it the effort required just kept ramping up to unexpected levels.

No.

From the very beginning, military and intelligence officials told political leaders that winning in Vietnam would require an immense commitment of troops. If we were not willing to do that, they advised, then we should cut our losses. Every damn time this happened, the politicians recoiled from the recommended force levels because they would be unpopular, they would be expensive, they would be distractions from other goals. At the same time, the politicians would not pull out because it never quite seemed like a good year to lose another country to the communists, not with Democrats seen as soft on the issue, not after Bay of Pigs, not after the Cuban Missile Crisis, not with an election coming up, not with the election after that coming up.

Time and again, political leaders chose to do enough to not lose anytime soon, but not enough to win. As the enemy adjusted to the half measures, more would be required to re-create the stalemate.

This narrative was so similar to the run-up to Iraq. Shinseki had stated his professional opinion about what force levels would be required to win the war and the peace, and he was overruled by the civilian leadership. In the name of political expediency, we invaded Iraq with a force too small to win the aftermath. We declared the mission accomplished when it was not. We would not even have a real campaign plan until Rubes and Colonel Storrie finished updating the initial version that had been created just a few months ago. All this was aimed at keeping the American public believing the war was no big deal. The public would not have supported what was known to be necessary.

The stalemate machine continued even now. We were not on a trajectory for success in Iraq. Our presence was part of the problem. Bush wanted to stay until the Iraqis stopped fighting us, and the Iraqis wanted to keep fighting us until we left. The withdrawal plan had at least offered a chance to change that trajectory or leave without more losses. But it had been rejected, more for its political optics than its merits.

Similar political concerns led to another set of assignments for me, again taking me away from analyzing an Iraqi election that was getting closer every day. The Vortex told me to evaluate a series of strategic surprise scenarios. Their premise was that the enemy may try to do something spectacular before the US election—something short of Red Team's Ramadan Offensive—to influence its outcome.

There were five scenarios. Another officer in Strategy was looking into the possibility that someone would hijack a plane flying in or out of Baghdad International and crash it into the Palace (real creative thinking there). I would address the other four: the assassination of Interim PM Allawi, a sustained and accurate indirect-fire bombardment, infiltration of improvised explosive devices into the Green Zone, and a hostage event in which senior military and Embassy leaders were seized by the enemy within the Green Zone.

Enemy attacks were, in fact, getting closer. A car bomb was detonated at one of the outer gates to the Green Zone, killing a lot of people who were trying to enlist in Iraqi security forces. It amazed me how many people were willing to risk their lives to fight for Iraq. This attack would be labeled as terrorism, but was it? Is an attack on the occupier's military and its local allies terrorism?

This evening, we had a tactical shooting lesson down by the Tigris. We noncombat folks got rudimentary training in how to deal with a sudden small-arms situation. First, because I have body armor, face up to the enemy. The armor would protect me even though I was presenting a larger target. Turning to the side would reduce my profile but leave me exposed. Second, this would not be like a training range where I could be calm and take my time. If the need to fire arises, I should advance toward the enemy or toward cover, wasting a round into the ground as soon as I unholstered my weapon. This might distract the enemy. Then fire a wild second shot in the general direction of the enemy for the same reason, then from the third shot onward take aim.

This was a lot of fun. It crossed my mind that if I fired high, over the backstop, maybe the round would cross the Tigris . . . On the other side, however, was Karrada District, which had few of our enemy.

My colleagues and I had many discussions about how to use round number fifteen, or round number thirty if we used both magazines. No one wanted to be taken prisoner.

> Tue 5 Oct: Finally a little bit of progress on the '05 review—COL [Vortex] agrees that we really need to go over it. Had me write a paragraph about what I think the message is to the CG; I wrote 2 paragraphs (Bad me) but also a 2-sentence version.

It took only a day to finish the Allawi assassination paper. Although it would look bad if that happened, the replacement process would be simple: The three-member Presidency Council would name someone without needing confirmation by the hundred-member National Council. The details could get touchy, but given the preexisting dysfunction in the government, the biggest problems would be psychological and pressure to delay the election past the UN-mandated deadline. It wasn't as if Allawi was such an effective leader that he couldn't be replaced. It didn't make it into my paper, but I wondered why we assumed it would be "anti-Iraq forces" that killed him rather than one of his colleagues. A similar process—unanimous consent by the Presidency Council—would follow if Allawi needed to replace the assassinated head of a ministry.

When I could find the time, I was still working on my primary election analysis duty. There was a rumor today in *Azzaman* (the top Baghdad paper) that the seven main parties comprising the IIG would form a unity list for the upcoming election. Although it seemed probable that there would be dozens of election lists, each seeking its own power, this seemed like bad news if true. Such a unity ticket would support American goals if it won, but during the election itself all opposition votes would then be pushed to radical Sunni or Shia Arab parties. Furthermore, if the new government were the same as the old one, which in turn was rolled over from Bremer's Governing Council, then it might be rejected as illegitimate by the Iraqis we hoped to get on our side.

Back in the United States, CNN reported Defense Secretary Rumsfeld told the Council on Foreign Relations that he had seen no strong evidence linking Saddam Hussein to al-Qaeda. He followed up by saying he had been misunderstood.

The next day, Charles Duelfer presented the Iraq Survey Group's final report: There was no evidence there were any WMDs. The whole war had been based on false premises.

CNN also reported Paul Bremer told an insurance industry conference that we didn't have enough troops in Iraq from the start. Of course, troop levels weren't Bremer's decision. Like us, he had been trying to clean up after other people's mistakes. Rumsfeld's mistakes. Bush's mistakes.

Now here we were, trying to clean up after Bremer's mistakes and wondering who would clean up after our own.

Chapter 5

Fear

There I was: working on a strategic surprise paper about the consequences of a bomb being infiltrated into the Green Zone when the swirling surf of rumors swept in with more substance. Security had found an improvised explosive device, an IED, near the café on Haifa Street beyond the Baby Assassin's Gate. Both the café and the market were now off-limits.

Was this in part an inside job, involving the squatters still living among us? Was it infiltrated over or through the walls, perhaps using the rumored gap down by the riverside? Or was it brought in by the day laborers, who were supposed to be checked at the gates?

A lot of Iraqis came into the Green Zone every day—the barbers, for example, until they all quit after receiving death threats back home. Fortunately, one of our new colleagues, Lieutenant Colonel Rutger Zuur, a Dutch marine, had brought a clipper kit.

For a while, date harvesters had been among us. The fallen overripe fruit created a mess on our boots and thus the Palace floor, so locals were invited to shimmy up the palms. This lasted until someone noticed they were tying ribbons high on trunks—one of them right outside my trailer—presumably to help their friends across the river target us better.

Worst of all, residents of Sadr City were stringing communication

The Baby Assassin's Gate at the head of Haifa Street

cables through the ceiling above the SPA offices. We treated the area as if it were a sensitive compartmented information facility, a SCIF, where computers of different levels of classification were lined up on desks (I had three!) and classified information could be discussed openly. This worked fine as long as we pretended the Iraqis didn't speak English, weren't recording anything, and weren't patched into the cabling. This situation pissed off the Vortex to no end.

Didn't the US military have its own people who could do this?

Rutger's arrival also complicated classified communication. Unlike stateside, very little material was marked "NOFORN" (no foreigners). Most "secret" material could be shared with Brits and Aussies, as well as with Canucks and Kiwis if they had not stayed out of the war. The Dutch, however, were not included in this Five Eyes arrangement, so we had to either exclude Rutger from conversations or pretend we didn't notice he was sitting next to us.

Thanks to turnover, I had a better desk assignment. I was no longer around a partition from Colonel Vortex in our main room but rather was stationed in a small adjacent room with Rutger and Neal Rappaport. This made it much easier to come and go without being noticed; the tradeoff was all three of my suitemates talked all the time.

The fourth in our room was a civilian newcomer, Gunner. The Vortex had asked him to join us from the Naval Postgraduate School and offer his expertise on counterinsurgency. Gunner had done something in Central America in the 1980s and had published on the Maoist insurgency in Nepal.

> Thu 7 Oct: Lots of noise after dinner tonight. A rocket hit someplace close to the palace around 7 pm, sending us all to the basement for an hour or so. . . . A mortar round landed in a Dyncorp-Blackwater tent but it was a dud. So the MWR rock-country dance was replaced by people waiting to watch the controlled detonation.

Rather than the usual desultory hangout by the pool, tonight we were going to have an actual professional concert. Alas, this was not to be. First a rocket hit somewhere nearby. Tom Ruby was in his office with the window open, talking to his wife on the phone; he was shaken up by the blast wave. This sent us all into the basement and canceled the planned farewell for my gloomy former colleague from Policy.

During the continuing bombardment, a dud mortar hit a contractor tent. Duds took longer to deal with than successful rounds, which blow up and it's over. The explosive ordnance disposal team was called in for a controlled detonation, which can take hours, and the concert was canceled.

Before this evening's disappointment, the two-star had asked me a tricky question: Who in Iraq was responsible for the election and whom did they report to? I had to research this. As it turned out, Bremer had created an Independent Electoral Commission of Iraq. It had the final say, and it reported to no one. It comprised eight Iraqis and the UN-appointed expert, Carlos Valenzuela of Colombia. As a group, they would decide the exact date of the election and develop detailed rules about how registration and voting would take place. The US had no say over any of this.

The two-star pressed me: Who were these commissioners, and what did we know about them? The Civil-Military Affairs Office was the coalition's link to the elections process, so I headed down to their area on the near side of the North Ballroom. They told me they didn't know even the names of the commissioners. Their identities were kept secret for their own protection.

This made sense to me. Such people would be prime targets for our enemy. The two-star did not like failure, however, and I didn't like giving him a chance to say he had stumped me. I was halfway to the Embassy anyway, so I decided to see if this once they might be useful for something. Jackpot! One of the FSOs in the Political section gave me not only a list of the Iraqi commissioners but also their pictures and professional biographies.

While at the Embassy, I popped into the Economics section to chat with my poker buddies. They were busy, but I noticed that the woman at the front of their office had some Wiccan symbols in her work area. Could she help me understand my daughter's new spirituality? No, she was too busy with a college algebra correspondence class that, she said a bit more loudly, none of the economists in the office would help her with.

I was an engineer and a teacher, so we made a deal: I'd help her understand factoring and the quadratic formula, and she would expand my understanding of my daughter's new spirituality beyond what I'd picked up from half-watching *Charmed*. We agreed to meet after work a few nights a week in the South Lobby, one of the quieter public places in the evenings.

Out in the Red Zone, it was anything but quiet. Ken Bigley, a British engineer, was beheaded by Zarqawi's Monotheism and Jihad. The two Americans who had been kidnapped with him, Jack Hensley and Eugene Armstrong, were already dead. Two female aid workers fared better: They were released after the Italian government paid about a million dollars in ransom.

> Sun 10 Oct: Tried to play bridge last night; probably asking [for time] off led to the extra work. I don't think I'll ever understand the game, nor will I probably find people to play with. I have run into some other card players, though.

I found a bridge group that met Saturday evenings on a balcony over the North Ballroom. I didn't know how to play bridge, but how different could it be from spades or hearts or whist or euchre? Very different. I could play the hands well enough but was baffled by the bidding conventions. Two types of people were in the group: those who took the game very seriously, knew what they were doing, and were impatient, and those who were trying to teach people how to play and love the game.

I didn't think this would develop into a post-Baghdad hobby, even though the group's organizer lived in Palmer Lake, about fifteen minutes away from my home north of Colorado Springs. But it was more entertaining than algebra and maybe a way to connect with people who played card games I was good at, unlike poker.

For once we got good news from across the river: Moqtada al-Sadr, tiring of the beating we were giving him in Thawra, offered a truce. Despite our policy of declining to negotiate with or even talk to terrorists, we reached a deal that might reduce the number of explosions we heard and felt every day. His Mahdi Army would stand down and allow economic reconstruction in his part of Baghdad if we would buy weapons that were the private property of his militiamen and stop attacking his forces.

To no one's surprise, this was a sham disarmament. Most of the weapons turned in as the week wore on were derelict or nonoperational. But his forces did stop firing at us, and he allowed coalition forces to begin working in the impoverished Shia Arab neighborhoods of northeastern Baghdad almost immediately.

No one thought this was a real peace with the radical portion of the Shia Arabs. Sadr had managed to stay a step ahead of us since the invasion, and he probably wanted to prepare for the aftermath of the upcoming election. Whether his political faction won or lost, he'd want to have his private army intact. Still, any break in the conflict was a good thing. Unfortunately, the Sunni Arabs had no similar single leader we could engage with.

Another of my mass-casualty scenarios almost came to pass. We captured two sets of rockets the enemy had daisy-chained to go off in rapid succession. One battery had seventy-two rockets; the other had sixty-four. They usually did not have time to fire very many rounds at a time. Once the enemy launched one at us, we'd get telemetry on the launch point and take out the site from the air. This time, they tried to throw several dozen rounds at us at once, but one of the launchers had dudded out completely and the other had failed after fewer than ten were fired.

Thursday and Friday nights were popular for this kind of attack, either before or after Friday morning services. Bad weather usually meant they held off on firing at us, since after all we targets would still be there next week.

On Thursday morning 14 October, we seemed to be in luck. Thick dust filled the air as we watched the final Bush–Kerry presidential debate on the big outdoor screen near the pool. A congressman was watching with us, stuck here because of the sand. He was the only one wearing a flak vest, but he took it off after about fifteen minutes. It was nice to see he was scared—especially if he was a Republican. They were the ones who most often showed up, eager to claim some national security credibility from the visit.

As it turned out, he was right to be scared. At about noon, they blew up the Green Zone Café. Blew up the hajjimall as well. This was the loudest explosion I'd heard since the rocket hit the dome back in August. The whole Palace shook.

It shook us all up, enough to get new orders.

We were directed to wear helmets and vests anytime we were outdoors. We were also supposed to pretend our nonsandbagged trailers offered us enough protection to allow us to de-armor once we got home. Colonel Vortex told me I could still swim in Saddam's pool, as long as I did it while wearing Kevlar. I'd have to resume going to the gym, which wasn't any more protected from incoming fire than the pool.

The Colonel also told us that if any of us broke the rules and got killed, he'd write a personal letter to our mothers explaining it was our own damn faults we were dead.

I believed him.

Thus, I needed to armor up to walk to the post office behind the Palace to mail my absentee ballot for the US election. I could have used an online voting service as long as I didn't mind giving up ballot secrecy, but I wasn't inclined to trust it. Too many people here saw Bush's reelection as imperative, and that was not how I voted.

Tonight's Embassy party was very subdued. The shark was out of town, so instead of playing poker, Stephen from the Economics section and I grabbed some late chow at the DFAC and then sat out by the pool till well past midnight, talking about work and women and the world.

I learned from Stephen how low morale had gotten among the State Department people. There was no precedent for having a fully staffed embassy taking hostile fire. Anywhere else, most personnel would have been evacuated. But appearances of normalcy had to be maintained, at least through the American election. Various criteria had been defined that were supposed to trigger an evacuation, but when these were met the red line had been changed to something even more dangerous.

No wonder so many of them had sour attitudes.

> Fri 15 Oct: Ate breakfast today with a girl who was at the Green Zone Café when the motherfuckers blew it up yesterday . . . [She] has lost a lot of hearing, has her lower legs all bandaged up—but she's going in to work. She told us in detail what it was like, from sitting down to people looking for their girlfriend, to getting pieces of plastic taken out of her ass at the CSH [Combat Support Hospital], to having to walk back to the palace.

While walking from my trailer to the Palace this morning, someone jumped on my back.

"Shit," I yelped, dipping a bit to the right to shrug off the weight while reaching for the pistol on my thigh.

"Did I scare you, huh? Were you scared?" It was the fucking Exec, now bounding off toward the Palace.

There was something wrong with this guy. Pretending to ambush armed people is never the brainiest idea, but doing it the day after we were reminded that the enemy was closer to us than we pretended?

Fucking moron. He'd gone from amusingly useless to aggressively annoying since he'd had to take the fall with the two-star about transitioning the militias work. Among other things, he'd been making snide comments about my algebra lessons, as if anyone cared what people did after hours.

I stewed on this through the checkpoint and down the hallway to the rear DFAC entrance—until I noticed the young woman in front of me in line had cuts all over her face.

I joined her rapt audience at breakfast. She had been at the Green

Zone Café yesterday, one table over from the people who were killed. One moment she was sitting at lunch, the next she was moshed into the chaos of people looking for their friends. After getting patched up at the hospital, she had to walk back—a good half mile, maybe more—on her own. The next day, here she was planning on going to work in the Embassy.

The four Americans who were killed there worked in Embassy security, as did most of the injured. Their office had placed the café off-limits after the first bomb was found last week.

In the evening, most everyone walked down to the interfaith chapel, blocked out of a foyer near the stairwell that led to the "other government agency" offices. Its ceiling was decorated with 99 cubes—I counted them—each inscribed with one of the 99 Revealed Names of Allah. An adjoining partitioned area hosted Islamic prayers, which as fall progressed and sunset came earlier had begun to overlap Catholic Mass on Sunday nights.

I'd been going. It was an acceptable way to get out of the office for an hour.

I even volunteered to do readings from the Old Testament, standing in front of the congregation with my holstered weapon visible. This wasn't as incongruous as one might think: Most of the readings described the Israelites wandering from Egypt to Canaan, fighting off and exterminating various tribes as they went.

The memorial service was somber. The chaplain had arrived a few days before. He admitted to me he wasn't mentally prepared for a funeral so soon—he had thought the Green Zone was relatively safe.

As had we all. We were more vulnerable to the strategic surprise scenarios than I'd thought. And this was only the first day of Ramadan. Every evening, we'd say "Stay safe" to each other rather than "Good night" or "See you tomorrow." This was now a salutation to take seriously.

> Sat 16 Oct: We all know this won't be the last one. I'm seriously thinking about grabbing a cot & sleeping in the office most nights through Ramadan at least.

Early this morning, a little tapping noise woke me up. My roommate Hank wasn't home, which is why I had been asleep and why I could hear something so soft. In some ways I appreciated having a bit of company in the evenings, but since he had moved in after getting evicted from the villa by the duck pond, I'd discovered he snored like a cement truck. Sometimes the only way I could get to sleep was to pound on the wall of the trailer to wake him up and then hope to drop off before he did. It was kind of funny and kind of mean because he thought my pounding on the wall was an incoming attack. I never told him the truth.

Tonight, all was very quiet except for this little noise.

What the hell was going on in the middle of the night? Digging? Someone trying to pry something open? I put some shorts on, retrieved my weapon, and slipped outside. Nothing to see, nothing to hear. I went back in, laid down, and there it was again: a tapping, either close and quiet or loud and far away. Pistol, shorts, door . . . Nothing but the breeze.

Then I saw it. It was the wind brushing a strip of hazard tape against my trailer.

Ripping off the tape brought no mental relief. Almost every night, I was awakened by the sound of a rocket or mortar hitting somewhere nearby. I knew the trailer walls wouldn't offer much protection, but now I appreciated how thin they were.

What was I to do? Sleeping under armor night after night didn't work, and you never knew when an attack would happen. Sometimes Giant Voice warned us to expect incoming fire, but as often as not, nothing happened after the alert. Sometimes Giant Voice urged us to seek shelter, and sometimes I did, but then what? A few of us huddled under concrete . . . for how long? The all clear wasn't a real all clear because it was never all clear. Yet staying in the revetment all night wasn't an option either.

I had come to realize that one morning I could wake up dead, as we put it. A man my age didn't usually think about living every day like it's your last, and the air force had not prepared me for this at all. My army and marine colleagues had a point: They were the real fighting forces; we and the navy were support. Air force people don't come under ground bombardment—not since Vietnam at least, not often. There were no live-fire simulations for air force people. Other than pilots, we were supposed to be safe behind the lines, eating fine food and playing golf while others took risks.

I considered sleeping in the Palace for safety. Cots were stashed somewhere in case we needed to take long-term refuge inside. But what a step to take! As far as I knew, everyone was sucking it up and hoping for the best.

The Saturday bridge group was more relaxed this week because the more intense people weren't there. One of the other newbies was a true civilian—neither military nor state nor any other government agency. She had come to Baghdad to make an as-yet-undefined film about the elections, the occupation, police training, civil affairs, whatever story needed to be told. She was interested in learning more about how the elections were supposed to work, so we made loose plans to talk about them sometime.

Given my own state of mind about risks, I was alarmed to learn she planned to walk to her trailer in a neighboring compound unaccompanied, unarmed, unarmored, in the dark. I more or less insisted on walking her "home"; she seemed amused by either the chivalry or the possibility that I had ulterior motives. She didn't seem to share my perception that the Green Zone might be dangerous. A lot of civilians, especially those in the Embassy, persisted in being complacent about the dangers.

> Sun 17 Oct: Woke up at 7:30 to a rocket hitting across the river. They didn't sound alert until I was in the shower; by the time I got dressed & out of the shower they were sounding all clear.

The bathroom in the compartment joining my trailer to its neighbor was broken again, so I had to use the communal shower. Unfortunately, we would only find out the latrine in the trailer had failed after someone shat in it. Too bad the little section with the latrine wasn't air-conditioned. The only thing worse than a pile of shit is a pile of steaming hot shit.

The communal latrine, on the other hand, the same one I'd used when I lived in the solo trailer at the beginning of September, was very clean. The contractor responsible for cleaning the showers and latrine was very diligent about standing at the end of the shower corridor staring at us as we undressed and toweled off.

Most of today was slow. I had dinner with Tom Duffy from the Political-Military section of the Embassy. Tom was a fellow Domer, and he tipped me off on how to join the Notre Dame Club of Iraq. I ordered a T-shirt from the club office in Irbil, shipped to me via New York. It wasn't safe to ship anything down the highway through Mosul, Baiji, Tikrit, and Samarra. The T-shirt would go well with my "Green Zone: The Ultimate Gated Community" polo I had bought at the hajjimart.

Then, as often happened when the day was slow, at 2045 Colonel Vortex called me over to spend the next two hours going over inserts for tomorrow's force posture briefing to the Commander. Whatever his other skills, the Colonel was a freakin' PowerPoint ninja. He had shape files for each Iraqi province. We filled them green, yellow, or red. Sometimes orange. Then, for extra precision, we painstakingly added intermediate shadings so we were not only assessing the likely risk at the province level but also which parts would be more violent.

This was a beautiful map when we finished. Nothing like graphics to add an extra veneer of credibility to complete bullshit.

> Mon 18 Oct [email to Jorge]: I haven't gotten blown up yet! It was so good to get an email from you . . . I will look forward to drinking that scotch with you in my favorite city.
>
> As wrong as the war was, the peace matters. You have spoken to me about the bravery of people you've known; now I respect it directly. You talk to the Iraqis who work here despite the danger to themselves and their families—the elaborate ruses they use to get here every day. You talk to Iraqi officials who are even greater targets for assassination—most of them have been shot at, or had family threatened or killed. Or look at the Iraqi police recruits—they still sign up, for the money but also so they can take their country back and we can get out of here.

Some of my friendships stateside shifted while I was in Baghdad. I treasured those people who would regularly email to check in with me. I didn't need much, just a reminder of the world outside the blast walls. But others back home, drunk on the neoconservative Kool-Aid, would argue with me. They would tell me I was wrong to be pessimistic: They knew from Fox that things weren't so bad. It was the liberal media trying to make Bush look bad.

Damn. I guess I could have done my job in Strategy while sitting at home watching TV. I hoped there weren't too many people like this—if so, Bush might get reelected. What a disaster that would be.

Neal and I got a glimpse of what they were seeing on Fox News, watching it on one of the monitors in our little office. A retired general was ranting about the volunteers who had flocked to join Zarqawi's jihadis from across the Arab world. He complained that the Iraqi people needed to be patriotic enough to rise up and expel these foreign fighters. I don't think it ever occurred to him or his viewers that the Iraqis were indeed patriotic enough to expel foreign fighters. We were the foreign fighters, you motherfucking moron.

At least Zarqawi's organization had the other day affiliated itself with Osama bin Laden, becoming al-Qaeda in Iraq (more precisely, al-Qaeda in the Land of Two Rivers). Al-Qaeda kept telling Zarqawi to tone down the violence. Maybe our original enemy would help calm things down a bit? Probably not.

> Tue 19 Oct: My decision last night to move into the palace, now that I stole a cot, has I think had a negative psychological effect on me. I can call it a move based on caution or prudence, but it is a concession to fear, which leaves me angry. At myself? At the insurgents? At Bush for not planning, not having a strategy and leaving us out here unprotected? Probably all 3.

I decided to sleep in my office. In addition to my own welfare, I worried about my daughters and the stress they seemed to be under. My photo of the injured duck had added to the stress. I meant well, but I hadn't thought it through with very much skill.

My fear wasn't just about the nightly rockets and mortars. After the café bombing and my work on the strategic surprise scenarios, I was skittish about our overall unpreparedness.

I especially worried about the infiltration scenario. What if the Green Zone were overrun and a lot of us were held hostage in the

Palace? What should Bush do? The premise for this scenario was something like the Iranian Hostage Crisis of 1979–1981, but that seemed like a poor analogy to me. As far as I could recall, the Revolutionary Guard hadn't wanted to kill the American hostages.

A better model was Beslan in Russian Ossetia. A few weeks ago, Chechens had seized a school, killed several hostages immediately, and mined the building. Hundreds were killed when the Russians stormed the building.

I also compared it to the 1985 seizure of the Palace of Justice in Bogotá, Colombia, by the M-19 organization. The guerrillas killed a lot of people early on, and then more during the rescue effort—by the end, half of Colombia's Supreme Court had been murdered.

Neither of these scenarios seemed hopeful. If the enemy got in here, they would have little intention of getting out alive or of letting any of us get out alive. They would hold people as long as they could, no doubt torturing and extracting confessions before executing some, and then massacring as many as possible when the futile rescue effort began.

My job was not bringing me joy.

Before I could sleep indoors, I needed to find the cots. The two-star had stashed them in the basement because he hadn't liked the clutter. I set one up and settled off to sleep in the small room I shared with Gunner and Rutger and Neal, embraced by those big thick stone walls.

The move into the Republican Palace did not solve my problems.

I slept better—deeply, in fact. It felt very safe and quiet with neither snoring nor blasts, and the cot was surprisingly comfortable.

Internally, however, I was beating myself up. I was a coward. Everyone else was out in their trailers hoping for the best, so why wasn't I? As word spread through the SPA, I got static from other air force officers in conversations that went something like this:

"Tom, is it true you're sleeping in the office?"

"Yes, yes I am."

"Why are you doing that?"

"I don't know, it seems like a good idea."

"Why?"

"All the rockets and stuff at night, I don't know . . ."

"So what are you going to do, Tom? Are you going to sleep here till you go home?

"I don't know. Tonight. Probably tomorrow. Then I'll see."

"What's your problem, anyway?"

Neal pointed out that whatever my problem was, his Red Sox had won two games after losing the first three of the American League Championship Series, so he was going to be in the office by 0530 to get online and watch Curt Schilling pitch in Game 6. And thanks to Schilling's fucking bloody sock, Neal was there the next morning as well. The one time in my life I wanted the Yankees to win, and they couldn't do it.

Curiously, I got no static from army officers, not even from the Vortex. Their attitude was matter of fact:

"Tom, you're sleeping here in the office?"

"Yes, yes I am."

"OK."

Maybe everyone was scared. Maybe the air force people were blustering their way through to avoid the stereotype of being part of a country-club service that couldn't handle war. Or maybe they refused to let themselves admit the danger. In contrast, the actual soldiers and marines figured you did what you needed to do to get through the night. If you were scared, you found a way to deal with it so you could still get the job done.

Or maybe I was kidding myself. Maybe the army folks had decided I was hopeless.

No, no, in fact my relationship with Colonel Vortex had become much more cooperative. The shift seemed to have begun when he and the Brigadier and I had been working on the withdrawal plan. Coincidence maybe—this was also about the time Rubes showed up, and the Colonel seemed to find him to be even more annoying than me. Or maybe I had absorbed enough of the Kentuckian's lessons about how to present things to the army. Or maybe I'd taken on and completed enough additional work to prove myself to be good enough.

Or maybe the Colonel was happy his friend Gunner, a Green Beret who knew his way around counterinsurgency, was around to balance out us purely pointy-headed intellectuals. Gunner was himself a Harvard PhD, which perhaps also reminded the Vortex that knowledge didn't automatically make you ignorant.

Gunner—a tall, gregarious, bearded man who was the opposite of the Vortex in every way imaginable—filled us in a bit on our unapproachable boss. They had known each other from Army Training and Doctrine Command. The Colonel had spent part of his boyhood in Thailand, where he was in a Boy Scout troop run by Green Berets. He was an infantryman, Ranger qualified, and proud of it. The Vortex had served not only in Desert Storm but also in peacekeeping missions in the Sinai and Western Sahara. When the war started, the Vortex was serving as a colonel at Joint Forces Command in what he thought would be his final assignment before retiring. When General Casey took over MNF-I, he requested the Vortex by name because he wanted to have smart people working on strategy.

Gunner told us not to take the Vortex's attitude personally: He talked bluntly to everyone, but he wanted the best for the mission and the people serving him. If he seemed to have no time for basic human decency . . . well, did he? The war wasn't going to be won with hugs and handshakes.

Today, for example, Margaret Hassan, the director of Iraqi CARE, was kidnapped. Irish-born, she'd been an Iraqi citizen for thirty years and opposed the invasions and the UN sanctions.

We also learned a young Japanese man, Shosei Koda, had left Amman, Jordan, on a bus to Baghdad. He wanted to see for himself what was going on in Iraq. We knew how his trip through Anbar Province would turn out.

> Thu 21 Oct: Talked to Laura—the film producer—about the Iraqi Islamic Party and the rest of the party landscape. Done teaching . . . algebra—except for the final—now she can offer me more insight into Wicca. May get into a bridge game over the weekend, and hopefully poker will start back up.

After three nights sleeping inside, I had to quit the Palace. I was feeling sick, and since my roommate had gone to Basra to check the security of the oil infrastructure in southern Iraq, I'd have a chance to sleep in on Friday morning—as long as the enemy allowed that to happen. Four rockets struck the area during dinner. Later, while I was tutoring the Wiccan, a dud hit a trailer near hers.

How many times would we keep getting lucky before more people got killed?

Despite the other nine projects on my list, I had made enough progress on how the elections might turn out that I could explain it to other people. Talking about the unclassified parts of this with a civilian was good practice for my upcoming briefings.

In a sense, building a model for the election had been simple. I only had to consider three questions: Who would vote, who would they vote for, and who would win?

OK, to be more technical about it: What share of the voting population would be from each of the major Iraqi identity groups? What percentage of each group's vote would go to which kind of party? How would the resulting blocs in parliament align into the two-thirds majority required to form a government?

My model could be simple because the elections would be conducted with a single national vote for a single legislature. The 275 seats would be allocated in proportion to the percentage of votes received by parties (or independent candidates) across Iraq. If a party or candidate got 1/275th, or 0.36 percent, of the national vote, it would gain a seat in parliament.

This system had been adopted because no credible census had been conducted in decades. Drawing single-member election districts like those used for the US Congress would have been impossible, but we couldn't even have assigned a certain number of seats to each province because no one knew their relative population. If we had tried, everyone would have claimed they were being cheated, rejected the results, and escalated the violence.

I started by estimating the share of Iraq's population held by different identity groups. The Sunni Arabs believed they were the largest group, maybe not quite a majority but at least 45 percent of the total. The Kurds thought they comprised 30 percent of the population. The Shia Arabs argued they were historically undercounted and had a solid

60 percent. Throwing in various small minorities, I could account for about 150 percent of the Iraqi population.

That was no good, so I turned to public CIA estimates: 15–20 percent Kurds; 60–65 percent Shia Arabs; 12–18 percent Sunni Arabs; and 5 percent Christian Assyrians, Chaldean Christians, Shia Turkomen, Yazidi, and other minorities. I fixed the relative proportion of eligible voters in each group at the middle of those ranges.

The first variable I could manipulate on my model was relative turnout. Would these groups vote at the same rate? A September Baghdad Poll suggested yes, with a suspiciously high 98 percent of Shia Muslims and 97 percent of Sunni Muslims saying they intended to vote—though the Sunni numbers were a blend of Kurds and Arabs.

A national poll conducted by the International Republican Institute (IRI) around the first of October showed a much bigger difference in the intention to vote: Yes, said 89 percent of Shia Arabs; yes, said 89 percent of people in the Kurdish provinces; yes, said only 73 percent of Sunni Arabs.

Were people in Baghdad more likely to vote than those in the rest of the country, or were the results skewed by differences in how and by whom the questions were asked? Was the Sunni–Shia gap minimal, as in the Baghdad Poll, or quite large, as in the IRI version? All I could say with any confidence was that Kurds and Shia Arabs seemed more likely to vote than Sunni Arabs. The Kurds had few obstacles to voting because their provinces were very peaceful. Shia Arabs expressed an equal desire to vote, and Grand Ayatollah Sistani was essentially telling them they would go straight to hell if they didn't vote; still, violence seemed likely to disrupt Election Day for some of them.

My baseline model placed the proportion of actual voters as 20 percent Kurd, 60 percent Shia Arab, 15 percent Sunni Arab, and 5 percent others.

I manipulated the proportions to develop specific outcomes. In one scenario, I supposed either violence or an election boycott depressed Sunni Arab turnout and dropped their share to 10 percent while bumping up the share of others. In another scenario, I supposed a blizzard hit the Kurdish mountains and depressed their rural turnout enough that their votes comprised only 15 percent of the total.

The second variable was whom the voters in each of these groups would prefer. I worked the information I had received from the Embassy about a month ago into an arrowhead diagram to describe the party landscape in two dimensions.

At the top center, I isolated the non-Arabs: the Kurdish parties—the Kurdish Democratic Party and the Patriotic Union of Kurdistan—and those associated with the Christians and Turkomen. They appealed to a different set of voters than the Arab parties did.

Immediately below them in the center I placed the relative moderates who were trying to appeal to all Arabs, such as Interim Prime Minister Ayad Allawi, a Shia, and Interim President Ghazi Yawr, a Sunni. They seemed to support Western democracy and did not place as much emphasis on incorporating Islamic principles into law. This group also included the Shia-dominated Communist Party and a Sunni group that sought to restore the monarchy. Only the Iraqi Independent Democrats led by Adnan Pachachi—a favorite of Westerners—was truly liberal.

I placed the exclusively Sunni Arab and Shia Arab parties on diagonals to the left and right, with the more extreme groups in the bottom corners.

To simplify the model, I classified the Shia Arabs on the right side into "religious" and "radical" parties. This distinction largely came down to this: The religious parties were already in the IIG, while the radical parties were conspiring against it, often violently.

The most prominent of the religious Shia parties were the Supreme Council for the Islamic Revolution in Iraq (SCIRI) and the three factions of the Da'wa Party. SCIRI was holding its Iranian-backed militia, the Badr Corps, in reserve, but they had to be considered part of the establishment. Its members and those of Da'wa served in prominent positions in the Interim Government, and they seemed to accept the democratic goals we had for Iraq.

The most prominent radical Shia party was the Office of Muqtada al-Sadr. Sadr was expected to participate in politics after the ceasefire and weapons buyback, but I didn't think we could count on him to be loyal to democratic principles.

I placed the Iraqi National Congress of Ahmed Chalabi in the

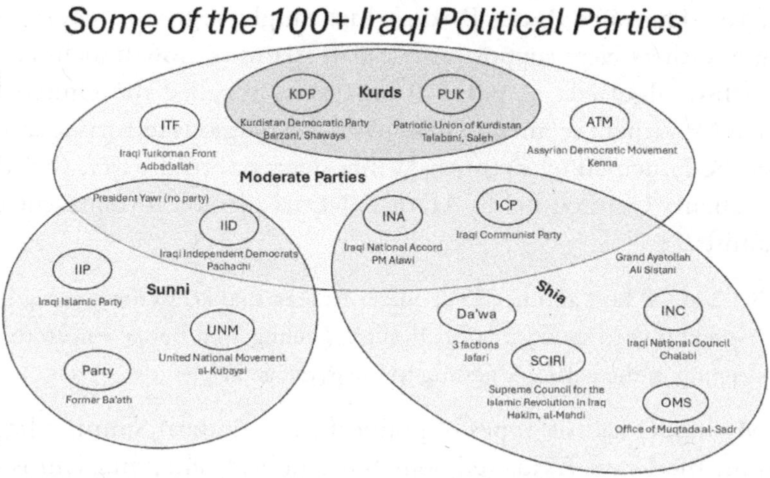

A replica of the political parties chart created by the author

radical Shia group as well. Chalabi had fallen far from his role as a Rasputin for the invasion, telling American leaders that Iraqis would welcome us with flowers as liberators. He was lying or at best misinformed. Although he continued to win love from warmongers in America, Chalabi didn't matter much anymore: In the IRI poll he was viewed favorably by 16 percent and unfavorably by 51 percent, by far the most negative rating of any prominent Iraqi politician. The military no longer trusted him, as he seemed to be working with the Iranians at least as much as SCIRI was.

The Sunni Arabs were less organized. Their only real political party was the Iraqi Islamic Party (IIP), which was the group Laura seemed most interested in learning about during our discussion. Of the major factions, they were the hardest to pin down. Despite its links to the Muslim Brotherhood, the IIP participated in the Interim Government and said it accepted the basic rules of the election and democratic principles. On this basis, I considered them religious rather than radical. Still, as with the Shia religious parties, it was hard to tell whether the IIP believed in a democratic process or was waiting to promote a radical agenda when the moment was riper.

Beyond the IIP were two types of radical Sunni Arabs who rejected the American project in Iraq. Some of these were the remnants of

Saddam Hussein's Ba'ath Party, which might regroup under a new name. Others were supporters of Salafi Islamists, now franchised as a branch of al-Qaeda. A political organization called the United National Movement seemed to liaise with the religious terrorists, though everybody denied everything. While not a political party, the Muslim Ulema Council led by Harith al-Dari seemed to represent true Islamists.

> Sat 23 Oct: Lost another $5 at poker. At least that keeps me coming back. A good way to spend 2 hours though. Feeling a bit better—need to start sleeping in the palace & getting to the gym again.

My model had six types of political party: radical Sunni, religious Sunni, moderate Arab, religious Shia, radical Shia, and Kurds and minorities. Based on polling, both Shia and Sunni Arabs seemed to support the religious parties more than moderate ones. This could change, so the other knob on my model (besides turnout) swung the vote within these groups. By adjusting these variables, my model would spit out a range of seats for each of the six party types.

My assessment of how those blocs would come together after the election was at the heart of the presentations I needed to finish up for the Vortex.

I assumed parties would ally with others within each group, except perhaps the radical parties, who might oppose each other as much as they did the moderates. The Kurdish parties would ally with each other and be joined by those of other religious or ethnic minorities, the Arab moderates would support each other, and so would the religious Shia parties. This assumption meant I didn't need to try to break down the votes for specific parties.

I further assumed parties would be willing to align if they were already working together as part of the Interim Government. Thus, a broad arc from the religious Sunni through all the different types of moderates to the religious Shia might be willing to cooperate. But they would not form a government broader than the two-thirds majority required—there were only so many cabinet seats to distribute, after all.

Finally, I assumed the radical Arab parties would only be willing to join forces with their coreligionists. Sadr would not ally with the

Muslim Brotherhood, and no front group for Sunni al-Qaeda would ally with the Shia Supreme Council for the Islamic Revolution in Iraq.

I expected the Kurds and minorities to control 25 percent of the National Assembly seats, which would make them difficult to exclude from the eventual government. This put them in an inflential position unless that blizzard hit the mountains on Election Day. If that happened, and if the Sunni Arabs also did not vote, the Shia Arabs could comprise 70 percent of the electorate.

In that case, a purely Shia Arab government might form, one including everyone from moderates like Allawi to radicals like Sadr. I didn't think this result was very likely—it required two strikes against voter turnout and cooperation among a wide variety of Shia Arabs—but I adopted "Shia-dominated government" as one of three possible outcomes because its implications were dire: The Kurds would probably declare independence, and the Sunni Arabs would fully rebel against Baghdad.

A more likely outcome was a "national unity government" that mirrored the one we had created for Iraq. If the Kurds and minorities won 25 percent of the seats, they could form a government with any groups that combined to win another 42 percent of the seats—in other words, with any groups that combined to win 56 percent of the Arab votes. To express it another way, this outcome happened if the Sunni and Shia radicals did not get more than 44 percent of the Arab vote.

A fully moderate government, one that excluded religious and radical parties, was too unlikely to include as an outcome. This would require parties led by people like Allawi, Yawr, and Pachachi to win 56 percent of the Arab vote. It would require a stronger turnout among Sunni Arabs than other groups and an increase in the popularity of the incumbent leadership.

In fact, the relative popularity of the religious and radical parties made it more likely the outcome could be what I called the "Kurd-religious Shia partnership," a government that excluded all the Arab moderates and all the Sunni Arabs. This would require 56 percent of the combined Arab vote going to Da'wa, SCIRI, Sadr, and so on. It was easy to tweak the election model to get this outcome: It just required drops in Sunni Arab turnout and in the popularity of the incumbent prime minister. It would also become more likely if Grand Ayatollah Sistani endorsed a list of religious candidates.

Colonel Vortex blessed these scenarios and gave me my next task: assess what each of the three probable outcomes would mean for our goals in Iraq. As a rough first look, it seemed like under any scenario the violence among Sunni Arabs would continue unabated, perhaps even increasing if all Sunni Arabs were excluded from power by the Kurd-religious Shia partnership. Setting aside the catastrophe of a fully Shia government, the wild card was whether Sadr would return to armed opposition in the Shia areas if excluded (under a national unity government) or would maintain his recent peace as a member of the next government.

> Mon 25 Oct: State Dept guy got killed at Victory at 5 am yesterday; turns out Saturday's noon attack killed two KBR Iraqis in their camp just outside the palace. It would be nice if they at least put out some sandbags . . . I suppose I should at least try not to sound so bitter—no one died today! (Yet.)

The indirect fire was getting more accurate or more lucky. I felt good about moving back into the Palace, though that was no assurance, not after what had happened to Ed Seitz.

Ed had been meeting some people at Camp Victory, across the lake from the al-Faw Palace I had visited with Colonel Storrie last month. The sunset came earlier now, so he decided to sleep over in temporary quarters rather than risk Route Irish after dark. He was in the latrine the next morning—or taking a shower, stories varied—when the shell hit.

Shit. What the fuck are you supposed to do to stay safe?

Ed's death bothered me than the others. I knew him a bit. He'd helped me understand how unprepared we were for some of these strategic surprise scenarios.

His death bothered me because he was being careful. The four killed at the café weren't supposed to be there—their own office had placed it off-limits for Americans. Others had been killed by indirect fire while going about their daily business. It happens.

Ed had done all the smart things. He had stayed safe. He had been careful. He had made the sensible decision not to risk being caught on the road after dark. And it did him no good.

The short version of this irony is to note that when the bullet has your name on it, it's going to find you wherever you are. For those with a more literary inclination, this called to mind "Appointment in Samarra," an old Iraqi or Babylonian story retold by W. Somerset Maugham that goes a bit like this:

> A servant is visiting the marketplace in Baghdad one morning, where he encounters Death, who he believes is threatening him. He begs his master leave to flee to Samarra, where surely Death would not find him. The master agrees with this plan, and the servant takes off on a fast horse. But the master is pissed that Death has scared off his servant, so he goes downtown himself and finds Death still loitering around the market. Death tells the master he had not intended to frighten the servant; rather, Death was himself startled to find the servant there in Baghdad . . . for Death had an appointment to meet the servant that night in Samarra.

At this rate, I figured, I'll probably have a rocket hit my office window while I'm sleeping there. And it won't be a dud.

Death was keeping its appointments in Diyala Province, east of Samarra. The enemy stopped a bus full of Iraqi soldiers and massacred all fifty of them. Why were they on a bus? Because Iraq had no functioning banking system. The only way these soldiers could get their pay to their families down south was to take it to them in person (or give it to a courier they really, really trusted).

Interim Prime Minister Allawi blamed the United States for the tragedy. He said we should have provided more security for the Iraqi soldiers. I supposed it was in his interest to seem as independent of us as possible to position himself for the election, but how about focusing on your own fucking failures, buddy?

I spent a lot of quality time with the two-star today, preparing him to go to a Central Command meeting. This produced more work. He liked my analysis of the Iraqi opinion polls, so he told me to turn it into a formal paper. He also wanted a declassified version of the political process briefing I had been working on with Mike Lewis. The Vortex chipped in to order up another decisive point analysis.

In the evening, I played spades with some people by the pool. Around dusk, six mortars flew over. It was very pretty, kind of like shooting stars.

Later, I laid awake in my office wondering, along with Iraqis, why it was taking so long for the big American hyperpower to get Fallujah over with. We kept making excuses for delaying what everyone knew was coming. The latest was we needed to move some British unit to Iskandariyah. Could we have realized a large force will need to be brought over, but Bush can't announce this escalation until after his own reelection? If so, maybe the operation would be put off until after the Iraqi election. I could only hope. No one told me anything about the plan we strategists had recommended against. But it had gotten far too late in the year for an attack on Fallujah to do more good than harm.

The next day was relatively quiet. With the two-star having left town, even Colonel Vortex was more relaxed. The only bad news was that 380 tons of explosives were missing from a depot at al-Qaqaa. The bad guys weren't going to run out of ammunition anytime soon.

Everyone but me headed home right after dinner. So, there I was, alone in my office, sitting on my cot with a computer screen as the only illumination, when the Exec startled me by popping into the doorway. He laughed at my reaction and started up with the same crap as other air force officers about my sleeping choices: "So are you scared, Tom?"

"No," I said, "not really, not right now. How about you? Is that why you're inside?"

He ignored my shade. "You're sleeping here. You must be scared."

I'd been over this with others, with him. "I gotta do what I gotta do. This is what I'm doing."

"So, you're scared? You know, no one else is here."

"No, I guess not. Except you. You're here for some reason."

"None of your friends are here."

I started to agree but paused. Was this guy defining himself as not a friend? Or just separating himself from people I more often talked and ate with? Come to think of it, today at lunch he had been embarrassed in front of some of those closer friends.

He had been questioning again why I was doing nothing but teach algebra to the Wiccan in the evenings. What kind of man was I? After all, he said, he was fucking several women regularly.

Although none of us knew what each other did at night, his

bragging struck me as a bit unlikely. There was plenty of sex going on (a few days ago a very disheveled female officer had joined our table and volunteered: "Freshly fucked hair. It was a good morning!"), but given the gender ratio, a woman could demand monogamy in return.

Apparently, it had struck the Kentuckian as unlikely as well. I almost lost my drink out my nose when she calmly told him the people who were getting some were not the people who were talking about it.

"Hey!" the Exec said, bringing me to the present. "You should be scared right now."

OK, what the fuck? Is he trying to threaten me?

I stared at him, and he stared back.

I recalled an incident with a Russian in Salzburg.

He had been big. And drunk.

He had been accused of sexually assaulting two women in just the first few days we had been there.

The Russian had pointed at the young Bulgarian sitting next to me in a booth in the *Bierstube* in the palace basement and said, "You. Come with me."

I put my arm around her shoulder and said, "No, she wants to stay with me."

He looked at me for the first time and said, "No. She wants to be with me."

I stared at him across the corner of the table. He stared back. My friends got quiet.

He took my glasses off and set them on the table. My friends somehow got quieter.

This is going to hurt.

I stared at him, and he stared back.

Then, after a bit, the Russian walked off.

Here in Baghdad, the Exec, after a bit, broke gaze and left my little office.

This didn't keep me awake long. I had enough to deal with in my life to spend too much time trying to figure out what the fuck that was all about. Was he insecure as the most junior officer, doing secretarial and valet duties for a very difficult person while the rest of us were setting policies and strategies? Was he still hanging on to a grudge after I sold him out for not doing his job on the militias handoff? Was he just a weird dude?

The next morning, I was awakened by Neal, back in the office for Game 3 of the World Series, which thank god the Red Sox were sweeping so this would end soon. I headed to my trailer to shower and get a very early breakfast.

When I got back, the SPA was in an uproar. Several rifles belonging to the two-star's security detail were missing. Its members were going to be in big trouble. Losing your weapon for any reason is a serious infraction in the military. I think most of us had found a pistol in the bathroom and quietly asked around to get it back to its owner. I'd left my own M-9 behind once and gotten it back that way. If you were less fortunate, or less liked, the pistol would get turned in to a senior officer and the guilty party would be vigorously chewed out.

Come to think of it, this had happened a few days ago to the Exec. No wonder he flexed when he could.

Beyond the personal consequences, however, a loss of this scale raised the question: Who took the rifles, and where were they now? Had someone stashed the weapons as a precursor to the hostage situation I'd been writing about, with the US election now only a week away? I joined an informal search party, hunting through unused parts of the Palace and up on the roof. We found nothing, but the Civil-Military Affairs Office told us some of their weapons had gone missing a few days ago too. They hadn't reported it because it would have gotten them in trouble.

As we gave up on the search, the obvious hit me: When the rifles were taken, I had been sleeping in a room a few feet down the hall from where they were stored.

FUCK!!!

Fortunately, the enemy hadn't been looking for people. They didn't expect anyone to be there (and I must not snore), so they didn't open the door to my office and find me.

Now I really didn't know where I should spend my nights.

Chapter 6
Anger

There I was: sitting on my cot late on a Thursday night. My trailer and the rest of the Palms had been evacuated because of a possible bomb, so we were having a party in our office—music, movies, even popcorn!

The Embassy had scheduled a Halloween party for tonight, 28 October, out by the pool behind the Palace. They publicized it well, so no one was surprised when an indirect fire attack began about fifteen minutes after it started.

The military had been ordered to stay away, so I had instead met again in the South Lobby with filmmaker Laura Poitras, to explain more of the unclassified nuts and bolts of the election process. By the time we finished talking, the explosive ordnance disposal team had found a suspicious item near my trailer and ordered everyone to stay inside.

Although she could have gone back to her own trailer, Laura and I kept talking for a long while about how each of us had gotten to be in Iraq. It was delightful to have a conversation with a true civilian. It reminded me why I had chosen to come here. I wanted a good outcome to this war, even if it would vindicate Bush's decision to invade. I wanted the sacrifices of Iraqis, of those trying to engage in a form of democracy, of those signing up for the new Iraqi security forces, of those commuting into the Green Zone to help us—I wanted all those sacrifices to be redeemed. I wanted all the kidnappings, the bombings, the rockets, the massacres, the death, the destruction to somehow lead to a good end.

Laura helped me remember my purpose after I had wandered in fear almost all the way through October. What I was doing mattered. I could find a way through.

I decided not to spend another night sleeping in the Palace. After tonight.

Fri 29 Oct: 4 more nights, then wake up to the election results.

Shosei Koda, the Japanese man who never made it to Baghdad by bus from Amman last week, was beheaded today. None of us were surprised, but we remained baffled by his choice.

We still hoped Margaret Hassan of Iraqi CARE might be released alive. Her kidnapping had been denounced across the socioeconomic spectrum: by Grand Ayatollah Sistani, by the Fallujah Shura, even by Zarqawi. Whoever was holding her wasn't listening to any of them.

Sat 30 Oct: The missing guns reappeared.

No one divulged what had happened to the rifles that had vanished on the night of 26 October while the two-star was out of town. The enemy had not brought them back. It must have been an inside job. Perhaps some idiot wanted to get the security detail in trouble or thought it would be funny. The perpetrator may have planned to return them sooner, but the uproar upended their plan.

There was no cache of weapons hidden somewhere for use by hostage takers. Probably.

With the US election a few days away, soon there would no longer be any extra reason to kill a bunch of us at once. Everything was looking up.

It helped my mood if I appreciated things like that. Sure, there was indirect fire almost every night, sure we were exhausted, but we could tell dark jokes about the situation and make the best of it. And

The author in his office during the Halloween party evacuation

if tonight's poker game was canceled, at least I wouldn't be losing all my money to that shark once again.

Meals had become more enjoyable. The new people in the SPA were more gregarious, more open to wide-ranging topics, than some of the quieter or gloomier people who had left. Some of the change was in me. I was no longer moping around worried about all those strategic surprise scenarios.

When I wasn't with my friends, sometimes I used meals as an opportunity to converse with strangers or eavesdrop on them. I met interesting people in the DFAC—troops rotating through the Green Zone from a forward operating base who could tell me what was happening in another part of the country or people from different sections of the Palace.

I felt so starved for information that I craved anything I could learn. I could not do my job well enough, relying as I was on intermittent public opinion surveys and what the *Mosquito* culled from local media. I tried to find Iraqis in the DFAC and engage with them to learn their perspective. Their views may have been biased in our favor given their willingness to make the dangerous, secret trip to the Green Zone to work for us and with us. But they knew what was happening around their homes every night. And we didn't.

Today, for example, I sat down for lunch with a couple of Iraqi women, one of whom was an orthodontist in her real life. She advised me it would be a waste of time for me to try to refix my teeth, crooked again from my ineffective teenaged braces.

After a bit, I asked what they thought about the Iraqi election. Her companion said there were posters and campaign activity around where she lived; the orthodontist said people would be killed if they tried to do that in her neighborhood. Her partner said, "Oh, you live in Adhamiyah?" and the orthodontist shushed her about that detail.

This was helpful, though troubling, intelligence. Adhamiyah, a middle-class Sunni neighborhood along the Tigris north of downtown, was an area that could be a bellwether for whether enough Sunni Arabs supported the electoral process rather than our enemy.

In the afternoon, I got chastised by some senior officers over this: I shouldn't be talking to Iraqis, or at least not be seen talking to them, or don't mention the election when I'm talking to them, or something. This pissed me off. These same officers were eager to hear and use whatever insights I picked up.

Maybe they thought I was at risk of fraternizing with the locals, or maybe one of the women complained about me to someone. I tended to disregard how my position as an occupier could skew anything I was told, not that I had much confidence in official intelligence.

Beyond that, my actions might put people more at risk. Although these women would have already been labeled as collaborators by any infiltrators observing them at lunch, maybe chatting with an infidel man might have been a yet greater offense.

Sun 31 Oct: My brief went very well and there is very little to change tomorrow.

Today I presented the first full draft of the postelection strategic review that had been developed over the past month. I didn't brief often, never above the two-star level and rarely above the full colonel level. Most of my work got rolled into the official input from the Strategy, Plans, and Assessment Directorate, and I was not the SPA briefer. I had only met the Commander and the Ambassador a couple of times. Most of the time, I interacted with a group of officers a step or two down from them.

This probably was for the best. I enjoyed giving PowerPoint presentations to any audience, but I also struggled not to interject my own personal views. I also tended to get very nervous when challenged by people who held positions of power over me, a habit carried over from my childhood.

Today's briefing went more smoothly than the withdrawal plan idea I had presented to the Smart Guys a month ago. They only wanted a few tweaks before sending it to the four-star Commander for final approval and incorporation into our plans.

This was a relief but, as always, completed work begat more work. My next assignment was to predict how contentious issues—such as federalism, oil revenue, the role of Islam, and the status of Kirkuk—would be addressed in the constitution by each of the three projected coalition governments and how this would affect future political violence in Iraq.

Later in the day, as morning approached on the East Coast, we learned our work had attracted interest beyond our blast walls. Today's *New York Times* published an article by Eric Schmitt about what military headquarters was up to. One topic was the campaign plan, which with their usual accuracy they attributed to the two-star as its "main author." It noted without apparent concern that the assessment team presented 215 separate measurements every week.

I had not appreciated how ridiculous this was until I saw it in print. Over two hundred indicators, subject to revision every couple of weeks. A daily drumbeat briefing on every accomplishment of the past twenty-four hours, in which "no accomplishment is too minor to mention." This helped explain why it was getting harder and harder to find Mike Davis and the other members of the Assessment team.

A primary concern among the leadership was electricity. Polls showed 70 percent of Iraqis were "extremely disappointed" with power availability. Yet in the same polls, more than half the Iraqi population said they had more electricity now than under Saddam.

How could this be? One reason was most Iraqis relied on portable generators to supplement what was sometimes available from power plants. They had power, satellite TV, cell phones, and so on, but they were disappointed they had to generate it themselves.

Another problem was distribution. Transmission lines paralleled major highways. This was great for maintenance in peacetime and great for enemy attack in wartime. Even if electricity production was up, its delivery was down. Beyond attacks by the real enemies, from time to time people realized if they blew up the lines to other parts of the country, their community would get to keep all the locally generated electricity.

Rubes and the Kentuckian pointed out a deeper problem. The measurements didn't have much meaning. It wasn't clear what was being measured when electricity was boiled down to a single number. Did electricity at 60 percent mean that 60 percent of Iraqis had power all day or that 60 percent had power for at least part of the day, even if only a few minutes or an hour? Did they have power 60 percent of the day? Did the number mean different things in different briefings on different days? So many measurements, so little understanding, so little relevance to the actual war effort.

The *Times* also wrote about the Iraqi election. It seemed our leadership had absorbed the main point of my strategy review: The election, in particular an election in which Sunni Arabs participated, was crucial to achieving economic and security progress. However, the leaders did not quite seem to grasp the impact of the pending invasion of Fallujah, now public knowledge. As an example that fit the headline of "In Iraq, US Officials Cite Obstacles to Victory," Schmitt wrote that they thought "Iraq cannot hold meaningful national elections if militants still control major Sunni cities like Falluja."

The *Times* presented this as if it were a real dilemma, but as I and others had pointed out, Fallujah was not a "major city." Only about 4 percent of the Sunni Arab minority lived there. It would be a shame if violence prevented them from voting, but the bigger risk to "meaningful national elections" was that the operation might trigger a full boycott of the election by the Sunni Arab religious leaders who called themselves the Muslim Ulema Council (MUC). Such a boycott is what would hurt our goals. As shown in the elections analysis I'd just presented, it would make it less likely a moderate government would be elected.

I spent Halloween (Samhain) evening with the Wiccan, preparing for her algebra final and trying to learn more about what this set of beliefs entailed. My daughter, it seemed, was now lighting candles in her room, and neither her mother nor I thought burning down the house was a required part of spiritual practice. Perhaps she could light them outside?

> Tue 2 Nov: Election Day. In a few hours we should find out if we'll have to have 4 more years of Bush or not. I still have a gut feeling that Kerry will win, even though the numbers disagree.

I refused to believe people were falling for the lies of the Republican Party. Bush and Cheney and Rumsfeld and Wolfowitz and *The New York Times* lied us into the war, did a half-assed job with the occupation, had no plan for success other than hoping it all worked out, and now were lying to our citizens about how it was going. Surely people would vote for a change!

> Wed 3 Nov: That sure turned out poorly.

Election Day—Wednesday morning in Baghdad—started out with a very early trip to a colonel's trailer. The outdoor screen by the pool wasn't going to be turned on until after 0500 (as a courtesy to those sleeping in nearby trailers), so she invited the remnants of the Kerry cell to come over and watch her TV as soon as polls closed, about 0300 local time.

This was my first visit to a senior officer's lodging. It wasn't much different from my own, except she didn't have a roommate and she didn't have to share a bathroom with another unit. Watching it together was a bit awkward, though, as we didn't know each other very well and no one else was geeky enough to show up. It was a relief to leave a little before dawn and join the group outside.

The early results went about as expected. It became clear it would come down to all those people in Ohio waiting in long lines in the rain to use too few Diebold voting machines. The mood was tense, as many had invested a lot of emotion in supporting the commander in chief despite the obvious failings of his war policy. Not that those of us favoring Kerry expected him to solve the problems he'd inherit. As the returns dragged on, the need to get to work became more pressing. Could this end up like the 2000 election and not be over for weeks?

Right about the time the election was called in the Buckeye State (about 0815 our time), we heard a big car bomb, a VBIED, out on Route Irish, toward the airport. The blast fit my mood. Later, I found myself getting into an argument with some moron who insisted Saddam was directly responsible for 9/11 and the Europeans had begged us to invade Iraq. There is no point in arguing with people who make up their own facts. I went to the gym and rowed for a long time to try to work off my anger.

My roommate Hank harshed my postexercise mellow in the evening. One of his friends, an oil ministry official, was assassinated today. Fuck all this death. Is there any hope?

Maybe with Command's top goal (Bush's reelection) accomplished, we could start taking reasonable measures to improve things in Iraq. High on that list would be calling off anti-Sunni kinetic actions like the attack on Fallujah and instead trying to engage with the MUC. Bush would never admit his errors and take responsibility for this war, but changing course might be enough.

> Thu 4 Nov: Laura took me down to the *Mosquito*'s rumors & atmospherics meeting down in the riverside compound—the one with the ponds & big villas where Gen Casey lives now & Martha & [Hank] used to live. Walked past the hajimall, now off limits, and the ruins of the Green Zone Café. Which blew up on a Thursday at 1215 so of course Laura was only two blocks away. She went to the scene but decided she just couldn't film that.

Colonel Vortex gave me permission to leave the Palace compound and walk a whole mile up palm-lined Haifa Street. He thought we were all excessively locked down by the two-star anyway. I told him if that civilian woman who's walking around with a camera all the time could get there and back alive every Thursday, so could I.

I was still nervous. This was the first time I'd left the immediate vicinity of the Palace since the suicide bombing three weeks ago, and the first time I'd ventured away without full military convoy since my trip to the same area with Martha Boyd back in September.

The remains of the café were like every other pile of debris, and they were completely different from every other one because they were fresh. One wall remained intact, with beams somehow cantilevered forty feet over the rubble that had buried the victims. How had more people not been killed? Remnants of roofing material dangled from what looked to have been a two-story building. The establishment's sign was still partly attached to one of the posts flanking the parking lot. A young man in a tank top with bandages on his chest, arm, and hand sat at the base of the other post, looking dejected. He attracted no attention from the two men in military gear standing in front of their Suburban.

Laura and I stopped for a moment and moved on to the house on a side street that hosted the *Baghdad Mosquito*.

As a daily compilation of open-source intelligence collected from local TV, radio, and press, the *Mosquito* contained clues about the actual mood of Baghdadis. Once a week, the translators took a break to discuss the word on the street, the buzz beyond what was in the media. Laura and I were the only visitors for today's session, and because her film technique was to observe but not directly engage, I got to ask a lot of questions.

The *Mosquito* staff present included seven young people. Attendance was lower than usual because one of their colleagues had recently been beheaded in Ramadi, and he'd had his cell phone (complete with his friends' contacts) with him. Their demeanor was more relaxed than that of the Iraqis I'd met in the Palace or those at the TRIC meetings back in August. They looked like young people from more or less anywhere, in casual Western dress, laughing and joking and teasing. One of the women was repeatedly "accused" of being a Persian, based on her facial features. Behind their camaraderie, there was a tinge of whistling past the graveyard of their country, a little too much

The ruins of the Green Zone Café

insistence on keeping things light. Or perhaps I was detecting what I expected to see.

I learned a lot that afternoon.

They said people did not understand how the election was supposed to work, but they were sick of the constant TV ads about voter registration that interrupted Ramadan entertainment. People were not convinced the election would be allowed to happen, nor that it would change much in Iraq if it did. Most people did not want an exile as the next leader, not someone who was taking it easy—especially in London—while they had been suffering under Saddam. This comment seemed to be directed at the centrist interim prime minister we had selected, Ayad Allawi, who'd spent more than thirty years in England.

I pressed on this: "Hold it, isn't it a bit heroic that Allawi survived an ax attack?"

This got a good laugh. "No," one of them said. "Everybody's had a brush with death. He's not special." And, he added, repeating a conspiracy rumor I'd first heard back in August: "It was probably a fake attack anyway. He lived."

I pointed out that almost everyone in Iraqi politics had been an exile at one time or another—if not in Europe, then in Iran or Turkey or an Arab state. "Ruling out exiles leaves just about no one but Sadr. Somebody has to win."

Less laughter, then: "That's why nobody cares."

What did people care about? Their daily needs and not getting blown up in the next traffic jam. Traffic jams were terrifying because they made great targets for suicide bombers.

Speaking of traffic, the translators said people were alienated by how Americans drove around the city. The Americans seemed to have no regard for personal property, as they would destroy cars parked on the street rather than driving more carefully and safely. The Iraqi police, they said, were worse: driving around with mirrored sunglasses, shooting into the air all the time, and acting like the "idiot little brothers of the Americans."

Americans were also accused of chopping down trees—so many that "now it looks like a desert here." I was not sure whether that was meant as a joke.

This gave me a lot to think about on the walk back to the compound and a lot to write up for the next day.

My work was cut a bit short because the two-star decided to transform our Thursday night movie into a form of officer professional development. Instead being entertained by *The Best of Chris Farley*, we would all watch *The Battle of Algiers* and attend a discussion session led by one of the other officers.

This was a powerful movie. It was filmed as if a documentary, despite having been created after the events portrayed, after knowing the French would lose Algeria despite winning all the tactical engagements. Every French action, no matter how effective or justifiable or immoral, created more opposition. In the end, the Algerians would always be there, and the French paratroopers would go home.

The same was true of us, trying to plan coalition action toward a strategic goal. The Iraqis would always be here, and someday we would go home. Were we undermining our strategy with our every seemingly needed action? Was this how it had felt to be on a base in Algiers, in an unsafe refuge amid the even less safe Red Zone outside the blast walls?

Fri 5 Nov: Talked to Dave Sacko about replacing me—not clear if CENTCOM will let that happen. He wanted to know about safety, what there is to do after work, how much chance he'd have to write.

Dave was a civilian, which I worried would complicate things a bit. By now, Central Command had gotten wise to the drug deals that had gotten us to town—we called ourselves the Doctors Without Orders; it was better than the two-star's Brainiacs label—so any future arrivals would need deployment orders. Still, if Gunner could be here, why not Dave?

I spent plenty of time writing here, but not for my own purposes other than my journal. Dave and I had begun working on a new book over the summer, in which we would be arguing that once a single country became as relatively powerful as the United States had, it would make more sense for other countries to join with it than to actively oppose or balance against it. This state of affairs could last as long as the unipolar power didn't overreach and do really stupid things that diminished its own power.

The primary constraint against doing stupid things in international politics was the prudent fear that others would take advantage of your failures. Fearless belief that we could remake the world might lead us to drain national power and create new enemies. Then, before we knew it, our advantage would be gone—not because anyone "balanced" American power but because we would have pissed it all away.

My writing projects here were more practical. Today, for example, I wrote a short paper exploring the idea of setting up a truth commission like the ones in post-Apartheid South Africa and in Latin American countries after they returned to democracy. Such commissions were useful when the crimes of a prior government were so widespread that judicial punishment was unrealistic, yet those crimes were also so severe that amnesty was rejected by the victims.

The typical deal offered by such commissions was this: Perpetrators, at least up to a certain level of authority or certain degree of atrocity, would confess their deeds and reveal what had happened to those who had disappeared. In exchange, they would receive a minimal, often probationary, punishment.

If implemented in Iraq, this could be a step toward bringing some former Ba'athists back into public life, thereby increasing the chance they and their families would accept the new regime. I pointed out, however, that as a rule such commissions were created in peacetime—either after a democratic restoration or as part of a ceasefire—not while war was ongoing and new crimes were being committed, some of them by the new government.

They also required a population willing to forego punishment. Saddam's horrors far outstripped those of most countries with truth commissions. In any case, whatever its merits for trying to reconcile the Sunni Arabs to the new order in Iraq, the coalition could not conjure a truth commission on its own. It would have to be created by the next Iraqi government.

I was also working on a series of letters to be sent by the four-star to his subordinate commanders regarding our strategy toward engaging the Sunni Arabs. We cleverly called this the Sunni Engagement Strategy (SES). Its bottom line was that a legitimate election was the campaign's key decisive point. We could not drive a wedge between our enemy and the rest of the population until after the election. Sunni Arab buy-in would set conditions for gains across all lines of operation. This would set the stage for successful completion of the MNF-I mission.

> Sun 7 Nov: While it's been quiet here, other than the jets flying over on their way to Fallujah, there was a SVBIED [suicide vehicle-borne improvised explosive device] at a checkpoint around dinner yesterday, and something hit near the Tigris as I was heading back after PT.

Deputy Secretary of State Richard Armitage was a legend of sorts among the military, so he drew a crowd when he dropped by the Palace on the apparent eve of Fallujah. He had done some interesting, heroic, clandestine, and perhaps illicit stuff in Vietnam; now he was regarded as a moderate within the context of the Bush administration. He offered little insight. Most of his talk involved bragging about his physical strength, how many push-ups he could do, and how few fingers he had to have touching the ground while he did them.

Mon 8 Nov: And the battle has begun in Fallujah.

I did not often visit the battlefield update and assessment theater located below our offices, but I did so today to watch the operation unfold. Maps, telemetry, video, audio: Those details meant very little to me because strategy is completely different from tactics. Especially in this case.

Tactically, it was already clear the operation would be a success. To no one's surprise, it looked like we would be able to take over the town, kill all the bad guys we could find, and wreak righteous revenge on people who themselves had nothing to do with the four contractors who had been killed and mutilated in March. Hoo-ah!

Yet even on the first day, it was clear the operation was worse than pointless. Because we had delayed the move for weeks, in service of the strategic imperative to make sure Bush would be reelected, the enemy leadership and many of its best fighters had left town. Those left behind in Fallujah were civilians (about to become internally displaced refugees) and dead-enders bent on becoming martyrs for their cause and taking a lot of us with them.

In the meantime, the enemy took advantage of our focus on this small city by launching offensive operations of their own. Right here in Baghdad, today they stormed and ransacked several police stations, running off with weapons, gear, and uniforms they could use to infiltrate the Iraqi security forces. There were also troubling reports of organized violence in Mosul. Whatever operational security was being gained in Fallujah was being offset by losses elsewhere in Iraq.

The bigger problem was the strategic damage, which unfortunately I was recognizing far too late. I'd spent about a week on that final piece of the elections analysis, assigned to me back on Halloween, and it was becoming clear a national unity government similar to the current Interim Government would be likely to govern in a way far more favorable to our goals than would a partnership between the Kurds and the religious and radical Shia Arab parties (a Shia-only government would have too many internal differences to form even if the numbers allowed it).

A Kurd–religious Shia partnership would be likely to integrate militias like the peshmerga and the Badr Corps and even the Mahdi Army into the security forces, against the wishes of moderates and against the best lessons learned from past demobilization efforts. Because they lived where most of the oil was, the Kurds and Shia Arabs would be likely to let local areas retain more oil revenue rather than share it on a national basis with Sunni Arab areas. They would be unlikely to create some sort of province-based upper house of the legislature that would give Sunni Arabs more say in governance. Finally, they would be less likely to favor continued coalition presence and more likely to have a government deeply informed by Islamic principles that might not be compatible with our democratic goals. All of this could end up in the new Iraqi constitution.

This outcome was not inevitable. Such a government could keep an eye on the deeper future and offer the Sunni Arabs prizes they could not demand, such as federalism, a senate, or limited amnesty. But it would take strong engagement by the United States to try to shape such a compromise constitution. Given the continued attitude in the Embassy that it was not their job to worry about the future, there was no guarantee such active diplomacy would develop; if it did, it was not certain to succeed.

Thus, it would better for our long-term goals if a national unity government were formed after the election. This would become more likely if the Sunni Arabs participated in the election and if the current moderate-led government looked strong, deserving of reelection by the Iraqi people.

The attack on Fallujah, contradicting the Sunni Engagement Strategy that was to be implemented soon, was making the better outcome less likely.

> Tue 9 Nov: There was some kind of alert tonight—stay in your trailers & take cover—and two pretty loud incoming rounds about 0100 last night.

As if I could take cover in my trailer, which was still unguarded by sandbags.

Those of us living in the Palms had learned of a possible solution to the force protection problem. There was a stash of bags and a pile of sand; all that was needed was labor to put the sand into the bags and pile them up. And permission to use that labor.

Colonel Barlow, the USAFA officer who'd taken me on the Green Zone tour way back in August, had become the "mayor" of the compound. General Casey had been so impressed with his work that he had made him commander of the Joint Area Support Group. Colonel Barlow was responsible for all support systems in the Green Zone, including security at the gates. Because we were not allowed to use explosive-sniffing dogs at the gates (they would offend Islamic sensibilities), officers had been tapped to act as backup for the security forces in case something went wrong. Mike Lewis and I took a turn getting trained in how to yell "stop" in Arabic. We were so relieved when our day at the gate was canceled because there was an increased level of perceived threat and no one was allowed in.

Neal and I figured if officers could act as blast absorbers at the gates, then we could fill sandbags and protect ourselves. We visited Colonel Barlow and offered—begged—to do the work. It wouldn't be so bad. The fall weather had moderated into being tolerable. It rained from time to time, and flowers were blooming in the patches of dirt around the Palace.

No, he told us, that work would be considered too undignified for officers to perform. Also, it would create inequities if we didn't also provide sandbags for the foreign service officers, who could not be allowed to do manual labor. We'd have to wait until local workers could be hired to do the work.

I suspected the real problem was that Halliburton subsidiary KBR, or a company like it, had a contract for procuring the sandbags. If we did the work, it might cut into their profits from the war.

As if the nightly shelling wasn't stressful enough, I was feeling a lot of responsibility about the outcome of my work. The Vortex had confirmed that my assessments of the election, its results, and its aftermath would be the guidance for the 1 December strategy brief to the four-star. Then they would feed into the rest of our work. I was becoming more and more terrified as I realized I had no real backstop, no one here who could challenge my analyses. What if people listened to me and I was wrong?

The Colonel seemed to share this concern. He expressed frustration about the implications of my work, though he didn't have any alternative to turn to. He would look for flaws or weaknesses, and I would parry them by doubling down on my position. For example, today he dropped by my desk and asked, "So, Tom, who's going to be the transitional prime minister?"

That level of detail was a bit beyond the scope of my project, but I looked him in the eye and said, "Ibrahim al-Jaafari of the Da'wa Party."

He scowled back at me and said, "You fucking better be right about all this, or we'll haul your ass back here so fast . . ."

Dude was right. I fucking *better* be right about all this.

Come back? People were saying I wouldn't be allowed to leave, but I needed to get home to my family. What would be the point of staying? Once my current work was done, all we could do was wait for the election (whenever that would be—the Electoral Commission still hadn't set a date). It would be a while after that before I were shown to be right or wrong. Surely, I would be able to get out of here.

After all, a month before I was scheduled to leave, I was not getting any major new projects. I was still working on the Sunni Engagement Strategy and on daily updates on political news or intelligence assessments, but my main new assignment was to transfer State Department cables from their classified system to ours for distribution. This kept me in another office a couple of hours every day, kept me a bit better informed about what State was doing and thinking, and left me feeling as isolated as I had in those first few weeks in Policy.

I also felt isolated by my new short-term project, which involved watching a movie over and over. The two-star tasked me with leading the discussion of the next installment of his professional development film series: *The Fog of War*, Errol Morris's documentary about Robert McNamara that had won an Oscar earlier this year. Gunner and I had both suggested this—he had used the movie in his classes at the Naval Postgraduate School, and I had learned of it through conversations with Laura.

During those conversations, I had also learned how she was collecting footage for her own film. I had imagined she was filming here in the Green Zone, watching Carlos Valenzuela and his United Nations team and the Iraqi Electoral Commission. Maybe she was going out with civil affairs on patrol to registration sites.

She was, but she had also met up with a Sunni Arab doctor, a member of the Iraqi Islamic Party who was standing for election. She was following him on the campaign trail and staying overnight with his family. Few people knew about this, as I suppose slipping in and out of the Green Zone wasn't part of whatever arrangement got her a trailer here in the first place.

I don't know that many other Westerners were making frequent trips into the city, protected only by whatever heft this Dr. Riyadh had in Adhamiyah. "Swimming with the sharks" is how she described it. That was why she'd found it so amusing in October when I insisted on walking her home from the bridge game out of concern for her safety within the Green Zone.

> Thu 11 Nov: Lots of explosions in the general area for Veterans Day, but nothing too close. This is the Shia "Night of Power," the last of the many days in Ramadan when it is extra good to kill infidels.

Veterans Day in Baghdad was different than back home. For the first time I felt like a veteran, like I was part of the day. Stateside, it was just a day off; at the Air Force Academy, not even that. They arranged the academic calendar to have classes on Veterans Day and get an extra day off at Thanksgiving.

Here it was also a day of work, without much formal recognition beyond the moment of silence at 1100. What transformed the day was the presence of the British officers among us. I doubted most Americans knew why Veterans Day is when it is. World War I does not have the cultural impact of other wars. One cannot teach political science without including history, but cadets thought Franz Ferdinand was a band and the Red Baron was Snoopy's nemesis or a frozen pizza. At most, they had a vague sense that the United States had rescued Europe from its problems.

By the time the Yanks arrived, the Germans were already near the breaking point, and the years of trench warfare were coming to an end. World War I for the US was exciting aerial dogfights and a steady advance across France. Americans were not murdered on the Somme, ground into the mud at Passchendaele, or exposed at Gallipoli. When it was over, rather than trying to deal with the aftermath, we went right back to our traditional isolationism, affected more by the flu pandemic than by the war.

Although we had no Germans, French, or Canadians with us—and the Dutch had managed to avoid World War I—the memory was rather different for the British and Australians. Their Great War lasted four years, not just one, during which millions of young men died in pointless assaults directed by arrogant leaders who had no strategy for victory beyond the brutal logic of attrition. Armistice at last at the eleventh hour of the eleventh day of the eleventh month was worth somber remembrance. They wore cloth poppies, the flowers that bloomed in Flanders Field, and shared them with us out of solidarity.

Remembrance Day was a time for stories of unit history. The British officer who had replaced Simon Tustin explained it was not an odd two-tone feather that he wore in his cap. No, it was the hackle of the Royal Fusiliers. Its members had celebrated their victory at St. Lucia in 1778 by taking the enemy's white plumes and dipping them in French blood.

The two-star arranged a lunch today for his air force officers with the three-star deputy commander of Central Command, who was here on a fact-finding visit. He was about to testify about the war to Congress, and he certainly needed to find some facts to replace what he believed to be true.

Our conversation centered on Iraqi politics and the upcoming elections. He kept asserting things about the election system, the people involved, and the timetable for the ensuing year that were so wrong I found myself feeling angry.

I did not like confronting people far senior to me. My habit, of which I was a bit ashamed, was to back down before authorities I didn't know well. I still found Colonel Vortex intimidating, though I had spent enough time working with him that I gave up during arguments more because I knew he was never going to listen to me rather than from any fear of having another cluster of F-bombs dropped on me.

But this guy couldn't talk or even think clearly about the war if he didn't know what was going on. In correcting his ignorance about the details, I went about as close to the edge of insubordination as one wants to go. Somehow, I found myself doing this without the usual queasiness I felt in such situations. He was wrong, I was right, and this mattered.

The three-star heard me out, then pitched what he said was the hot idea in Washington: postponing the elections, something people thought had worked well in Afghanistan. He said Interim Prime Minister Allawi was urging this. I told him I supposed he would: as things stood, Allawi would lose his position and be out of power. The best Allawi could hope for would be to serve on the three-member Presidency Council.

Setting Allawi's motives aside, I laid out why delaying the election would be a bad idea. Polling, however sketchy it might be, said Iraqis overwhelmingly opposed a delay, even in the Sunni Arab areas. A delay would break yet another promise to the Iraqis (especially to the Kurds and Shia Arabs we'd betrayed under W's dad). It would feed the cynicism I'd seen at the *Mosquito* meeting. More specific to our strategy, a delay would jeopardize Grand Ayatollah Sistani's support, prolong the period of preelection violence, and postpone the critical decisive point when the Iraqi people might start supporting their government more than the enemy. Finally, it wasn't up to us: The election date would be set by the Independent Electoral Commission of Iraq under its UN mandate.

This felt exhilarating. I didn't know this guy, he had a lot of power and authority, and I was too angry about how we were waging this war to give a fuck about any of that. I knew what I knew, and one of the things I knew was that having him pitch these stupid ideas to Congress would be very bad. As I did this, I realized my colleagues were backing me up with additional details and points I was omitting. They trusted me enough to follow me into the verbal battle. It felt a bit like leadership.

The two-star was smirking through most of this. He may have been happy to have one of his Brainiacs show up a senior officer, especially one from Tampa. If there was anything we all agreed on, it was that the ten-thousand-mile screwdriver micromanaging our actions from Central Command Headquarters added no value to the war.

If the two-star had minded, he would have had every chance to tell me the next evening, when I had dinner alone with him. I'd gone to the DFAC a bit late, and I ended up in line right behind him. I tried to ditch him at the salad bar, but he sought me out and let me know he'd saved me a seat. This was just awesome. Besides having authority over me, he had his own special brand of unpredictable scariness.

But the meal was OK. Civil. Some of the best mentoring I'd had in the air force, not that I had much to compare it to. We talked about what my air force future held, and his view confirmed what I already figured: After two tries at promotion to lieutenant colonel, it wasn't going to happen based on my deployment here. Some of the choices I'd made had left me with a career that was difficult to measure. Furthermore, my choice not to extend in Baghdad past the original four months demonstrated that my priorities were not what they needed to be. Maybe that decision was what my family needed, but as the old military saying went, "If we'd wanted you to have a family, we'd have issued you one."

The next day, I learned Dave Sacko had been vetoed as my replacement. With my luck, I would end up with an extended assignment without getting any credit for it because I'd shown my lack of dedication to the mission.

Not that it was easy to show dedication. During our dinner, the two-star had also said he would not permit me to visit Baghdad University to talk to some professors about political issues. The two-star told me this would be too dangerous. Maybe, he said, I could send some written questions to them or set up meetings with politicians at the Convention Center, where the Interim Government was meeting inside the Green Zone. He was not going to let me go out into the city.

When I told Colonel Vortex about this, he erupted in a stream of curses that was impressive even for him. This was a fucking war. People are supposed to take risks from time to time. Air force people are so fucking soft and don't know a damn thing about war anyway. And who the hell did the two-star think he was, anyway, deciding what the Colonel's people could do?

The Colonel seemed to appreciate my metamorphosis from sleeping in the Palace two weeks ago to now wanting to take an optional trip across the river.

My attitude surprised myself. It wasn't as if anything had gotten safer. The Fallujah operation was still going on, and violence had increased in Baghdad as a result. This was true throughout the country. The enemy had captured several police stations in Mosul over the last couple of days and taken over large swaths of the city against minimal resistance.

In part, I was motivated by realizing I had only left the Green Zone once since my arrival, on the trip out to al-Faw Palace with Colonel Storrie. Shit, I'd hardly left the immediate confines of the Palace. My tasks hadn't sent me outside, but was my only experience with the war outside the barricades going to be a single drive to Camp Victory with the Brits? Maybe I needed to manufacture an adventure!

And, to be honest, I was motivated by knowing this civilian woman was venturing out all the time. Laura had put the idea in my head in the first place when she mentioned that Baghdad U was in the area patrolled by the civil affairs unit she rode with from time to time. She found Karrada District safe enough. Competitiveness, pride, they lead you to do strange things.

In the meantime, I was hiding inside and working on a paper about voter registration problems. Every adult was automatically registered, a policy used by almost every democracy except the United States. There might be errors, however, so at the beginning of the month, forms had been sent to the food distribution warehouses in each province. Food agents would pick them up and distribute them to clients along with rations. Family members could correct mistakes at one of the 542 voter registration centers (VRCs) nationwide.

However, violence in Anbar—Fallujah, Ramadi, and the rest of the Upper Euphrates Valley—was so severe that no forms had been sent there, nor had any VRCs been opened. In Nineveh (Mosul), things had progressed smoothly until the attack on Fallujah, at which point violence was threatened against election agents. Security problems, sometimes including direct threats, had prevented distribution of voter forms in northern Babil, western Baghdad, and Baqubah, where violence was now also on the increase after Fallujah.

The Electoral Commission hoped things would get better. Its backup plan was to allow same-day corrections on Election Day, when security could be at the highest level.

In other Sunni areas—including Tamim (Kirkuk), Salah ad-Din (Tikrit), and the rest of Diyala Province outside Baqubah—registration was proceeding without any real difficulty. The same was true in Kurd and Shia Arab areas, including eastern Baghdad. It seemed so smooth, in fact, that we worried election officials who didn't want to look bad were covering up problems.

Based on this information, we concluded that the Sunni Arabs as a whole were not rejecting the election, though violence was hindering their participation in some areas. The Electoral Commission thought the six-week registration window would be enough, and free and fair elections could still be held by the end of January.

> Sun 14 Nov: Finally got the ½ day off—first good night's sleep/rest in a long time—since I got up early on election day, it was a week & ½ before that. It would have been better sleep if it wasn't the first day of Eid. The prayer calls were very loud at dawn. I've never heard them inside before. And these at times angry chants were punctuated by an explosion nearby. There were several incoming rounds last night early, & also coming back from the gym yesterday. There have been a lot of firefights & bombs & protests in the city that we barely even hear about. Since Fallujah began, it's been even riskier in the Red Zone. Leaves you much more worried about the people . . . who are out there every day.

It had been three weeks since I'd had a chance to sleep in on a Friday, and for the first time I was awakened by the morning call to prayer. It was Eid al-Fitr, the day of feasting at the end of Ramadan. I rarely heard the prayers at any time of day, but today they were loud. Without knowing the words or the meaning they seemed both melodic and dangerous. To what extent were the mosques endorsing the explosions I could hear?

At a mosque in Fallujah, an American marine had shot an Iraqi. Video by an embedded NBC reporter showed a unit walking through the mosque with a few bodies lying on the floor. One of the Iraqis started moving and groaning, and a marine shouted, "He's fucking faking he's dead!" Another concurred, "Yeah, he's breathing," and the first shouted again, "He's faking he's fucking dead!" Then he shot the man in the head at close range. One of the other members of the unit observed, "Well, he's dead now."

We were all disgusted, including the Vortex, who had often reminded us that winning wars required killing people. This looked and sounded like an execution. On the other hand, how could the marine have been sure the enemy was not hiding a weapon or a bomb? After five days of battle, of being shot at and wounded himself, how much time could he spend assessing the threat? This was not, after all, some noncombatant prisoner. Still, even if this might be justifiable, why did he do it right in front of the cameraman?

Our anger turned also to the media. Like in other places, as enemy hideouts were cleared in Fallujah, we found caches of drugs and alcohol and pornography kept by these righteous Islamists. This got no press.

The execution was less shocking to Iraqis, according to the *Mosquito*. This was more or less what people thought we were doing all the time. The same had applied for Abu Ghraib. Iraqis had assumed all along that we were torturing people there—that's what Abu Ghraib was for, after all. It was Saddam's prison, now under new management. In fact, they assumed we manipulated events to our own choosing, which is part of the reason they were upset about power outages. If there was an insurgency, it was because we wanted it. Why, they did not know, but we could control the violence if we tried. The looting, the assassinations, the bombings: They all must fit some master plan of the Americans.

Or, some Iraqis claimed, a master plan of the Jews. During my *Mosquito* visit, one of the translators had relayed stories that the Israelis were funding Zarqawi and al-Qaeda in Iraq. Chaos and war in Iraq were good for the Jews, they thought. After Yassir Arafat died a few days earlier, the press reported he had a lot of cash hidden away in Switzerland. This led to rumors in Baghdad that he had been funded by Mossad. Because, apparently, the only way he could have had money was if it came from the Jews.

This shooting, the whole Fallujah operation, could not have been timed much worse. It was Eid, after all, so throughout Baghdad and the rest of the country, people were gathered with friends and family to share big dinners and watch television, the only diversion when it wasn't safe to go outside. The execution video gave credence to other stories being told by refugees. With fighting wrapping up in Fallujah, a flood of the dispossessed had poured into Baghdad, only a few dozen miles away. They told their big-city friends and family about atrocities they had witnessed. Some of their tales may have been exaggerated, but the NBC report bolstered it.

Fallujah had been followed by increased violence throughout northern Iraq. It had endangered the security of the elections process. It was turning Sunni Arab opinion toward the enemy rather than against them. And it was leaving allegedly moderate factions among the Sunni Arabs with little room to maneuver. None of this struck me as having been worth it.

> Mon 15 Nov: This is the third day in a row we got hit at about 8:20. Spent 45 minutes last night in a bunker—with a lot of others. Tonight I was in the palace, this one hit close. We figure they're walking them in night by night. Tomorrow could be bad.

We had a six-hour cultural awareness presentation today. It was a neoconservative pep talk, full of errors of fact and interpretation, but I didn't feel like intervening. It wasn't like with the CENTCOM three-star, when speaking up seemed necessary and I was surrounded by friends. Ignorance was widespread among people in headquarters. I was just as angry now, but nothing I could say would change anything.

The highlight of the event, so to speak, was a discussion of Islam by a Sunni man and a Shia woman. This went fine through a description of the Five Pillars of Islam, the key beliefs and practices required by the religion: There is one God and Muhammed is his prophet; prayer, five times daily; give alms to the poor; fast at particular times, especially during Ramadan; and the hajj, the pilgrimage to Mecca. These had always struck me as light demands on believers, at least compared to what Christians are expected to accept (the Trinity of a unitary God with three Persons; the virgin birth of Jesus, Jesus both fully divine and fully human; the Resurrection).

Then the presenters started talking about the principle of jihad. Jihad, the Shia argued, did not mean going to war against non-Islamic peoples. Its primary meaning was the internal jihad, the constant struggle within oneself to resist temptation and seek closer contact with Allah and His wishes. There was also an external jihad, which she said meant moving beyond oneself to build a society in accordance with Allah's will. The Sunni retorted, "Why are you lying to these people? I know that is not what you people really believe." Things escalated from there, soon switching to Arabic. The encounter perfectly fit the theme of the day: Arabs are crazy violent people. I wondered if it had been staged for that purpose. Surely two professional-looking people could talk rationally about differences in their beliefs?

Our lack of understanding of Iraqi culture, Arab culture, and Islam was pathetic. It would have been funny if it weren't so harmful to our efforts. We used Saddam's prison as our prison, we fenced off the patriotic memorials in the Green Zone, and we ruled from Saddam's official Republican Palace. We had imported a foreign ideology, just as he had imported secular socialism. We seemed hostile to religion, just as he was until his later years.

Another example of this was Camp Victory itself. The al-Faw Palace was built to commemorate the key Iraqi victory in its war with Iran, after which the Iranians retreated from the Basra area. Iraq had started the war in 1980 by invading Iran during the hostage crisis; for some reason, the Iraqi plaque at that palace omitted its own aggression and said the war started in 1984 when Iran invaded Iraq. With tables turned, Iraq faced losing access to the sea and its most productive oil fields. After a long struggle, it expelled "the Persians" and recovered its territory. Soon after making peace with Iran, Iraq invaded Kuwait and was defeated in the First Gulf War. Throughout the 1990s we bombed Iraq regularly to enforce UN sanctions. We tended to forget

Iraq had been at war for twenty-four years, with no end in sight. That had shaped Iraqi society.

The Battle of al-Faw was a patriotic event for Iraqis, perhaps their greatest military victory in centuries. After we invaded, we renamed the area around it Camp Victory. Our victory. This was yet another disrespectful or tone-deaf move on our part, a literally thoughtless error. I'm sure no one thought about the impact it might have on our image among Iraqis.

At least we hadn't needed to rename the Republican Palace.

I was ashamed of having casually used terms like the hajjimart for Ghazi's Market. Maybe I needed my own internal jihad to cleanse myself of this casual bigotry.

My recognition of how our actions and attitudes were undermining our aims spurred me into advocacy beyond my subordinate role as I worked on this Sunni Engagement Strategy. If we were going to encourage Sunni Arab participation in the upcoming elections, we needed to refrain from kinetic action (killing people and breaking things), except for direct attacks against active insurgents and helping defend the elections process against attack if asked.

I was also calling for us to find ways to work with Sunni Arab leaders. The Muslim Ulema Council, led by Harith al-Dari of the Umm al-Ma'arik mosque in western Baghdad, had suggested things we could do to make it easier for them to advocate that Sunni Arabs vote. These included allowing coalition detainees to vote while awaiting trial, expediting the detention process, withdrawing US forces from city centers, transferring the election from the Electoral Commission to the UN, and setting a March 2007 withdrawal date. These would not all be possible, but they could be a starting point for discussion and maybe some could be implemented.

Of course, it was not clear how serious the MUC was or whether they could deliver on promises of Sunni Arab participation in the elections. They had no equivalent to Grand Ayatollah Sistani, no one who could bring everyone along. We didn't know how to connect with the Sunni Arabs as a group.

Even their cluster of various leaders seemed to have no power. Despite their appeals for mercy, it was announced that Margaret

Hassan, the kidnapped director of Iraqi CARE, had of course been murdered.

To try to improve our understanding, the SPA had obtained its own cultural advisor, a Christian exile from suburban Detroit. He would from time to time get in touch with his extended family and his old neighborhood and report back on events from their highly representative perspective. I suppose it was useful to learn that the Christians he knew weren't thrilled about a future under a more or less Islamist government of whichever sect ended up on top. Christians had done OK under Saddam, as they posed no threat to him. While working on my current project, I asked him how we should engage with the Sunni Arabs. He stared at me for a while and then shouted, "Chop off their heads!"

He and I were going to spend some more time together. After four days of lobbying by the Vortex, the two-star reversed himself and approved my trip to Baghdad University. It would no longer be just my trip, however. We would turn this into an excursion for other interested parties, including our cultural advisor and someone from the State Department. This approval by the two-star was contingent on my being able to make arrangements with the university, working through a captain in civil affairs.

> Wed 17 Nov: Gotten very busy at work. Paper on engaging w/ coalition partners that want to withdraw—please wait until after the election. Also a big project on engaging the Sunni. The good guys. The key is figuring out the Iraqi Islamic Party. A lot depends on whether they can be trusted or not.

The withdrawal of our allies from the "coalition of the willing" had become a real problem. Over the course of the year, eleven countries had announced they would be removing their troops from Iraq, and the commitments of nine more were set to expire in early 2005. This had created the uncomfortable but accurate impression that the coalition was falling apart in the face of domestic opposition, lack of capability, and the deteriorating security situation.

My recommendation to the four-star was that he approach coalition partners and encourage them to at least delay announcing troop withdrawals until after the Iraqi election was held. That way withdrawal could look more like "mission accomplished" than "get the heck out of here." This suggested yet another reason to not delay the elections. Asking partners to hold off for another month or two was one thing. Asking them to stay quite a bit longer probably would have been too much.

On Thursday, my second possible replacement from the Air Force Academy was vetoed. She had received a medical waiver from the US side, but the waiver was denied on the Iraqi side. The two-star grabbed me in the corridor and asked me what the fuck the Academy was thinking in trying to get this person here. Did they not understand this was a deployment into a combat area that could not treat an acute medical incident without evacuation? I admitted I had no idea what the fuck they were thinking. Maybe they were listening to Bush and watching Fox News and figured the war was an office job. Both of us were rather pissed about how long the Academy was taking to identify the next officer. They were supposed to be here in less than a month. The two-star told me I would need to stay until a replacement arrived. How long might that be? I had been keeping these ups and downs from my family, but before long I would need to break the news that I was not coming home on time.

The two-star then proposed what seemed like the nuttiest idea of the whole deployment so far. He wanted to send me to Fort Bragg, North Carolina, at the end of the month to talk about the current situation to troops who were about to rotate to Iraq. I'd return to Baghdad for a week or so, then go home if I had a replacement.

This made no kind of sense to me, and it made less and less sense the more I complained about it to anyone who would listen. For starters, why would the full contingent of soldiers need this presentation? The officers, maybe the most senior NCOs, but this seemed like something that could be disseminated down the chain of command.

Second, why on earth should I be the one to do this? I had no credibility among soldiers as a barely combatant airman. Granted, I might know more about Iraqi politics at this moment than just about anyone else in the world, but that level of detail was not required.

And if somehow you could argue I would be the best presenter, you are going to ship me across the Atlantic and back to do this? I could present the same information after they got here, or someone could come up to Fort Bragg from Central Command in Tampa or down from the Pentagon who could do about as well, while I stayed here doing work no one else could do.

And if I had to go, how about sending me the rest of the way home early after I was done rather than going in and out of theater three times in two weeks? Or send me to North Carolina a week later, so it was on my way home?

Some of this could be explained once I calmed down a bit. The trip timing couldn't change because the unit would be deploying out of Fort Bragg before I was set to return to the States; once they got to Iraq, they would be busy moving out to their various operating bases and there would be no good time or place to get everyone together. They thought it was a good idea to go direct to the troops so the story didn't get muddled or watered down or de-emphasized as it went down the chain of command. The new unit would be getting here as the election season was heating up, and we wanted to make sure no one did anything stupid without knowing it. And no, no one from CENTCOM could do this. Hadn't I just shown up their three-star as clueless about the Iraqi political situation?

But some of my arguments registered with the two-star and, more importantly, with the Vortex. Fortunately, my push to visit the university in Karrada District inoculated me from too much suspicion that I was too scared to make extra trips down Route Irish—though I was. By now, the route to the airport was no longer open for regular vehicles. Travel was only in an armored rhino bus, which in theory could survive most attacks.

The most persuasive argument related to me as an individual. The Colonel agreed, somewhat paradoxically, that I was both too valuable to spare for a week or so and too ignorant about war to give a presentation to soldiers. They decided instead to send a marine lieutenant colonel instead.

With this bullet dodged, this evening I led two screenings of *The Fog of War.* My job was to introduce the film and lead an open discussion afterward. It would be a bit like teaching.

The session after the first screening was a disaster. Laura the documentary filmmaker had found the idea that we were watching documentary films in Baghdad intriguing, so she decided to film and document our discussion. This was awkward in a whole lot of ways. We had to pause after the credits rolled so she could mic me up, which dissipated any initial reactions. Worse, though a few of us knew her, for the most part the reaction was: Why is this woman pointing a camera at us? Who is going to hear what we say? Are we cleared to talk with her around? Commentary thus was limited to trivial statements of finding it interesting. I had failed at the one thing I ought to be good at: leading a group discussion.

The second screening discussion was much better and more reflective because we had privacy—Laura had headed into town. It's such a brilliant film. McNamara's opening line grabs you: "Any military commander who is honest with himself, or with those he's speaking to, will admit that he has made mistakes in the application of military power. He's killed people unnecessarily—his own troops or other troops—through mistakes, through errors of judgment." From there, the film offers biography, history, and a series of lessons—many of which could apply to what we were doing now in Baghdad.

"Empathize with your enemy." Did we appreciate how the Iraqis, especially the Sunni Arabs, viewed us and our occupation and destruction of the social order they had been living in? If we could not understand their goals and feelings, then how could we hope to establish a lasting peace? Fallujah was only the latest example of taking military action without concern for the psychic consequence.

"Never say never." We were so stubborn about "not negotiating with terrorists," so stubborn about "staying until the job is done," that we were not willing to explore options for peace. Could engagement with the Sunni Arabs lead to a settlement? We ruled it out. Only unconditional surrender, or death, were proposed to our enemy. We could think about the effects of a withdrawal plan at our level, or in a Smart Guys meeting, but not where it mattered. Yet at some point the war must end, and we may not always be in as strong a position to sculpt that end as we were now.

"Get the data." "Rationality will not save us." "Belief and seeing are often both wrong." McNamara's lessons were contradictory! Without data, without real information, there was no hope for crafting a successful strategy. Yet not everything could be measured with data; not all questions had a statistical, quantifiable, rational answer.

"Be prepared to reexamine your reasoning." As my time grew short, I wondered how much I was stubbornly refusing to reconsider arguments I'd been making. Was I captured by the process, unable to step away from my conclusions?

> Sat 20 Nov: Sitting in the conf rm yesterday assigning colors to provinces post election by scenario, this whole quantified project seems ludicrous. . . . We don't understand Iraqis, we don't understand the Sunnis, we make assumptions just as we have all along. [The two-star's] "brainiacs" are just McNamara's "whiz kids" forty years later.

The contrast between the Sunni Engagement Strategy and our actual operations was infuriating me. We had established that the decisive point in the campaign was the upcoming Iraqi election. Only after it was held and its results were accepted as legitimate could we hope popular loyalties would adhere to the Iraqi government more than to the Islamic insurgency or the Ba'athist resistance. Furthermore, we had concluded it would be best if Sunni Arabs voted in the ensuing election. We had issued policy letters discouraging kinetic operations in city centers, urging respect for important mosques, and for co-opting opposition clerics rather than confronting them.

Nevertheless, early yesterday afternoon, just after the conclusion of Friday prayers, US and Iraqi forces raided the Abu Hanifa mosque in Adhamiyah, north of downtown Baghdad. We had in the past tried to intimidate people there with low-altitude flyovers. Today, we killed three people and arrested the imam and forty others. We found a few small arms at the mosque, as one would in any building in Baghdad.

This was stupid.

The mosque was the burial site of Abu Hanifa, one of the primary early scholars of Islam. It was perhaps the most important religious site for Sunni Arabs in Baghdad. It was also in the heart of a relatively professional, middle-class neighborhood. Its residents had been required to overtly support Saddam and thus they had been hit hard by de-Ba'athification, but they were not fans of Salafi jihad. Now, however, they were outraged.

The Abu Hanifa raid came right after the arrest of a member of the Iraqi Islamic Party—the second vice president of the National Council, in fact. Together with Fallujah, this seriously undermined the Sunni Engagement Strategy. It was such a colossal fuckup that Prime Minister Allawi started claiming he had nothing to do with it, that American forces had worn Iraqi uniforms to cover up what he said was entirely our operation.

Meanwhile, there I was, sitting in the Palace, trying to figure out what we knew about a list of 270 Sunni leaders. Did they support or oppose the occupation? Would they be persuadable? This was a fucking useless exercise. We knew nothing. Even when we knew better, our actions were undermining our goals. This had to stop.

Sun 21 Nov: We are about to lose the fucking war.

I wrote a lot more, then laid awake for a long time repeating, "Oh fuck oh fuck oh fuck."

Chapter 7

Action

There I was: lying awake within the wafer-thin walls of my trailer on a Sunday night trying to develop a more useful response to what I'd learned today than a stream of obscenities.

The day had started out like most. After breakfast I went to the Vortex's Morning Prayers stand-up meeting, then spent the rest of the morning at the Embassy transferring State Department cables to our system. The big news in the afternoon was that the Electoral Commission had scheduled the election for 30 January 2005, one day short of the UN- and Sistani-endorsed deadline. Meanwhile, northern Baghdad was still enraged about the Abu Hanifa raid two days ago, and our partners in the Iraqi government were still denying they had been involved in the operation.

Then I found out what we were planning to do next.

We were going to raid the other top Sunni mosque in Baghdad, Umm al-Ma'arik (Mother of All Battles), and arrest Harith al-Dari, the spokesman for the Muslim Ulema Council.

This was an absurd idea. The MUC, the political front for the Sunni Arabs who were fighting us, was our only channel of communication with that enemy. Did we really fucking think that with Dari gone there would be no more calls to violence? Hell, Dari was almost a moderate: he opposed vehicle-borne improvised explosive devices

(VBIEDs) because they caused too many civilian casualties. Were we going to arrest all their imams? That wasn't possible, because any Sunni can step up and lead prayers.

Besides having no operational purpose, this would eviscerate our Sunni Engagement Strategy. So far, the MUC had not called for a boycott of the election. After this, they certainly would, and it would be difficult for the Iraqi Islamic Party to not follow along. This would reduce Sunni Arab participation in the election, shrink their representation in the ensuing government, and mean their interests would not have to be considered when the new constitution was written. Any hope the Sunni Arabs would eventually view the Iraqi government as legitimate would hinge on concessions from the Shia Arabs and Kurds who would comprise the new government.

It got worse.

We were also going to arrest two of Moqtada al-Sadr's top lieutenants.

As with Dari, these were not good guys. But this would break the October ceasefire with Sadr and renew the war with his Mahdi Army. Sadr had kept his side of the bargain for the most part. Northeastern Baghdad had become safe enough for us to begin a lot of public works projects. Even if Sadr were inclined toward a restrained response, the unemployed and angry young men who followed him might not be inclined to listen.

Whatever these two guys were personally involved in, arresting them now seemed gratuitous. The only justification would be some sort of twisted evenhandedness: engage with the Sunni Arabs by showing them we're not just against them, we're against the Shia Arabs as well. We're against all of you!

And that is what would result: renewed war against all of Iraq, north, south, center.

Supposedly, Interim Prime Minister Allawi was backing these plans while denouncing the Abu Hanifa raid. The only motive I could ascribe to him (if this were true) was that provoking violence would be a way to get the election postponed, which would keep him in power. I could not think what his endgame was, beyond clinging to power a bit longer.

This was a massive failure of strategic patience by our military. At the highest levels, we were saying, "Wait for the election, don't stir anything up, be patient." Armies aren't good at patience. Dari is a problem, take him out. Bad guys are around Abu Hanifa, go get them. Sadr's no good, it's time we did something.

What was the point of what I was doing, these strategic assessments and PowerPoints and letters for the Commander's signature, if we were going to take actions in direct contradiction to them?

If we want to be stupid, we can be stupid without my help. Send me home, don't bother with a replacement, fight the fucking war the way you want, leave me out of it.

No, that wasn't an option. Nor was staying quiet as I had with Fallujah and so much else.

I had to take action to try to stop this from happening.

I started within my chain of command. As I expected, Colonel Vortex dismissed my concerns. I had not been asked for my opinion on these raids, so I had no business offering it. Whatever he might think of my sudden desire to go into the city, I was still one of those possibly pacifist professor types. My concern was high-level strategy, not operations. Even, apparently, if those operations ran counter to the strategy signed off on by the Commander.

I had already decided not to let that stop me. The two-star had said I could jump the chain and go directly to him if the Colonel was impeding things. I told the Exec I wanted to talk to the two-star. Before leaving the SPA offices, I described the situation to Colonel Storrie, knowing he would run it up his own Brit chain of command.

Next, I sought other ways to bring attention to this problem. I met with one of the senior foreign service officers in the Political section of the Embassy, in the same dim rooms where in late September I had been shocked to learn the State Department had no interest in thinking about the future. He was polite, he listened, he agreed this all sounded very serious, and he said there was nothing State could do about this. It was up to the Iraqis, or maybe the military, to decide about opening new fronts in this war.

The subtext: None of this was their idea. When Secretary of State Colin Powell said if we break Iraq, we own it, he didn't mean his own department. State was going to watch, talk to each other, and write cables for me to download and transfer to our system. The FSO said he would pass the concerns up his chain within the Embassy, but I doubted it would happen quickly enough to make a difference.

A more hopeful route was through Matt, senior advisor to the Interior Ministry. A joint American–Iraqi security operation would involve him. Furthermore, he was smart, effective, and connected. Allegedly connected. The link to Condi Rice was only a rumor, though it was part of his mystique.

Matt's desk was in a more secure area on the far south end of the second floor, beyond where I had to turn around when I would walk the interior perimeter to clear my head. But he was nowhere to be found. I couldn't call him, I couldn't email him, I had no way of reaching him except by leaving a note and hoping he would find a way to get back to me. Our disarticulated communications systems were crushing my hopes.

After dinner, I finally ran into the two-star in the SPA corridor. His opening words were not what I had hoped for: "I hear you're talking about these raids. Tom, this is very sensitive. You shouldn't be talking about it."

Someone, probably the Vortex, had passed word to him along with a conclusion contrary to my views. Fuck it. I looked him in the eye and said, "Yes, General, it's sensitive. It's also very important. We're all cleared for it, we all have a need to know, and I think we can talk about it all we want."

The two-star stared at me, looking shocked. Nobody ever talked back to him. Not since Colonel Haith had back in August, and no one had seen him since.

Then he backed down. Physically, as well as verbally. He wasn't a very big man in the first place (fighter pilots can't fit in the cockpit if they are large), but his bluster inflated him. The gas seemed to bleed off, and the two-star seemed less imposing than usual. He mumbled something about how this was not our area; this was for the MNC-I, the operational arm of the military. I told him I understood—that's why I was trying to find someone who could take action.

I turned my back to him and walked away.

> Tue 23 Nov: Heard the jets flying over a little before dawn, and bombs being dropped—sounded like to the NW. I guess in a few minutes I'll know if we took out al-Dari, and lost the war.

I had the next morning off, so I tried to sleep in. An aerial attack woke me up and I worried. But wouldn't the raid on the mosque to get Dari be land based? I went back to sleep.

I was reawakened at 0800 by the sound of digging around my trailer. At last, I was getting sandbags! Well, for the moment I was getting a huge pile of sand. The bags were being carted first to the far end of the Palms.

The weather was cool and crisp, with lows in the thirties. I could see my breath as I hurried to the Palace to see if anything had happened. No, not yet. There was still time. I tried to focus.

Near dinnertime, I finally met with Matt. We sat outside his offices in the corridor beyond the back stairs to the DFAC. As hundreds of people filed past to eat, we addressed this sensitive matter people shouldn't be openly talking about.

I relayed to him how this raid contradicted the Commander's guidance and what I thought were the likely consequences. I described my failure to get anywhere with this in either the military chain of command or the State Department. I told Matt his clout was the only thing that could stop it.

Matt said he agreed it would be best if this didn't happen, but he wasn't sure what could be done. The raids had been ordered, and they were going to happen. This, he said, was outside his influence as senior advisor anyway: Prime Minister Allawi had made it clear that he, not Interior Minister Nadiq, would have the final say on the raids.

The only good news Matt offered was that Allawi had ordered a formal investigation of the Abu Hanifa raid while still denying Iraqi involvement. Maybe the prime minister would realize that if these new raids happened, he would have no good options. If he tried to blame them on the Americans again, he would look ineffective at protecting Iraq's sovereign interests. If he took credit, he would own a backlash similar to what he was now trying to hide from and would undermine his current denials of responsibility.

Matt said he'd see what he could do, but he wasn't optimistic. It was more than anyone else had offered me. I could do nothing but wait.

> Wed 24 Nov: COL Storrie . . . said he now understood why I was now more gloomy about our prospects—I had just put the pieces together more quickly than everyone else. It just helps to have more information on what's happening than anyone else. In the kingdom of the blind, the man with a seeing-eye dog is King.

The next day brought no news. No raid yet, nothing canceled, nothing new planned.

The release of the First Cavalry Division's latest poll of Baghdad gave me something to do besides wait: analyze it for distribution within the SPA, and beyond as leadership might see fit.

Although the poll had questionable validity, I could compare it to the one from 16 September. However legitimate either was in isolation, they should suffer from the same weaknesses. The change from that one to this—taken on 8 November, so before Fallujah, before Abu Hanifa, but after the ceasefire with the Mahdi Army—might give me some insight into changes in Sunni and Shia Arab thought.

Shia and Sunni Baghdadis alike said they supported democracy and voting, but the gap between them had grown. Shia intention to vote had held steady at 91 percent, but Sunni intention had plummeted from 86 percent to 71 percent. The Shia liked Prime Minister Allawi more than before, but the Sunni did not. Furthermore, both groups had shifted toward radical politicians and away from moderates, especially from the liberal Adnan Pachachi.

As bad as this seemed, the crosstabs masked a deeper problem. This poll did not distinguish Kurd from Arab. Although no one really knew, we believed Baghdad's population mirrored the nation as a whole: about half Shia and half Sunni (and a few Christians), with the Sunni population half Kurd and half Arab. National polls had found Kurd views were similar to Shia Arab views on top-line issues like the elections and security. I had no reason to think this would have changed, so I deduced both Shia Arabs and (mostly Sunni) Kurds would vote at a 91 percent rate. This meant to get to the aggregate

Sunni finding, participation among the Sunni Arabs would have to be 51 percent.

A 40-point gap. None of our—of my—election projections imagined a gap so big.

Sunni Arab turnout would barely be half that of other groups, before Fallujah, before Abu Hanifa, before Umm al-Ma'arik (hope not), and before their leaders called for a boycott.

A 40-point gap in Baghdad, where the security presence was much stronger than out in the Sunni Triangle, out in Anbar and Nineveh and Salah ad-Din.

How the fuck would we get a legitimate Iraqi government if the Sunni Arabs didn't vote?

My analysis included some unsolicited advice on finding ways to improve Sunni Arab opinion. If we were able to co-opt Sadr into the political process, I wondered, why not give Sunni leaders the same courtesy? Furthermore, we must limit kinetic action against Sunni Arabs to true necessity, balancing any military gain against further damage to voter participation. In other words (while I didn't say so directly): Don't Fucking Raid Umm al-Ma'arik and Arrest Dari. That said, arresting Sadr's people might have an upside: another way to close the 40-point turnout gap would be to reduce Shia Arab participation in the elections.

After reading this, Colonel Storrie grabbed me and said he now understood why I was so pessimistic. It had taken some hard numbers to start convincing people.

> Thu 25 Nov: Thanksgiving actually was nice. . . . It marred the day a bit to have a rocket hit the compound just before the group photo, killing 4 gurkhas and injuring 17.

Much to be thankful for today. The Umm al-Ma'arik raid had not happened, no one had been arrested, and both the Brits and the State Department (thank you, I should have had more faith) were making noise about what a colossal fuckup the Abu Hanifa raid was.

Maybe I could be hopeful as well as thankful.

Close-up of the base of the sabers on the Parade Grounds

I was thankful for a slow, relaxing day. I reviewed the intelligence updates, received no new tasks at Morning Prayers, and transferred some State Department cables.

I was thankful the DFAC served a fine midday dinner to share with my colleagues.

I was thankful the SPA took a field trip in midafternoon. The first stop was the Parade Grounds, the long avenue gated by arms rising out of piles of captured Persian helmets, holding sabers as an archway. Rumor had it someone had crawled into those helmets to pose for a picture and gotten stuck so tightly a rescue was needed.

As we disembarked from our vehicles, ordnance hit the Palace area. The pillar of smoke was still visible behind our group picture. Only after we returned would we learn it had killed some of the Nepalese Gurkhas who manned the checkpoints.

The two-star gave us a pep talk as we stared into the setting sun. The usual kind of thing: service, duty, and how important our work

The author at the Parade Grounds on Thanksgiving

was. Then he started name-checking people. He pointed out Colonel Storrie as "the Gloomy Brit," and then me: "There's Tom, his silent sidekick."

I took offense. I was pretty damn vocal about my gloominess. I was nobody's sidekick.

This was gratuitous for a happy occasion, but it sent a clear message. Pessimism was not appreciated. Realism was not appreciated. I wondered how much I was losing effectiveness, slowly over time and maybe now all at once over the stink I'd raised the past few days. People did not want to hear what I was saying.

Should they want to hear what I was saying? I was confident, but I wasn't confident about my confidence. Dammit, now I sounded like Rumsfeld and his unknown unknowns!

Next, we went to the Iraqi Tomb of the Unknown Soldier, a bizarre collection of modernist monuments. It was a strange destination. Whatever solemnity it should evoke was absent because we understood none of the symbolism and these were our enemy. It was a great setting for photos with friends under the clear afternoon sky, but nothing more.

Our final stop was shopping at the al-Rasheed Hotel. A lot of people had decided to invest in rugs and have them shipped back home, as if they had any idea of value or quality, other than what they were told by the salespeople. This seemed as wise as a prior mania for currency speculation. I limited myself to small trinkets, like a tiny rug to use as a mouse pad.

A final moment of gratitude: We were ordered not to work this evening. I went to my trailer and worked on other research projects. I may not yet have a replacement named, I may not be sure when I'm going home, but the end must be near. Time to start reentry to my prior life by working on a book chapter called "NATO, the Balkan Crises, and European Security and Defense Policy." NATO, the EU: That's what I'm confident I know something about. Not Iraq.

> Fri 26 Nov: A fairly frustrating day, really. The work is starting to pile up on me a bit—not getting much info on the Sunni, DIA analysis of the election is really bizarre.

At Morning Prayers, Colonel Vortex told me to evaluate a new election analysis from the Defense Intelligence Agency (DIA) and see what it meant for our strategy and plans.

Mostly it meant DIA didn't have a fucking clue about the electoral laws and Iraqi politics. Garbage in, garbage out, as they used to say when I worked with software. DIA's conclusions were wrong because the information they based them on was wrong. Their conclusions weren't very good even if you accepted the faulty assumptions. I told the Vortex to tell the two-star to tell the Commander no, there was nothing we should do differently. We should stick to our strategy of waiting for the election.

I spent so much of my time raising the "Bullshit!" flag on different ideas. Based on what the two-star had said yesterday at the Parade Grounds, I suspected my immediate chain of command was not thrilled. On the other hand, they kept giving the work to me rather than to someone more amenable.

The most irritating aspect of this, however, was that DIA had provided a different election analysis only a week before. That one had been based on a different set of erroneous assumptions and had reached the opposite conclusion from today's. This was a big ass-covering exercise. With all the details classified, no matter what happened, DIA could later claim to have predicted or warned about it while suppressing the analyses that predicted the opposite.

I was thus excited to sit down with someone sensible this evening. In the run-up to the invasion, Tom Warrick had orchestrated the Future of Iraq project within the State Department, the only real attempt by any American official to try to figure out ahead of time what we should do during and after the war. The project was a better attempt to systematically design a strategy or plan for success than anything the Defense Department had devised.

To my dismay, Tom was bearing bad news. He said a consensus was developing in Washington to delay the Iraqi elections. People believed doing so would enhance Sunni Arab turnout because security would be better in a few months.

What I'd hoped would be a happy chat turned into yet another round of flagging the bullshit (though Tom was careful, as a good diplomat, to not present his own views—he was the messenger, letting me know, strategist to strategist).

Although the Sunni Arabs might calm down from Fallujah and Abu Hanifa if we didn't take any more inflammatory actions, there was no reason to think security would soon be much better in general. Whatever the effect might be on the Sunni Arabs, this idea, much like the DIA analyses, waved away or ignored other critical facts. The election date had been set by the Independent Electoral Commission of Iraq, which was outside our control. A delay of more than a single day would violate the United Nations mandate.

If we ignored those facts and imagined the Sunni Arabs were happier, what would the Shia Arabs think? They, especially their more radical elements, would be unlikely to agree to a delay and might return to violence.

Finally, what was the endgame? What if violence increased instead? Would we delay the election indefinitely? There would no longer be any structure for that, no date at which we might hope to bend Iraqi support toward their elected government rather than the enemy.

Worse, Tom also said some people in Washington had become interested in "managing" the election so the moderates would win—people like Prime Minister Allawi and President Yawr. He said they were worried the Da'wa Party was too Islamist, so they shouldn't be allowed to have much influence after the election.

How Iraq could form a government after the election without including the most moderate and most popular of the religious Shia Arab parties was beyond me. Who among that group was better? Did we prefer the Supreme Council for the Islamic Revolution in Iraq, which was funded and armed by Iran? Did we prefer Sadr's Mahdi Army? Were we going back to Chalabi's Iraqi National Council, despite him being a liar who had cast his lot with Iran?

If we wanted a more moderate national unity government after the election, we needed to manipulate two variables in my election model. The first was turnout. We needed to make sure the Sunni Arabs voted in numbers similar to everyone else so they would have fair representation on the committee that would write the new constitution. The second was support for the current moderate leaders. Delaying the election might improve Sunni Arab turnout, but it would probably make the current government even less popular.

It was too late to massage the political situation in Allawi's favor. That had been a point in favor of the withdrawal announcement scenario two months ago: It would help him look strong and patriotic. Instead, our actions had enraged the population and left Allawi complicit.

No, at this point the only way we could manage the election results would be to rig the paper ballot boxes, and surely the Bush administration would never do such a thing. We'd most likely get caught and thus sabotage the point of the whole invasion and occupation. Allegedly, after all, we were fighting to allow the Iraqi people to select a government of their own choice.

> Sat 27 Nov: Went to the Memorial for Jim Mollen, murdered a few days ago as he was taking his soft car alone to the ministry. He had a week left here.

We held another memorial service today, this time for Jim Mollen, the foreign service officer who had been the senior advisor to the Education Ministry. We'd worked together back in August on the militias project. He had been making one last trip into the city.

I would have been on today's rhino bus to the airport if I had not been replaced on the trip to Fort Bragg. The convoy was hit by a VBIED. The armor worked; no one was seriously hurt, but the bus was disabled. Future travel to the airport would be by helicopter.

We in the Green Zone were cut off by land from the rest of the world.

Things were getting dangerous out there.

Nevertheless, I was still trying to set up a trip to Karrada District with civil affairs.

I spent most of the day reacting to last night's meeting at Adnan Pachachi's house. Several unpopular political leaders were calling for a six-month delay in the elections—longer than what Tom had been discussing with me at the same time. Prime Minister Allawi attended but said he did so "only to observe." Both President Yawr and Deputy Prime Minister Barhim Saleh (a Kurd) said such changes would be illegal, and the Electoral Commission rejected them.

The IECI also rejected holding several days of voting or staggering voting by province. I agreed these were bad ideas. Violence on early days would discourage voting on later days. Let's get this done and over with already!

> Wed 1 Dec: Been sick for days now.

Too sick to work, too sick to leave the trailer much. Worse than the usual feeling like crap. It was hard to stay well in Iraq, but this was the worst I'd felt since the day the rockets hit the dome back in August. Decongestants made one sleepy, which was the last thing we needed given how tired we always were; extra nasty coffee to counteract them made one sick in another way. I ate spoonfuls of Tabasco to open my head. That gave me instant wicked hiccups.

In between naps, I read from my roommate Hank's excellent collection of books. He had brought over Al Franken's *Rush Limbaugh Is a Big Fat Liar* and *Lies and the Lying Liars Who Tell Them*. I also reflected on *April 1865: The Month That Saved America*, about the last days of the Civil War. Of particular interest to me was the debate among Lee and his generals about surrendering versus continuing a guerrilla war, a debate settled on the side of surrender. A different choice had been made here in Iraq: The Ba'athists had gone underground and kept fighting, adopting Salafi Islamism as needed to find compatriots.

Lee was able to make this choice in part because Lincoln and Grant allowed the Confederate enemy to keep its weapons and its leaders to remain in place. A similar dilemma had confronted Bremer right after the invasion, whether he'd drawn the parallel or not. Bremer could have offered terms similar to Appomattox, allowing Ba'ath Party members to remain influential and absorbing the old Iraqi army into the new one.

That might have tamped down the resistance we faced now, but what of democracy?

The price of peace in 1865 turned out to be the restoration of the old order after incomplete Reconstruction in 1876, the Klan, lynchings, segregation, and Jim Crow. Would the price of a different choice by Bremer have been repression of the Shia Arabs and Kurds under a new Sunni Arab autocrat?

Perhaps not. History never truly repeats. Perhaps the Shia Arabs and Kurds were too numerous to be put back down. Still, something to think about while feverish.

Being sick also gave me a chance to catch up on magazines sent from home. The news was weeks old by the time I got it, and I'd had little time to review it until now, but perhaps it would be good to see what's happening back in the States before I got there. A washed-up pop-punk band from the mid-1990s had a hit called "American Idiot"? Maybe there was hope after all.

Getting home was now a correct statement. The Academy had tapped Lieutenant Colonel Greg Rose as my replacement. As a Middle East specialist, he would have been the best choice to come here in the first place. He was due to arrive the day before I would leave, so the two-star had greenlighted my own preparations for the trip home—redeployment, it was called.

> Fri 3 Dec: I was so wiped out on Monday that I took two 3-hour naps and then slept 14 hours that night. Only really today did I feel at all back to normal.

It took almost a week for me to feel well enough to be working. I was still trying to wrap up the Sunni Engagement Strategy, despite my inability to figure out who we would talk to. One of the MUC's demands had been to allow detainees to vote, and I was advocating for that. It was their easiest demand to meet, and it wouldn't make a substantial difference in the results.

Another issue we struggled with was how to measure or evaluate the success of the election. Some metrics focused on turnout. Higher turnout would be better than lower, but how high would be good enough? First democratic elections usually have a high turnout, but they usually are conducted in peacetime. We thought 60 percent would be great and 40 percent would be terrible. Equally important would be the turnout difference among provinces. Ideally, no province would have a turnout more than 10 percent lower than the national; if any were 40 percent below the national, that would be a sign of problems.

We also looked at political violence surrounding the election. Given that hundreds of people were killed during each election in India and we had a hot war going on, we expected people to die. The enemy would try to destroy the election. Would a few hundred dead be OK? A thousand? We never settled on a number, deciding instead to hope 90 percent of the polling stations would be able to remain open nationwide, including at least 80 percent in each province. We also hoped there would be a sharp decline in violence after the election.

A third set of metrics looked at the distribution of seats. We assumed the Kurds would get their 20–25 percent, barring bad weather. In a good result, the Shia Arab percentage would not exceed 60 percent, while the Sunni Arab percentage would approach 20 percent. Regardless of how the next government would be formed, such results would at least approximate national demographics.

Fourth, we would consider the election successful if international statements were positive and if allegations of fraud were scattered nationwide rather than concentrated in certain areas. It would be even more successful if those allegations were disproven.

Finally, a successful election would have the ballots counted and results announced within a week, with the Transitional Government formed and ready to work on a constitution within a month—by the end of February.

These criteria were for internal consumption. In public, no matter what happened, we would declare the election successful.

> Sat 4 Dec: I think this wild idea about putting together a book on the elections was misguided and foolish from the start—I don't have the contacts & it's far too late to start to cultivate them now. Far better to write a longer version of this journal—all the crap we do every day.

I was scheduled to leave in eight days, after Greg got here. As my departure date got closer, I thought about what I was going to do with this experience, as an academic, as a citizen. What were my skills? What did I have that was unique? I could write! If Laura could make a movie about the election, why couldn't I write a book about it?

Well, for one thing, I couldn't write that book because unlike her I wasn't doing much with the election. She knew the people; I didn't. She'd been following it on the ground; I wasn't. Laura was rather insulted when I suggested she could help me build a network, by . . . yeah, by gifting me what she had built up over months. Yeah, that's what I was asking. Not a very good way to treat a friend.

If I wasn't going to be able to write about the election, maybe I could take my journal and write a book describing what it was like in the Green Zone during this time. That shouldn't take too long. Rather than having any deeper meaning, I could write about the ups and downs of being here.

I could write about today, for example: I finished the Sunni Engagement Strategy, so I was happy. Then the Vortex assigned me a bunch of what I wrote down in my journal as "stupid projects." I was depressed. I was being wrung out as much as possible before I go. But I finished all of them, and I was happy again. Maybe I needed to work on my own emotional stability—how to stay on an even keel or learn how to more quickly come back up after being down.

Tue 7 Dec: I finally escaped the [Green Zone] for a day.

There I was: walking around the back lot of a civil affairs compound, waiting for the unit's commander, Captain Khris Scarcliff, to get our convoy ready.

In five days I would be on my way out of Baghdad and Iraq. Five days, and I'd have survived my four months, assuming the chopper or the C-130 transport aircraft didn't get shot down. Instead of relaxing at the SPA with no new work to do, instead of having some last talks with friends and colleagues I'd probably never see again, I was taking a gratuitous trip into the city to meet some specialists on Iraqi politics and society from Baghdad University.

Khris's little base was on the west side of the Green Zone, near the north end of the 14th of July Bridge, which commemorated not Bastille Day but the very bloody coup that had ended the Iraqi monarchy in 1958. The base's main structure, which looked like it might have been a fire station before the war, had been converted into a combination garage, office, and sleeping area.

Civil affairs units patrolled sectors of the city with the goal of establishing friendly relations with the citizens by establishing a normal pattern of routine interaction. They functioned a bit like beat cops in a sense, or undisguised spies. They would get to know what was going on in a neighborhood and provide early warnings about something changing for the worse. They were like beat cops, except for being fully armored and driving through urban neighborhoods as if the citizens were their enemy.

Khris's base seemed more relaxed than other compounds I had visited. When not patrolling, he and his team took care of their weapons and vehicles and just lived. They were inside the Green Zone walls, so they didn't have to worry as much about security as soldiers at forward operating bases in the rest of the city did. That said, it wasn't any safer from indirect fire than we were back at the Palace. One of the troops told a story about everyone sitting out front one evening when a rocket came in low, hit the parking lot near the road, and skittered across the pavement toward them. A dud.

The gravel area behind the building was full of palm trees and old Iraqi vehicles. Up against one of the low walls were the daisy-chained rocket launchers that had been captured after the failed October attack. Allegedly, this was where the giant Saddam heads from the Palace had been taken. They were no longer here. I would have liked to have seen them.

As I walked around this area alone, waiting for the convoy to be ready, I wondered why the hell I was going through with this trip. It had made sense when I first proposed it in mid-November, when there would have been time for me to take whatever I was about to learn and work it into our strategy or at least our situational awareness.

This assumed, of course, that I was going to learn anything. What would Iraqi political science professors know about politics in Iraq? There had never been elections; there had never been campaigns. These people's opinions may be no better informed than my own.

By taking the trip now, however, I would have four working days, tops, to assimilate this. I could write up a trip report, but its integration would fall to someone else, probably Greg when he finally got here, and he wouldn't have the background to immediately understand it. It was far too late for the information to be useful. The election would be what it was going to be.

It's five days until I leave. This is when the retiring cop gets shot in the movie. I should be staying safe, not taking risks. This was arrogant, this was cocky, and it had become a pattern. Yesterday, there had been a midday warning on Giant Voice to take cover for indirect fire.

I grabbed some boxes to take to the post office to mail home because I figured the lines would be shorter during the alert.

Maybe I didn't want to go home.

As much as I wanted to get out of this place, away from the mortars and the F-bombs and the rockets and the two-star and the exhaustion and the Vortex and the stress and the isolation and the clogged latrines, I knew I would miss the dark humor and the frenzy and the card games and the respect and the sudden friendships and the common purpose and the togetherness. Most of all, I would miss doing something real, a hundred hours a week.

What was I going home to? Instead of working on actual policy, on things that mattered in the real world, I would be going back to teaching cadets. They wouldn't be any more disengaged from world events than before, they wouldn't be any less intellectually curious than before, but I knew I would be more annoyed by their attitudes than I had been.

What was I going home to? The same problematic marriage Jorge had forced me to confront over the summer in Brussels. I'd come to Iraq in part to avoid having to deal with it. My feelings had not changed with time and distance. I needed out. I needed to stop going along for one more day after one more day.

What was I going home to? Daughters who were in distress. There were many ways to interpret what was going on; my version was they were calling out for help I was not around to provide. Not all the updates about what was going on at home were from home. Those from relatives and friends and neighbors had me worried.

I needed to get home and build a better future for me, for all three of us, despite my dread of what it would take to create it. I could not keep avoiding this. Once I left this conflict, I could enter the final stages of resolving the conflict my life had become.

I had no idea what lay beyond the inevitable divorce, but the hope for something better gave me good reason to want to stay alive for a few more days.

But how could I guarantee my safety? Sure, I could stay in the Palace and avoid getting killed like Jim Mollen had ten days ago. We'd heard he had not been on an official trip, which would have been enough of a shame, but had instead been paying a social visit to friends and colleagues in the city. He had taken a last, unnecessary trip. Someone betrayed him, or he was very unlucky.

I could also stay in the Palace and get killed like Ed Seitz, out at Camp Victory back in October. He had been excruciatingly careful, staying overnight rather than risking the drive back down Route Irish in the twilight. It did him no good.

If there was a bullet out there with my name on it—if I had my own appointment today in Samarra—nothing I did would make any difference. I may as well go out and see part of the city. Otherwise, all I'd have to talk about when I got back would be making PowerPoints and trimming position papers to a single page. I didn't want to spend four months here without actually being in Baghdad. Route Irish didn't count. I had very little sense of place.

I didn't want to have to admit I spent all my time hiding in the Green Zone.

So: Let's go.

I didn't pay much attention to the details of Kris's pretrip briefing to his unit. They didn't mean anything to me—a bunch of acronyms and code names for locations. As on the trip to al-Faw, this would be a two-vehicle formation, but in up-armored HMMWVs rather than street-standard British SUVs. I would be in the lead vehicle, sitting behind Khris rather than the driver. Khris started to tell me to ready my weapon for use, then he thought better of it and advised me to keep it holstered. Embarrassing, but fair. I was air force, after all.

Laura joined me in the back seat to film Khris on his beat as she often had. Above us was our turret gunner. The three civil affairs troops in the other vehicle were joined in the back seat by someone from the Embassy and our cultural advisor, Dr. Chop-off-their-heads.

Had I paid attention to Khris's briefing, I would have known this wasn't going to be a routine trip over the 14th of July Bridge to the district council building. The bridge's southbound lanes were closed to repair shell damage, so we needed to route around to the next bridge downstream and approach Karrada, a neighborhood enveloped on three sides by a meander of the Tigris, from the west rather than the north.

But I had not been paying attention, so I only realized this when, a short distance from the civil affairs compound, Khris tapped his driver, pointed, and we turned right onto a dirt double-track atop a levee separating the river bottom from . . . a farm?

I didn't know what to expect to see on my journey into this city of seven million people, but this wasn't it. Squash? Melons? Did the DFAC source fresh local produce from here?

We bounced atop the levee for a while with the Tigris below us to the left. As the river curved away, Khris pointed in that direction, and we angled off-road down the face of the levee. There was so much side differential I worried we might roll down the hill. The only good thing was our route was so random, so unlikely, no one could possibly have planted IEDs here.

Once we reached level ground, we drove along some farm lanes and stopped under a bridge. I was nervous again. The farmers knew we were here. Were they calling the enemy? Khris and the driver pored over maps, trying to figure out how to get from the bottom of the bridge to the top so we could cross the river. Around us, only chickens. There were lots of chickens in Baghdad. Laura had told me Dr. Riyadh had a flock in his backyard.

After some circuitous driving, we made it over al-Jadriyah Bridge. At last, I was headed into the actual city. Just over the river, we passed a low, domed building that looked a bit like one of the silos highway departments use to store salt for snowstorms. Laura, having been in this neighborhood with Khris before, told me this was a mosque. Its grounds hosted refugees from Fallujah, huddling under improvised shelters after we had destroyed their city.

Karrada District, on the south side of Baghdad, was a peninsula about four miles long but less than a mile wide. It had the reputation of being one of the safest, most diverse, and most prosperous parts of Baghdad. Here Kurds and Arabs, Christians, Sunni, and Shia commingled in relative peace.

It was kind of a dump. Clearly, twenty-five years of war, fifteen years of sanctions, and the more recent looting, violence, and complete breakdown of civil order had taken their toll on the commercial streets. Many buildings had three or four stories, with shops at street level and residences above. But trash was everywhere, and many windows and doors were boarded over. Given the style of architecture, the palm trees, the disrepair, I was reminded of a crappy section of San Diego. Nevertheless, it was so exciting to be on the ground in the city.

Our destination was in a nicer part of Karrada, a civil affairs operating location that had been the palace of one of Saddam's daughters. The district council was meeting there today, which meant extra security. The faculty members were going to drive over and meet us here.

The place didn't look much like a palace. It was a nicely designed, nicely decorated modern villa with a couple of big meeting rooms. It fit with the other buildings on a residential street.

Unlike in the Green Zone, we weren't required to armor up. The operating location was considered safer than the Republican Palace. Khris didn't even wear his helmet when he left the vehicle. It was safer because it was less likely to be the target of a mortar or a rocket. As inaccurate as such fire was—they still had only managed to hit the damn Palace once the whole time I was there—at least if you fired at the Green Zone you'd hit something. Aiming at this location, you'd probably hit someone else's house.

The professors were delayed because of some kind of security concern, so we settled in to wait. It was nice to relax a bit and walk around outside among the greenery, Kevlar-free.

After a while, people filed in for the council meeting. I wasn't able to attend, both because we didn't know when the faculty would arrive and because there wouldn't be much point in me listening to a discussion in Arabic. Still, it was interesting watching the different council members and citizens come in and engage with one another outside the meeting room.

The attendees were mostly but not entirely men. Some wore suits; others dressed like sheikhs. I wondered whether people wore the desert robes as part of normal life or whether they were pretending to be authentic, much as people in Colorado would sometimes show up in a cowboy hat and a bolo at a formal meeting to make a point. Some cowboys are real, some can pull off the look, and some (including me) look foolish. Were similar fashion errors being made by some city folk here? Were others laughing behind their backs and saying, "Ghazi—he's all robe and no camels!"

We ordered in some lunch. It took a long time for the lamb kebabs to arrive, but they were so delicious!

By midafternoon, it became apparent the professors were not going to show up. Khris apologized for the meeting falling through, not that it was in any way his fault, and said he'd see if he could reschedule it in the next few days. He told us he would make up for it: Against the two-star's direction, he would take us on a tour of the district. I was thrilled.

Our first stop was the university. The campus was a lot of brutalist cement buildings with lots of green space between them. A typical new public campus, in other words. No one was playing Frisbee on the quad, but lots of students were walking around. Almost all of them were in Western attire. Some women wore headscarves, but most did not. The dress was a bit more modest than what one would see on a typical American campus; on the other hand, it was also late on a December day.

How did these young people feel about having fully armored vehicles drive onto their campus, complete with a helmeted and jacketed soldier on the roof, manning an automatic weapon? Was this helping us? Were we spending any time balancing our understandable desire to protect ourselves from a very real enemy against the need to win over what during Vietnam had been called "hearts and minds"? Or did we even care anymore about making that happen? The next Iraqi government would need to win those hearts and minds, not us.

After leaving the campus, we drove through the neighborhoods. At one point, Khris directed his driver to stop near some sketchy-looking armed men. He said he didn't recognize these guys, so he wanted to see what was going on. He told me to stay in the HMMWV.

Yeah, like I was going anywhere. *Come on, Khris,* I thought. *There are lots of people with guns out here—leave these guys alone.* I wanted a joyride, not a firefight, though that would be a better story. If it wasn't an obituary.

Khris approached the men, talked with them a bit, then started laughing and came back. He assured us they were on our side, looking

Silhouette of gunner at Baghdad University

out for the wrong sort of people. Kind of like a neighborhood watch for the area, at least if neighborhood watches were made up of well-armed men who had given themselves the authority to shoot to kill as they deemed necessary.

This stop wasn't as risky as it seemed. If these were bad guys, would they want to shoot us here and now rather than waiting for a more opportune time?

It was almost sundown when we got back to Khris's base. This had been my best day in Baghdad. The cherry atop the sundae was finding my trailer protected by sandbags, at least on the wall next to my bed. I would have five nights of safe sleep.

> Wed 8 Dec: Finally reworked the Sunni Engagement Strategy into a memo for the CG, my last. Brigadier Smith has gone over it with me, and prepared [the two-star] for its conclusion—Don't lose the war. Hold your nerve. Tactical patience. Kinetic ops against actors, away from population centers, not talkers & mosques. Meet or at least entertain MUC demands.

Today, Secretary of Defense Rumsfeld mused, "You go to war with the army you have, not the army you might want or wish to have." It was kind of funny how he would talk about the war as if it were some abstract thing he had nothing to do with rather than something he chose to start. Like much of what he said, he wasn't wrong. He was a smart guy even if he sounded a bit like Yoda. However, his point was only relevant if war were forced on you. When you choose the time and place for an optional and unjustified war, the least you can do is check to see whether you have the right army. If you don't, maybe don't start the war, at least not until you develop the army you want.

I had nothing to report from my trip to Karrada, so I spent the day wrapping up the last bits of my part of the war with a final look at the election. It had become clear the Kurd–religious Shia coalition was a far more likely outcome than a national unity government. The moderate Arabs in the current Interim Government were more and more unpopular. Although we believed the Sunni Arabs were smart enough to know it would not be in their interest to boycott the election—the MUC, we thought, was bluffing to try to win concessions—they were still unlikely to vote in high numbers and unlikely to support the more moderate candidates. The last good shot at a moderate, cross-identity government had slipped away a few days ago when the largest parties met at Lake Dohuk in Kurdistan but failed to assemble a single national list on which they could stand for election. Just about the only way the less religious Shia politicians like Allawi would gain support was if Grand Ayatollah Sistani did not endorse other parties, like the Da'wa and SCIRI, or if he included the more secular leaders in an endorsement.

In anticipation of what we now realized was a suboptimal outcome, the final version of the Sunni Engagement Strategy went beyond the current situation to advocate for certain postelection actions. Our advice to the Commander was that the United States, especially the Embassy, needed to work hard to convince the Shia Arabs and Kurds that their own interests would be best served by policies that were acceptable to the Sunni Arabs. Concessions on oil revenue, federalism, militias, and partial rehabilitation of the Ba'ath could go a long way toward bringing lasting peace to Iraq. Otherwise, violence would persist and increase, perhaps drawing in neighboring Sunni Arab states.

With work done, I prepared to leave. I discovered offices in the Palace I hadn't known existed. Sure enough, we had a Travel Office. I would return on official redeployment orders even though no one could figure out how I had gotten here without them. I had a momentary fear they would not issue orders to go home if they couldn't match them with orders to arrive. Look, I'm here, aren't I?

I would leave the Green Zone on 12 December and then have a couple of days to find transportation to Kuwait. As long as I made it there by 16 December, I'd be fine. The rest of the journey home would be on scheduled military flights. If I didn't make it to Kuwait on time, those would have to be rescheduled.

After I packed up what I hadn't mailed back and turned in my ammunition, I had a lot of time. My being free, however, didn't mean others were. I'd been on the other side of that dynamic many times. At some point, the people leaving think about nothing but going home, while those remaining fight off resentments. You have nowhere near enough time to have final conversations with everyone you'd like to say goodbye to, nor do they have time to break away from their own duties.

I managed to have a last long talk with Stephen on a balcony off the Economics section of the Embassy. We'd not been getting together for poker as often nor interacting so much on strategy once I'd moved more into politics. He reminded me how unhappy foreign service officers were about being stuck in their offices, unable to do their jobs. For most, volunteering for Baghdad had seemed like a good career move: Check off this hardship assignment and maybe be sent to Rome as a reward! But balancing that line on the résumé would be a lack of tangible accomplishments. People felt they were targets, here to further a political message.

My hail and farewell on the balcony over the courtyard turned out to be great fun. As an extra treat, we celebrated the 350th birthday of Rutger's Royal Dutch Marines with a cake. Several of us were leaving, as always, and more were arriving—though not Greg. My replacement's travel to Baghdad from USAFA had been delayed, so we would get no overlap. My own plans had progressed enough that I would still leave as scheduled.

Thank goodness. Maybe I didn't want to go home, but I wanted to go home.

The two-star said a few nice words about me and the work I'd done and gave me a campaign flag. It had a typo: "Operatin Iraqi Freedom." This was disappointing. I'd hoped to get the one I'd seen hanging at Ghazi's that said "Operation Iraqi Freedoom."

The Vortex was very laudatory. For all our differences, I'd developed an appreciation for the work he did. It must have driven him a bit nuts trying to juggle a bunch of free-spirited, independent-thinking scholar-soldiers. Although he pushed back on me hard, all the time, that was his job. If he disagreed, well, I was there to advise, not to direct our actions. He accepted what I was doing well enough that he had kept giving me more to do right up until the end.

I was a better officer after working for Colonel Vortex. He had taught me to strip away illusions of how I might like things to be and to focus on how things really were. That would be a valuable skill as I moved on with my life.

I expressed nothing memorable about how grateful I felt for this opportunity to serve, to try to advance the mission, and to share fun times and scary times with good people.

I would miss the guys in the SPA. They had been my life, my lifeline, for months, and now it was coming to a close.

The night before I left, I stayed in the office late, saying final goodbyes. I closed my time out by sending a final email to all my colleagues in the Multi-National Force–Iraq's Strategy, Plans, and Assessment directorate.

Saturday, December 11, 2004 10:57 PM

Friends and colleagues,

I said my piece at the hail and farewell, so I don't need to say much more about how privileged I feel to have been able to share this mission with you. This has been the best professional experience of my life, and I'm glad

I came. I'm glad you are here as well, because, it is very important that we help Iraq get itself back together after the war.

A lot of people back home ask me if things are better or worse in Iraq than they seem—I'm not going to get caught up on that; I think the answer is yes, both those things. I think the focus rather should be on the Iraqi people. Many of them resent our presence, which is understandable. But the vast majority agree that they want a democracy, and they are bravely fighting to achieve it. It takes tremendous dedication for Iraqis to get up in the morning and work on reconstruction projects, or work as police, or work on government staff, or assemble a political slate for the elections—knowing all the while that they and their family are targets for intimidation and murder. Yet they do it because they believe that their sacrifice would ultimately make Iraq a better place. We owe it to them not to shortchange Iraq, not to undermine their achievements. A successful election—meaning one in which most Iraqis, Sunni and Shia, vote—may well turn the corner on the war here. It won't end our shared task, but it will be a step on the right path.

I hope we can stay in touch beyond Baghdad. We have shared an important mission, an opportunity that most people don't get to have. Stay safe, and get to your homes when you can.

I also sent an email to the friends who were my lifeline to the real world. It was much like the other, then I added:

I leave in a few hours to begin my trip back to Colorado. Thank you for your messages of support while I have been here in Iraq. The contact I've had with friends has made it much easier to get through my time here. I'm sorry my messages back have often been a bit less interesting—I can't tell you the "good stuff," and the rest of it doesn't change very much.

Before leaving, I told you why I volunteered to do this: despite my belief that the war was a bad idea, once it happened it was important to help Iraq get itself back together. Working in strategy, looking at the political process, I think I have made a contribution to this cause. It has been hard work, at times unpleasant work, but it has been valuable work. I think this has been the best professional experience of my life, and I'm glad I came.

Then it was off to bed for one final night as a target for indirect fire.

Sun 12 Dec: Hard to believe it's really over.

Redeployment day dawned very unlike Iraq. It had rained much of the night, so puddles were everywhere. I dragged my stuff from my trailer through the Palace and on to Landing Zone Washington (a parking lot along the route to the PX) to wait for a Blackhawk helicopter. No one saw me off. Once you were gone, you were gone. By coincidence, the Wiccan, my former algebra student, was there, on her way to a bit of mid-tour leave.

The lines for the helicopters were long. With Route Irish closed, this was the only way from the Green Zone to the encampment at Baghdad International. There was only so much room on each helicopter, and there were only so many aircraft devoted to this mission.

They landed in pairs, were loaded in pairs, and took off in pairs. The day dragged on, until I—and the Wiccan and a colleague she was traveling out with—made it up to the barriers and were next.

Blackhawks are not passenger aircraft. We strewed our suitcases and duffels and gear in the rear of the helicopter. Then I crammed myself between the cargo and a window on the starboard side. We were traveling west, so I would get to look north, away from the river and Karrada District.

A soldier spent the flight with his rifle pointed out an open door. What was his mission? Who would he hit, air to ground, from a turbulent aircraft? Did he have the same goal I had when I traveled by land on the same route in September: to shoot as needed and just keep their heads down?

We passed the traffic circle near the Palace, which I remembered from my trips to TRIC meetings in one of those towers off to the right. How long ago that now seemed. I thought my whole tour of duty would be spent listening to Iraqi bureaucrats argue with each other while drinking that wonderful tea. I never got any more good tea, except at Tammy's party at the al-Rasheed.

Before long, we passed over Mansour District, a well-off area, more so than Karrada, but strictly a Sunni Arab neighborhood. Professionals lived here, but how many of them were also with the enemy? The neighborhood looked nice. Everyone had a rooftop where they could seek refuge from the summer heat. Did anyone on the rooftops also have small arms or rockets to fire at us?

A bit farther away was a crazy-looking giant mosque, surrounded by construction cranes. Was this Umm al-Ma'arik, where Dari and the Muslim Ulema Council were headquartered? Was this where the raid had not yet taken place? It was in the right general direction in this unbelievably flat city, but no, Umm al-Ma'arik was farther to the northwest. This was the al-Rahman, still in Mansour.

Finally, water. We were over the lagoons surrounding al-Faw Palace and Camp Victory. The airport was only a little farther, adjacent to Victory but across a highway, the highway that was the source of the attack on the fuel depot my first day, the highway that led to Abu Ghraib and Fallujah.

Upon safe arrival at Baghdad International, the Wiccan and her friend and I had two choices. We could drag our gear to Camp Striker to get billeting for a specific flight tomorrow, or we could wait around the flight line and see if space became available. I chose the latter, despite the risk that I might spend the night sleeping on a folding chair in a tent.

Chapter 8
Acceptance

There I was: reclining atop a seaside villa watching the horns of the new moon follow the sun into the industrial haze of Kuwait City.

I had been lucky. I didn't have to wait long at the airport before I found a C-130 transport to Kuwait with an open seat. After an uneventful flight, I took a government-chartered bus to the Hilton Resort, which the US military had rented out. By 0200 I was sharing space with four strangers, trying to adjust to sleeping without the white noise of small arms fire in the distance.

I slept till noon, then sat on the roof all afternoon writing in my journal, trying to capture my state of mind on my first day at peace.

Coming out had been far more disorienting than going in.

Going in had been a slow boil. Nothing unusual about the commercial flight to Frankfurt, or even the military charter to al-Udied and then walking around a cool desert base all night with new friends. Then it began: the humid hell of a Qatari morning, a C-130 to Baghdad, the fuel depot explosion, the fast drive to the Palace, the fire, the mortars and the rockets and the missing guns and the bombings until I found myself hiding in the Palace all night. Over time, it came to seem like concrete shelters and Kevlar and hundred-hour workweeks and the Vortex were all normal.

Coming out was a flash. Landing Zone Washington was still Iraq and flying out of the Green Zone on a Blackhawk was still Iraq and milling about the airport was still Iraq and getting onto the final C-130 was still Iraq and now it was not Iraq at all. I had slept in a real bed in a real building with real walls, and now I was sitting on the roof with a view, not of concrete barriers and shipping containers and garbage stretching to the Palace looming over everything, but of the sea all the way to a horizon broken by two docked oil tankers. No rockets or mortars were going to hit this compound, the Vortex was not going to give me more work, and I could go outside and walk along the beach without protection.

The next day, Tuesday 14 December, I wanted to see part of the Middle East from the ground after four months behind barriers. I didn't know of any tourist attractions in Kuwait, but I could visit a nearby commercial district, Fahaheel, and experience how an urban Arab area looks and feels without the constant threat of violence.

No one was willing to go with me. Some people asked me why I would want to do this. Others said their commander had forbidden them from leaving the hotel grounds because it was too dangerous in this peaceful, prosperous, allied country. I found that disturbing. It was possible to get in trouble anywhere, but if any part of the Middle East ought to have a positive view of Americans, it would be the country from which the American-led coalition had expelled Iraq fourteen years ago.

I went anyway, alone. Many people here spoke English, any cabbie would know where the Hilton was, and I could always walk back. I hailed a cab and rode a little way up a parkway to a traffic circle that seemed to be a town center.

It was dull. Quiet. Calm. Safe. Wonderful.

I spent quite a while wandering the streets. It was nothing exotic, nothing one wouldn't see in any downtown. As in Europe, the streets were narrow, though the skyline had minarets instead of steeples. Signs were in a language I didn't know, but the important ones had universal symbols. There wasn't much pedestrian traffic in the middle of the afternoon on a weekday. I looked around some stores and bought some intricate gold jewelry for the kids at what seemed a good price. It had been a while since I'd gone shopping.

Fishing boats at Fahaheel, Kuwait

I ventured farther up the parkway. Soon I came upon a large mosque set back in expansive grounds, and there didn't appear to be much of anything built up beyond. It was still quiet and calm, but it no longer felt safe. There were few people and little traffic in this direction. No one knew where I was, and no one would miss me for quite a long time, not until I didn't show up for my flight home tonight—if then. I was on my own.

I went back to the traffic circle and walked to the Gulf. An array of boats, a mixture of modern and traditional designs, were tied up in a harbor next to a commercial structure with a boardwalk alongside. This al-Kout Mall had an open floorplan with one establishment seeming to run into the next, or perhaps I was in the Kuwaiti equivalent of a Walmart Supercenter. Groceries dominated the central area—fresh produce in display after display. After the limited selection at the DFAC, I gawked at the bounty. I needed to adjust, more than I had realized.

Someone, maybe an employee or a manager, called out to me, asking if I was an American, an American soldier. I said yes, hoping that was OK, and he urged me to take some fruit—no charge! I didn't know what to do. Was I supposed to accept this gift or was I supposed to insist on paying? I was alone, ignorant, and worried. I got the heck out of there.

My flight was scheduled to depart at 0500 the next morning, so a shuttle took us to the airport at 2200. There was no place to sleep, lie down, or get comfortable. I stayed up all night playing spades. As much as I enjoy card games, this all-nighter just about worked it out of my system.

The aircraft didn't leave until 0700. At the stop in Italy, I was shocked to see snowy mountains on the horizon after months of desert heat and humidity. I had not realized Aviano was so close to the Alps. As we stretched our legs, a lineup of local base folks congratulated us on finishing our tours of duty and thanked us for our service.

Then the military flight continued to Baltimore, which, like Frankfurt, has military and civilian operations. I got to a hotel at 2100, twenty-three hours after pickup in clock time, thirty-three hours after pickup in real time, and forty-four hours after waking up. Given jet lag, sleep was a series of short naps before I dragged everything back to the airport for a commercial flight back through Atlanta.

Security lines snaked through the terminals forever. While waiting, I channeled Bilbo Baggins: What do I have in my pocket? A lock. The lock to my gun safe. Why was it in my pocket? Somewhere in my bags was my weapon, unlocked. I had no magazines, but it might not be a great idea to have an unsecured weapon in an airport. While kicking and pushing my duffels down the line, I felt around each of them until I found the box, verified my M-9 was still in it, and locked it up. To my relief, no one asked what I was doing, and I was able to present my secured weapon to the security screeners.

When I got home to Colorado late in the afternoon, I was damn tired. All the reunion pictures one sees after deployment seem to involve happy-looking people. I look bad in my picture with my daughters. Maybe the people in the reunions shown on television had been given a chance to rest first. Or maybe they were people returning to better situations than I was. I had escaped a foreign conflict only to return to a domestic one.

I filed for divorce first thing in the new year. It got messier and more expensive than I wished, but it needed to happen. No one was happy, and no one was going to ever become happy. The deployment to Iraq did not cause the divorce. If anything, it delayed it because I couldn't file papers from Baghdad. But the experience had hardened my resolve. I was not yet forty, but I had become aware that life was too short and too unpredictable to sit around and wish things would get better.

Eventually, things got better.

My daughter got better.

I got better.

My general style and demeanor changed for a while. "Edgy Tom," my marksmanship mentor Deron Jackson called me. I spoke veryrapidlyandverydirectlyalmostinamonotone much of the time. I was dropping F-bombs right and left, which seemed to deeply offend some of the more pious officers—including my medically denied prospective replacement. Ah, to have seen her try to confront Colonel Vortex over his foul language. That would have been worth staying in Iraq for.

It took a while for this to wear off, for me to detox to something like normal. This incredible intensity left me impatient with those who did not understand. For many years, if someone asked me what I thought of the war, at a social event, for example, I would snap back into it. After ten minutes or so I would realize I had been monologuing and everyone except my now-regretful interlocuter had slipped away.

I was especially annoyed the war seemed to have had no impact on anyone's lives. When someone would walk up to me at a gas station and say, "Thank you for your service," I would reply, "You're welcome," rather than say what I was thinking: *Maybe if you weren't driving that motherfucking giant SUV with the W sticker on it, we wouldn't have to have so much goddamn service for you to be thankful for.*

It was worse in the classroom. Cadets still didn't give a shit about the war. They weren't going to be on the ground, and no doubt the war would be over long before they would be flying over it. Where and when it made sense to talk about the war as part of a lesson, cadets would challenge my understanding by pointing out how it differed from what they saw on Fox or heard on Rush. They had no interest in the human toll, certainly not on Iraqi civilians but not even on American personnel. They were like almost everyone in this country.

There I was: driving back from Denver with my daughters from a performance of *Oedipus Rex*, listening to public radio report that voting had begun in Iraq. So far, their morning had been peaceful. Were we, unlike Sophocles's protagonist, going to be able to overcome our fate?

I was no longer involved. I had no easy, secure means of communication from the Air Force Academy, and I had duties to perform—but I was still interested. I still cared.

The early signs were good. Only forty-four people were killed on Election Day, fewer than we had dared hope—fewer, in fact, than on the average day in Iraq. Furthermore, nationwide turnout was 58 percent. A bit low, but that might minimize disparity in turnout.

Once the results began coming in, however, I knew I had been too optimistic. It was fortunate we never formalized our metrics, as otherwise we would not have been able to execute the fallback plan of declaring the election a tremendous success no matter what happened.

A month before the election, the Iraqi Islamic Party had joined the Muslim Ulema Council's call for a boycott. Fewer than four thousand out of over two million people voted in all of Anbar Province (where Fallujah is located). I estimated only about 10 percent of Sunni Arabs voted nationwide.

This was worse than I'd ever imagined. Only 17 of the 275 seats in the National Assembly (6 percent) were won by Sunni Arabs, far below their share of the population. Twelve of these winners had served in Saddam's sham legislature; the Shia Arabs and Kurds blocked them from any leadership positions. Three of the remaining five Sunni Arabs in the assembly had been elected as part of the otherwise Shia Arab "Sistani list"; the Sunni Arabs rejected them as traitors to their community. Only two Sunni Arab members of the National Assembly were acceptable to both sides: Interim President Ghazi al-Yawr and Interim Industry Minister Hachim al-Hassani, who had resigned from the IIP rather than honor the boycott.

The moderate cross-sect Arab parties had done three times as well as the Sunni Arab parties, winning 18 percent of the seats. Almost all of these (15 percent of the total) went to the "Iraqi List" created by Interim Prime Minister Ayad Allawi; the rest went to either the "Iraqis List" created by Yawr or to the Communists. Despite the love shown him by Western media, the only true liberal, Adnan Pachachi, could not even get 1/275th of the vote.

The election winners were the Kurds and the Shia Arabs. The two main Kurdish parties had formed a united election list that included Christians living in areas under Kurdish control; they and a minor Kurd party ended up with 28 percent of the seats in the Assembly, far exceeding their share of the population. On the Shia Arab side, Grand Ayatollah Sistani had assembled an election list from the religious and radical parties, everyone from SCIRI and Da'wa to Sadr's people and some Shia Turkomen and Kurds. The Sistani list won 51 percent of the National Assembly seats, and smaller Shia parties won another 3 percent.

We had assumed a result like this would be welcomed by the Kurds and Shia Arabs but rejected by the Sunni Arabs. As they formed a government and wrote a constitution, it would be up to the US to encourage concessions to the Sunni Arabs in the name of national unity.

With the political line of operations now dominant, this task belonged to the Embassy and the State Department in general. But they were distracted. On 17 February President Bush nominated Ambassador Negroponte to become director of national intelligence. His successor, Zalmay Khalilzad, did not get into place until 21 June, nearly five months after the election.

Even if there had been full attention from the Embassy, there's not much the United States could have done without undermining the legitimacy of the results. The only way to get a broader national government would have been to have almost half the Sistani List defect from its coalition and join the Kurds and moderate Arabs. It's hard to see how the Iraqi parties could have been manipulated to that degree—and it still would have excluded most Sunni Arabs.

At most, the United States could have sped up the inevitable. The Iraqis did not form a new government until the end of April, three months after the election. As I had predicted to the Vortex, the National Assembly selected Ibrahim Ja'afari of the Da'wa Party as transitional prime minister. The Kurds insisted one of their own, Jalal Talabani, be elected transitional president by the National Assembly. Talabani's deputies on the Presidency Council would be Adil Abdul Mahdi of the Iranian-influenced Supreme Council for the Islamic Revolution in Iraq and outgoing Interim President Yawr as the token Sunni Arab. The only acceptable Sunni Arab left, Hassani of the Iraqi Islamic Party, was given the post of speaker of the assembly. All groups were represented, but the power was with the Shia Arabs.

If this had happened more quickly, the new transitional government would have had more time for its main task: writing a constitution by the 15 August deadline. As it was, the constitutional drafting committee did not begin meeting until June. It included only two Sunni Arabs among its fifty-five members. Once Ambassador Khalilzad assumed his duties, the Embassy tried to involve itself in this process, but it was unsuccessful in doing anything except fail, in the eyes of the Sunni Arabs, and meddle, in the eyes of the rest. The only American accomplishment during this period was to make sure the drafting deadline was met, even though there was a provision for a six-month delay built into the Transitional Administrative Law. A delay would not have made a compromise much more likely in any case.

Not surprisingly, the new constitution favored Shia Arabs and Kurds and offered little protection for the Sunni Arabs, neither federalism nor an upper legislative house. The Kurds would continue to control their own oil, and it would be possible for the Shia Arabs to form a similar region that would control most of the rest of the oil. The only thing given the Sunni Arabs was that legislative seats would be distributed by province, which would mean that disparity in turnout would not matter. This was pretty much what I'd predicted back in November, but it would have been nice if the Sunni Arabs had been given more reason to accept the new constitution.

There was one last chance to derail this train wreck: The draft Iraqi constitution was subject to a referendum on 15 October 2005. In addition to the need for a national majority, the constitution would be rejected if at least three of the eighteen provinces voted against it by a two-thirds margin. This had been conceived as a Kurdish veto because there were three Kurdish provinces: No constitution could be approved unless it was acceptable to the Kurds. This provision also offered a possible Sunni veto. As expected, the twelve clearly Shia Arab and Kurd provinces supported the constitution with at least 94 percent of the vote. Baghdad, Diyala, and Tamim had mixed populations, but they also all voted in favor.

This left the three largely Sunni Arab provinces. The no vote in Anbar was 97 percent, and in Salah ad-Din it was 82 percent, but in Nineveh (Mosul) the no vote was only 55 percent, 12 percent short of the threshold that would have vetoed the constitution. Nineveh had just enough Kurds, Turkomen, Christians, and Yazidi to allow the constitution to be ratified. The Kurds and Shia Arabs promised that some provisions of the constitution could be reopened after ratification. These promises may have helped carry the referendum in Nineveh, but they were not kept.

The constitutional government election was held on 15 December 2005, exactly a year after I flew out of Kuwait. This was the third national election during that calendar year. The Sunni Arabs turned out this time, and together with the provincial allocation of seats, they and the moderates gained enough representation to deadlock most of Iraqi politics for years to come. The Sistani List broke apart, and the Kurds advocated for their own interests rather than worry about the rest of Iraq. They barely considered themselves part of the same country.

After the full cycle of elections was over, coalition forces raided Umm al-Ma'arik mosque on Sunday 8 January 2006. Harith al-Dari was not the target. He had fled into exile.

There I was: waking up on my forty-first birthday. The morning news informed me the enemy had blown up the al-Askari Shrine in Samarra, which was on our short list of places that must be kept safe. From there, Shia believe the Twelfth Imam (the Mahdi) occulted himself. He was to return, along with Jesus, at the end of days.

This attack enraged the Shia Arabs, and the civil war came.

Until now, the conflict had been a resistance to American occupation or an insurgency against the American-installed government. The Sunni Arab enemy was killing both Sunni and Shia Iraqis if they supported the government, not because of their faith. Likewise, though most of the people the Shia-dominated Iraqi government was killing were Sunnis, it did so because they were supporting the enemy, not because of their faith.

After Samarra, the conflict became a full-out sectarian civil war. Sadr's Mahdi Army attacked the Sunni Arab population in general. They were joined by Shia Arab militias disguised as regular Iraqi forces. The militia demobilization process had not even started. Instead of breaking up the militias and blending their members into other units, the Iraqi government incorporated some of them into Iraqi security forces as the Wolf, Tiger, and Scorpion Brigades. Under the leadership of the new interior minister, a commander from the Iranian-trained Badr Corps, they engaged in abuse and sectarian cleansing. Other militias remained independent through the rise of the Islamic State and beyond.

The Shia Arabs' indiscriminate campaigns of murder and ethnic cleansing, urban neighborhood by urban neighborhood, village by village, were met by an equal and opposite reaction from the Sunni Arabs. The Samarra bombing, and the Shia response to it, and the Sunni counterresponse, finally broke Iraq.

Early 2007 saw the publication of *Hope Is Not a Plan: The War in Iraq from Inside the Green Zone*. I edited it, Tom Ruby and I wrote most of it, and Gunner Sepp and Greg Rose were among the contributors. This being near the peak of the Iraqi Civil War, people were interested in "what went wrong," so I was interviewed on some public radio programs. PBS's *Frontline* flew me out to Washington in February for an episode, "Endgame," that was broadcast in June.

That was almost the last of my involvement with Iraq. Soon enough, I lost contact with most of the people I served with, other than through the tenuous touch of Facebook. The Vortex went on to serve in a similar capacity in Afghanistan, and advanced to become a two-star in his own right. Colonel Storrie was promoted even higher, to three-star in the British Army.

Simon Tustin turned to another kind of service after his military career was over, leading a Christian nonprofit dedicated to transforming lives in African countries. Colonel Wenger, with the help of others (but not me, despite saying I would), rejuvenated not only the Iraqi Boy Scouts but also the Afghan Scouts during a later tour—service for which he received international scouting recognition in 2016.

I met up once with Gunner, in Monterey, where he had gone back to teaching at the Naval Postgraduate School. During the last two years of the Bush administration, he served as deputy assistant secretary of defense for special operations, working on counterterrorism worldwide. The media often quoted him on the lessons of counterinsurgency he had drafted a few desks over from mine in the Palace.

Neal Rappaport became head of the Economics Department at the Academy, but he spent as much if not more time serving again in Iraq, and then three times in Afghanistan, before retiring and moving to Uruguay. Mike Davis was recognized by General Casey for his work in Assessment setting up the monthly commander's assessment/synchronization board; he served out most of what would become a thirty-five-year career on the faculty and staff of Air University and National Defense University.

My roommate Hank stayed in Iraq through 2006, having all sorts of adventures working on oil facilities, and he never gave up our trailer. He kept the key so he always had a roof over his head when he cycled back to Baghdad. He made colonel, then retired and returned to the oil industry. His colleague Martha Boyd, who led me on the tour of the villas where Hank used to live, left the military soon after getting back to the US and returned to private practice as an attorney.

Both military attorneys remained on active duty, eventually serving as staff judge advocates. Stephen got that posting in Rome and returned to Iraq in 2008; he and all of my poker group continued to distinguished diplomatic careers. Rutger entered the Dutch foreign service after retirement.

Colonel Barlow, the former mayor of the Green Zone, returned to being head of the Academy's Aeronautical Engineering Department, and then retired to become dean of engineering at Arkansas Technical

University. Khris Scarcliff, the civil affairs captain, transferred to psychological operations and spent several tours in Afghanistan and Africa before retiring to Texas and opening a brew pub featuring PsyHops beer.

Matt became a bit of a legend. He came back from Iraq in 2006, unhappy about how the militias had become death squads for interior ministers who no longer listened to American advice. He went back for the surge in 2007–2008, then to Afghanistan for most of the time from 2009 to 2016.

Upon leaving the Policy Division, Colonel Haith became the senior advisor to the operations and training staff within Iraqi Army headquarters. He retired from the military, but Petraeus brought him back as a civilian to first develop a basis for assessing the quality of Iraqi forces and then implement those concepts via a leadership center for the Iraqi Army. He repeated this work in Afghanistan before fully retiring.

Tom Ruby returned to Air Command and Staff College, eventually rising to vice dean. Later, he spent two years in DC working on counterinsurgency. He retired as a colonel to farm and write in Kentucky.

The most momentous post-Iraq career was by the one person whose goal was only to observe and report. Laura Poitras released *My Country, My Country* in June 2006; I took my daughters to a screening in Denver in September, where they had a chance to meet her. After the showing, Dr. Riyadh, the Iraqi Islamic Party candidate who hosted her and is the protagonist of the film, called in from Baghdad to answer questions from the audience. Her movie lost the Best Documentary Oscar to Al Gore's film about a different crisis.

Laura continued making movies that the Department of Homeland Security didn't much like, and she became known as someone who stood up against the system. In 2013, after Edward Snowden contacted her as depicted in *Citizenfour,* she ended up in possession of his secrets. This drew me back in for a moment that August when *The New York Times Magazine* was writing a profile on her that would be titled, rather appropriately, "How Laura Poitras Helped Snowden

Spill His Secrets." Laura called me out of the blue from Berlin to ask if I could offer a character reference. Slanders had been made that she had been working with the enemy in Iraq. People claimed she had been on a roof in Adhamiyah right after the Abu Hanifa raid because she was acting as a forward spotter against American forces. I shouted my assurances to Peter Maass of the *Times* that she was routinely at Dr. Riyadh's home while I was sheltering under a tent at a nonprofit fundraiser during a horrendous thunder and hailstorm.

That was my last contact with events in Iraq.

There I was: sitting in the parking lot of Boonzaaijer's Dutch Bakery on Christmas Eve, 2014, talking to Tom Ruby on the phone. Before I took my apple strudel home, I needed to decide once and for all whether I was going to try to write about my experiences—and whether I would do so as fiction or nonfiction.

My life was feeling a bit adrift again. I'd not kept promises I'd made to myself on the roof in Kuwait ten years before, promises to stay engaged with national policy. As the two-star anticipated, I did not get a late promotion. I retired at the end of January 2008, just as I would have if I hadn't volunteered to go to Baghdad. Pursuing work in Washington or taking an academic position would have required me to give up shared custody of the teenagers. I chose to stay in Colorado Springs and be a parent.

That choice had been more than validated. By fall 2008, my other daughter had developed an eating disorder, though insurance would not authorize care until her health was in more danger. Her mother, my new wife, and I—all three of us—cooperated to check her into Children's Hospital in Denver while Barack Obama was taking his first oath of office. She remained there through her sixteenth birthday. This would be another long struggle that I could be present for but could not do much to solve. Eighteen months later, we were back at Children's, staring at a lot of tubes and wires as her heartrate fell to near thirty beats per minute.

Eating disorders are a lot like addictions, just in reverse and thus trickier. At least, that's the model the hospital staff taught me. I could not fix this. I had to learn to trust her to be OK as she pursued her college dreams in Hawai'i—having somehow managed in the meantime to be valedictorian of the first high school class in the country to complete an International Baccalaureate program from first grade. She had figured out how to make it work and was doing fine—as was my other daughter, now in Texas on her way to a doctorate in psychology.

Speaking of Hawai'i, that was where I had met the woman who had become my second wife. She had spent much more time than I had in a combat zone, living and working for over a decade in Colombia as a journalist and a researcher. My experiences had left me grumpy about fireworks and jumpy when a dumpster lid was dropped. Her experiences had left her making sure she always sat where she could see the restaurant door and had a clear path to a rear exit.

The day after I retired from the Air Force, I was appointed to run the office that oversaw all the foreclosures in my county. Governor Bill Ritter and his staff did not want to spend time worrying about that office. They wanted someone who could take charge, whip it into shape, and create no negative headlines. They warned me I would face a lot of hostility from the county commissioners, all Republicans. I told Ritter's people that as long as the commissioners didn't fire rockets at my office, I'd be good.

Now, for the first time, I was the one responsible for what happened. I reported to the governor, but neither Ritter nor his successor John Hickenlooper exercised close oversight. As in Baghdad, I was not prepared for what was ahead of me. I knew about as much about real estate, banking, and law as I'd known about Iraq. I inherited an office that was three weeks behind its statutory deadlines, and the foreclosure rate kept climbing as the Great Recession took hold.

Each foreclosure represented a life not working out the way someone had hoped. Some had planned to pay off their loan by selling investment property for a profit—a sensible plan until it wasn't. Many others could not sell their family home after a job loss, an earner's illness or death, or an emergency with a parent or child had hit at just the wrong time. So many people came through my office: rich, poor, connected, isolated, prominent, unknown. Friends.

I was not the cause of the loss, I could not prevent the loss, but I was the voice at the end saying "sold." All my deputies and I could do was treat people with equal respect, give them truthful information about their options, and try to protect them against the scammers who prey on the most desperate. Sometimes there was a happier ending when money was left for the homeowner after their debts were paid from the sale proceeds.

One woman, as she picked up that excess proceeds check a few weeks after the auction, let me know her husband had killed himself right after I sold their house.

That took a bit to come to terms with.

I had pushed myself outside my comfort zone by running for county clerk after being outraged by the incumbent's attitude toward students' voting rights. No Democrat had been elected to countywide office in El Paso County since Nixon was president, but 2009 seemed like a good time to take a shot. Going door to door in so many neighborhoods once again exposed me to lives I would otherwise have never seen. It had felt good to be out there trying to make a difference rather than sitting back and waiting for someone else to act, even if the rise of the Tea Party meant my campaign was a failure..

Setting up a campaign was similar to starting a new business, so I used those skills to stay outside my comfort zone and set up a side gig with my second wife. By the time of my call with Rubes, we'd wrapped up our most successful year: a whopping $7,000 in profits, bringing our four-year total to almost $10,000. Fortunately, Hickenlooper's reelection the month before meant we wouldn't have to rely on the business as primary income.

I was making the most difference in conservation. I had gotten involved with the Colorado Mountain Club, first mapping and expanding a roadless area in the Rampart Range and then leading a team to build a new trail up Ice Cave Creek canyon near Palmer Lake. Unlike everything else, this was tangible and lasting. It is quite satisfying to move big rocks and use steel tools to cut dirt until there is a safe, sustainable route through the forest, one people will be able to enjoy for years to come.

Despite all that was good with family, work, and service, I felt stuck when I called Rubes. The public trustee job offered no advancement opportunities, and any change would require a cut in pay, a reduction in prestige, or a loss of autonomy. I was helping a few people achieve their goals, I was helping a few people have a better experience in the mountains, but all of this felt trivial compared to what I had been doing in Baghdad. My thoughts kept going back there, in part because of how much everything in Iraq had gone to hell of late.

All of this—the public office, the business, the political involvement, the volunteer work—all of it was real. It was satisfying. It was trivial. It was something to distract me from how much Iraq had gone to hell in 2014.

By 2008, two years after the shrine in Samarra had been blown up, the level of violence began to drop. Some attribute this to the surge of American troops, some to General Petraeus's successful engagement with Sunni Arabs in the "Anbar Awakening"; I think the separation of Sunni and Shia Arab civilians that had resulted from successful ethnic cleansing also played a part. By this time, both the former Ba'athists and the al-Qaeda types were a diminished presence—Zarqawi had been killed in mid-2006—and the Iraqi government, now led by Nouri al-Maliki, felt more confident. The Iraqis required the Bush administration to agree to withdraw all American troops by the end of 2011, and the Obama administration was not able to negotiate an extension on acceptable terms.

With almost all American forces out, the Iraqi government, still dominated by Shia Arabs and Kurds, turned on the Sunni Arabs again, setting the stage for our enemy, now calling themselves the Islamic State in Iraq and Syria (ISIS), to return. In the first few days of 2014, Fallujah came under enemy control once again. In June 2014 Mosul fell with little resistance. It looked as if Baghdad itself was in danger. Soon after, ISIS began massacring the Yazidi population that I'd barely taken notice of while I was in Baghdad.

A few days before I called Rubes, the peshmerga, having endured as the military arm of Iraqi Kurdistan, had staged a counteroffensive that seemed to have rescued some of the Yazidis around Sinjar near the Syrian border.

Nevertheless, the overall situation in Iraq remained terrible. Had my actions in 2004 led to this? Could I have done better? What was my own part?

Tom Ruby convinced me to write it out as truly as I could, rather than as fiction. We had been discreet in *Hope Is Not a Plan* to get it past the military censors. The full story deserved to be told. Writing would also help me come to terms with the experience and my part in it. It would help me get this story outside myself and turn it into something I could look at and deal with.

It took a long time after that call before I could finish this book, during which so much more happened, good and bad. My daughters began to thrive in professions of their choosing, and I got a grandson. My second wife's chronic illness got worse and worse until it took her life in 2019. The business we had started did well enough for me to decide to leave public service and be a work-from-home entrepreneur before COVID-19 made it cool. Donald Trump won an election, lost an election, and won an election. ISIS was defeated. NATO and European security became relevant again.

Somehow, in the middle of 2025, Sistani was still alive, Sadr was still influential, and Iranian-backed Shia Arab militias were still independent.

I embarked on—and remain in—a new relationship with a woman who was attractive in part for how she engaged with the world: mindful, grounded, in the moment. We met doing service work on the trails in the Rampart Range. I would not be able to be a partner in this relationship if I had not done the work to engage with all that happened in these past twenty years, during my time in Baghdad most of all.

As I went through my journal to piece this story together, the first thing that struck me was how stressful and horrible it all had been. There were so many days when we took incoming indirect fire, so much heat and heated emotion, so much physical illness. Although the moments of real joy stood out in my memory, there was so much I had tried to forget.

Above all, I tried to forget the physical fear of explosives infiltrated into the Green Zone, the strategic surprise scenarios seeming a bit too close to real, the increased rate of bombardment that drove me into the Palace, and then the weapons disappearing for a few days. The turning point in that awful period in October was when we were evacuated into the Palace during the Halloween party because of the unexploded ordnance found near my trailer. My long conversation that evening with Laura reminded me of my purpose and inspired me to take action despite the weight of the questions I was being asked to resolve.

If I were more important—if I held a higher rank than major—at this point in the story I would assert I was right about just about everything and that things would have worked out just fine if people had listened to me.

Quite the opposite. People did listen to me, about everything from militias to election outcomes. At first, I feared I was too confused and unqualified to offer analysis; later, I feared my confidence, considering that I had not become much more qualified. As much as turnover of personnel broke the continuity of everything we did, at least new people brought fresh ideas to break the groupthink.

Fear, stress, heat, personalities: Those were the conditions under which I was offering advice. They were also the conditions under which everyone senior to me was operating. None of us had a handle on what we were doing because none of us had ever done something quite like this before.

Let's be fair to Colonel Vortex, as much as he was his own vector of fear, as much as I resented his attitude. He was in a very difficult situation. Whatever pressure we all felt from him, he felt the same and more from further above. All the crazy deadlines we had to meet were also his deadlines. He knew how messed up the war was, and he also knew what answers were acceptable to the two-star and the Commander. I think he was a bit bewildered about what to do with a bunch of academics with no operational experience who had infiltrated his cadre of action officers deployed from the regular army and marines. Why should he have been trusting my advice, especially regarding Fallujah, only a week into the job?

A week into the job in Strategy. That was the second thing that struck me in returning to this story and trying to tell it: how time passed as if it were in its own vortex. The whole strategic review of the campaign plan at the worker level took two weeks. How on earth did all that material get put together so fast? But then five and a half weeks later, on 31 October, I was briefing the review at the colonel level. How on earth did it take that long to get from my level through the Vortex to his colleagues? When was it briefed to the Commander? Was it before or after the invasion of Fallujah?

I spent all of September and October intermittently working on my alleged primary duty of projecting election outcomes—and that project, like the strategic review, was capped at mid-2005. As if time would stop then? As if the reverberations of kinetic actions would stop echoing within six to nine months? Only in November was this relaxed, as I was told to consider how the election results might influence the writing of the Iraqi constitution all the way out in August 2005.

Not, mind you, that I was straining to look at a longer time frame and being reined in. I accepted my own blinders as a way to keep myself focused on what was in front of me and not get spooked by side issues.

But the timetable of our work had real consequences for the mission. We weren't building the aircraft while it was flying; we were building it after it landed. I didn't develop a clear idea about how different election outcomes might affect our desired end state until 8 November, the first full day of the fight in Fallujah. Only then did we develop a framework for arguing that we preferred a return of the Interim Government over a coalition of Kurds and religious Shia Arabs.

Even so, we still saw advantages in containing the insurgency or resistance to the Sunni Arab areas rather than having a renewed fight with the more radical Shia Arabs who would be excluded from a moderate government. We somehow did not understand that it is better for peace in the long run to have part of each of two groups opposing us rather than all of one of the groups. How could we? Our experience with counterinsurgency in Southeast Asia and Central America was rooted in ideology, not ethnicity or religion.

There's more we didn't understand, but let's stay with this issue of timing for a bit first. We didn't have a basis for caring much about Sunni Arab participation in the election until we ran these scenarios, and I didn't wrap up the Sunni Engagement Strategy memo for the Commander until another month went by—I just flipped through my journal, and sure enough: 8 December. By then I was advocating for reopening the idea of an end date to the occupation, allowing prisoners to vote, and rehabilitating some former Ba'athists into public life. The actual engagement strategy was watered down into bland guidance to not do unnecessary things that would antagonize the Sunni Arabs.

This awareness had been enough for me to run around the Palace trying to find someone who could stop the Umm al-Ma'arik raid. If that knowledge had been at hand sooner, I could have used it as a reason not to raid Abu Hanifa earlier in November. I could have used it as an argument against attacking Fallujah in the first place.

Besides encouraging the Sunni Arabs to vote, the other way to achieve the election of a government similar to the one we had in place would have been to increase the incumbents' popularity. Beyond being yet another reason not to do Abu Hanifa and Fallujah, I could have brought that argument to bear on the withdrawal idea. I had two whole days to take Simon Tustin's idea and present it to the Smart Guys. I could not embed the idea in any strategic goal, so the discussion turned on its effects on the American electorate and W's reelection campaign.

This lack of time and my lack of knowledge was the most frustrating thing about my job.

Now, just as I cannot say people should have listened to me more, I'm also not saying everything would have turned out great if I'd presented better arguments. Let's imagine every bit of this analysis had been at hand in early September. Let's imagine that knowing this, we had not launched the Fallujah operation at all—let alone as our own Ramadan Offensive—and had helped the Allawi regime become popular enough that Grand Ayatollah Sistani never endorsed an electoral list and the transitional government elected in 2005 looked much like the one we had installed.

In that case, there would have been more unrest among the Shia Arabs, led by Sadr, and the Sunni Arab hard-liners would have still been fighting. Maybe the violence would have been less intense in those provinces, but violence would have spread throughout the country. I'd be describing a different kind of failure. I'd be wondering why we didn't take action in Fallujah to reduce the violence emanating from there and why we opened ourselves up to the claim among Shia Arabs that democracy was a sham because they got stuck with that same London exile we'd forced on them, Ayad Allawi. We'll never know whether this crisis in the alternate timeline was better than the one we got.

A lot of other things could have been done differently, not just these.

Bremer could have moved more lightly against Ba'ath Party members and the Iraqi Army—but what would have been the price in trust among Kurds and Shia Arabs? Would we now be claiming his failure to remove more of Saddam's state poisoned all hope of reconciliation and peace in Iraq?

A different electoral system could have been imagined—but could it have been approved against Grand Ayatollah Sistani's wishes?

We could have arrested or killed Moqtada al-Sadr on any of several occasions, but maybe that also would be seen in alternative hindsight as having removed the most unifying voice in Shia Arab politics.

We could have installed a dictator of our own as we had in Guatemala and Iran. Perhaps the real problem was that we chose a desired end state—democracy, unity, liberalism—that was not attainable in that society at that time. Would we not have then owned the failures of our new dictator, as we had in Iran? How has supporting murderous dictators in Central America worked out for the United States, let alone for the people who live there?

If we keep rolling this back, perhaps we should not have invaded Iraq at all. In that case, would some eventual atrocity of Saddam's or chaos into which Iraq later fell be blamed on our failure to follow through on what Rumsfeld had assured us would be an easy little war? We only know Rumsfeld and Cheney and Bush were wrong because we trusted them.

We tried the get-mad-but-do-nothing option in Iraq's neighboring Ba'athist state, Syria.

As McNamara, possessed of the wisdom of defeat that the architects of this war may not yet have grasped, agreed at the end of *The Fog of War*: Sometimes you're damned if you do, and you're damned if you don't. Our judgments are limited by our inability to either change the past or know the future. As the Vortex would have emphasized, there is no point in trying to fix the past. Let's close by returning to the real world, the actual chain of events, to consider our failures, many of which could be called failures of imagination.

One reason we were equanimous about the possible outcomes of the Iraqi election was that we imagined the State Department would have more influence over Iraqi political decisions. It didn't help that we took our eye off the ball during the change in ambassadors in the first half of 2005, but was it ever reasonable to think we could have convinced the Shia Arabs and Kurds to give away some of their short-term advantages to the Sunni Arabs? Neither of those groups had any reason to trust us. Did we have any credible leverage, or did they assume we would fight the Sunni Arabs on their behalf no matter what they did?

A bigger example of this was my failure to imagine how effective a Sunni Arab election boycott could be. I was confident the Sunni Arabs understood the consequences of a boycott and thus would not do it. But they did, silencing their own voices in the future government. I am still baffled by this. What were the Sunni Arabs hoping to accomplish by boycotting? I still can't imagine they thought, in December 2004, that the election would be postponed or called off.

Perhaps our most severe failure of imagination was the narcissism that the war would always be about us or about the government we had installed. I was—we were—believing sectarian war would not break out. I believed this because for the most part Iraqis got along with each other, lived together Shia and Sunni and Christian, Arab and Turkomen and Kurd. Of course, for the most part Rwandans and Yugoslavs had also lived together, until they no longer did. This danger never fully made its way into our analysis. We never quite grasped what would happen when the enemy kept its own appointment in Samarra by demolishing the al-Askari Shrine.

These failures of imagination were tied to a sort of failure of despair. Time after time, we always assumed there was reason to hope. If analysis projected a bad outcome, we disregarded the results and selected a more optimistic interpretation. In his final days in Iraq, Simon was telling anyone who would listen that we were a goal down in injury time, and thus desperate measures were called for. By my final days in Iraq, I was doing much the same, minus the soccer references. His imagination about how bad it could get was better than mine; after all, he was a Brit.

But Simon's views were disregarded when we discussed his proposal to boost the Interim Government by announcing a withdrawal plan. No one was willing to take seriously the idea that at some point a sovereign Iraqi government might pick the time and conditions of our departure, and then we would be forced to leave in haste and disorder. My November assessments of the need to engage with the Sunni Arabs to boost their turnout were dismissed by almost everyone except Colonel Storrie (another Brit!) as too gloomy. In fact, we were probably two goals down in injury time and I was not gloomy enough.

Maybe if we had accepted how awful things could get, we might have tried harder to do something to avoid that future, either by helping moderate parties gain popular support or by engaging with Sunni Arabs to avoid a boycott. The only thing we were good at imagining was that we would find a way to make things turn out okay. Holding on to hope, refusing to admit how bad things are, is a great way for an individual to get from one day to the next.

I know that all too well.

For a group, however, or for the long term, it's just another failure of imagination and a damn lousy way to deal with a crisis.

Aside from human nature, why did we have such failures of imagination? For one thing, we didn't understand what was going on. The rapid turnover of people—some there for a year, but many others for 60, 90, or 120 days—meant constant loss of continuity, constant assertion of unearned expertise by me as much as by anyone else. The pace of work meant there was little time to get back to or even remember ideas from the week before. There was always a new problem, and we were all so tired.

A deeper root of our failures of imagination was we never understood the Iraqi people. We had no empathy. We did not understand the feelings and motivations of our strategic enemy. I could not understand why the Sunni Arabs would boycott the election. I could not understand why the Shia Arabs and Kurds might refuse to compromise with the Sunni Arabs.

Most of all, I don't think any of us understood what it was like to live under occupation. It didn't register to me at the time, but the Strategy office was a bunch of White men, except for the psychologist, and her role was never very clear to me. We were almost all very highly educated Americans, and those who were not were Dutch or British. We knew counterinsurgency only from the side of the government, whether in El Salvador or Northern Ireland. Perhaps more diversity among our own experiences as Americans—more than one woman or perhaps a Black or Hispanic or Native American officer—might have increased the range of our imagination. Perhaps if we'd had a Polish officer working with us, one who had grown up under Soviet domination, we could have gained some insight.

Instead, our strategy treated our enemy—treated all the Iraqi people—as mere objects of our policies. I guess I did my best to try to understand the enemy but failed; others spent their time thinking about how our actions would look to Americans, especially before our own election. How would it look to Americans if we cut and run from this war? How would it look to Americans if we negotiated with terrorists?

How would it look to Iraqis if we showed we were committed to their freedom?

So here I am, sitting in my home office watching the sun set over Pikes Peak into a haze of wildfire smoke, much as it did so long ago over Kuwait City. In the end, of course, our failures had few consequences for any of us as individuals. I think we all knew that would be the case. Assuming we lived, we wouldn't have to face our failures. Indeed, most of us were promoted on the basis of the service alone, regardless of how we performed.

I suppose insulation from consequences is what allows me to look back on my time in Iraq, awful as it was, as an amazing experience. Not just the fear, the stress, the heat, the personalities: also the trust, the relevance, the endorphins, the friends.

It was real. It mattered. And this is how it happened.

True story.

Glossary

9/11: The date in 2001 when four aircraft were hijacked by al-Qaeda, who flew two of them into the towers of the World Trade Center and one into the Pentagon; the other was forced to crash by the passengers in a field in Pennsylvania.

Abu Ghraib: Prison in the town of the same name that had been used by Saddam Hussein for the torture of political and other prisoners. It was used by American forces to hold prisoners after the 2003 invasion. The April 2004 revelation that some American guards were abusing those prisoners was considered scandalous.

Abu Hanifa: A mosque in Adhamiyah that was perhaps the most important religious site in Baghdad for Sunni Arabs. American and Iraqi forces raided it on 19 November 2004.

Adhamiyah: A Sunni Arab neighborhood on the north side of Baghdad.

Allawi, Ayad: Interim prime minister of Iraq and leader of the Iraqi National Accord. A former member of the Ba'ath Party, he lived in exile in London for many years after falling out with Saddam Hussein.

al-Askari Shrine: Also called the Golden Mosque, a site in Samarra of great importance to Shia Arabs.

Ba'ath Party: An Arab nationalist and socialist political party, different factions of which ruled Iraq under Saddam Hussein and Syria under Hafez al-Assad.

Badr Corps: A Shia Arab militia backed by Iran, totaling about sixteen thousand fighters as the armed wing of the Supreme Council for the Islamic Revolution in Iraq.

Baghdad Mosquito: A collection of local media reports compiled so people would know the "buzz" around the city and country.

Bremer, Paul: Leader of the Coalition Provisional Authority.

Camp Victory: A military compound near the airport and surrounding the al-Faw Palace, home to many of the headquarters units.

Casey, George W.: Commander of the Multinational Force-Iraq.

Chalabi, Ahmed: Leader of the Iraqi National Congress and a significant advocate for the invasion and occupation of Iraq.

Coalition Provisional Authority: The UN-authorized governing body over Iraq from the beginning of the occupation through the restoration of sovereignty at the end of June 2004. Led by Paul Bremer, it among other things created the Iraqi Interim Government that ruled after it, established the Transitional Administrative Law, and set up the rules for the first democratic elections in Iraq.

al-Dari, Harith: Spokesman for the Muslim Ulema Council.

Da'wa Party: A religious Shia party with three factions that functioned independently; the main faction was led by Ibrahim Ja'afari.

decisive points: Key events, critical systems, or functions that would create an advantage in a war.

Desert Shield and Storm: Operations authorized by the United Nations to first shield Saudi Arabia from attack after Iraq occupied Kuwait in 1990 and then to expel Iraqi forces in early 1991.

drug deal: An informal manpower arrangement that bypasses official deployment and personnel channels so a commander can obtain the people they want.

Early Bird: A daily email of defense-related news and opinion curated by the Department of Defense.

Giant Voice: An alert system for incoming fire and other announcements, broadcast through loudspeakers mounted above and throughout military bases.

Governing Council: A group of Iraqi representatives selected by Paul Bremer to advise the Coalition Provisional Authority. After Iraqi sovereignty was restored, its members became the core of the Iraqi Interim Government.

Green Zone: Officially the International Zone, the Green Zone was several square miles along the Tigris, downstream from downtown Baghdad. It hosted most embassies and international organizations working in Baghdad, part of the military headquarters, and many aspects of the incipient Iraqi government. It was called "Green" to suggest a more relaxed security posture behind its barricades than in the "Red Zone" outside.

Gurkha: A Nepalese soldier.

hajjimart: The common (though disrespectful) name for Ghazi's

Market, an Iraqi shop located next door to the post exchange in the Green Zone.

Iraqi Constitutional Government: The government to be elected under the constitution that would be written by the Iraqi Transitional Government.

Iraqi Interim Government: The government established by Paul Bremer and the Coalition Provisional Authority to rule Iraq during the interim between the restoration of Iraqi sovereignty and the first democratic elections.

Iraqi Islamic Party: A branch of the Muslim Brotherhood and the only major religious Sunni Arab political party.

Iraqi National Accord: The political party led by Ayad Allawi.

Iraqi National Congress: The political party led by Ahmed Chalabi.

Iraqi Transitional Government: The government to be elected in the first democratic elections in Iraq to replace the Iraqi Interim Government. Its main task would be to write a constitution for Iraq.

Ja'afari, Ibrahim: Leader of the main branch of the Da'wa Party, a religious Shia Arab party.

Jersey barriers: Two- to three-foot-high concrete barriers used to block and channel traffic.

Karrada: A relatively safe neighborhood on the south side of Baghdad, across the Tigris from the Green Zone.

kinetic operation: One that uses force to achieve its ends.

Kurdish Democratic Party: One of the two major Kurdish political parties.

Kurdistan: Three provinces in northern Iraq that had been effectively autonomous from Iraq since the aftermath of the Gulf War (Desert Storm).

Kurd–religious Shia partnership: A hypothetical outcome to the Iraqi election in which the Shia Arabs and Kurds would hold all the power, to the exclusion of Sunni Arabs.

Kurds: One of the three major demographic groups in Iraq, comprising about 15–20 percent of the population. Concentrated in the mountainous areas in far northern Iraq, along the borders with Turkey and Iran.

Mahdi Army: A Shia Arab militia led by Moqtada al-Sadr.

Monotheism and Jihad: A radical Sunni Islamist group led by Abu Musab al-Zarqawi that later became affiliated with al-Qaeda.

Morning Prayers: A daily stand-up group meeting called by Colonel Vortex at which we would share progress and he would assign new tasks.

Multinational Force-Iraq: The American-led "coalition of the willing" that was occupying Iraq under United Nations Security Council Resolution 1546.

Muslim Brotherhood: A Sunni organization active (and also banned) in many countries in the Middle East, whose activities range from social welfare to political violence.

Muslim Ulema Council: An association of Sunni Arab religious leaders, whose spokesman was Harith al-Dari.

national unity government: A hypothetical outcome to the Iraqi election in which moderate and religious parties would hold all the power, to the exclusion of radical Sunni and Shia Arabs.

Negroponte, John: US ambassador to Iraq.

Pachachi, Adnan: Leader of the Independent Iraqi Democrats, the closest thing to a Western-style liberal party in Iraq.

Patriotic Union of Kurdistan: One of the two major Kurdish political parties.

peshmerga: Two groups of Kurdish militia, totaling about seventy thousand fighters, dedicated to the protection of Kurdish regions in Iraq.

post exchange: A government-run general store.

Ramadan: The Islamic holy month.

Red Team: A group whose role is to try to understand the motivations and future actions of an adversary.

Republican Palace: My workplace in Iraq, this building hosted the US Embassy in Iraq and part of the military headquarters, along with many other government and international offices. It had also hosted the Coalition Provisional Authority.

Rumsfeld, Donald: Secretary of defense.

Saad, Dr. (Saad al-Obaidy): Chair of the Transition and ReIntegration Committee.

al-Sadr, Moqtada: Heir to a line of Shia religious leaders and leader of the Mahdi Army.

Salafi: A fundamentalist strain within Sunni Islam.

senior advisor: More formally senior consultant, a civilian or military officer assigned as a mentor and liaison to an Iraqi government ministry, agency, or office.

Shia Arabs: One of the three major demographic groups in Iraq, comprising about 60–65 percent of the population. Concentrated in areas south of Baghdad.

Shia-dominated government: A hypothetical outcome to the Iraqi election in which the Shia Arabs would hold all the power, to the exclusion of Sunni Arabs and Kurds.

Shinseki, Eric: Former chair of the Joint Chiefs of Staff.

al-Sistani, Ali: The grand ayatollah who, as their object of emulation, functioned as the spiritual guide for most of Iraq's Shia Arabs. He did not advocate for direct clerical rule in Iraq.

Sunni Arabs: One of the three major demographic groups in Iraq, comprising about 15–20 percent of the population. Concentrated in areas near and north of Baghdad. They controlled Iraq under both the monarchy and during Ba'ath Party rule under Saddam Hussein.

Supreme Council for the Islamic Revolution in Iraq: A religious Shia Arab political party that promoted direct rule by religious leaders, similar to Iran.

Texas barriers: Six- to eight-foot-high concrete walls meant to fully surround an area and protect it from direct fire.

Thawra: A large Shia Arab neighborhood in northeastern Baghdad, more often known as Sadr City.

Transitional Administrative Law: Effectively the interim constitution of Iraq, written by the Coalition Provisional Authority under Paul Bremer.

transition and integration: The term used for the disarmament, demobilization, and reintegration of militias in Iraq.

Transition and ReIntegration Committee: An interagency Iraqi Interim Government committee tasked with disarming and demobilizing militias in Iraq. Chaired by Saad al-Obaidy.

Turkomen: One of the smaller demographic groups in Iraq, comprising less than 5 percent of the population. Historically concentrated near Kirkuk.

Umm al-Ma'arik: The mosque of Harith al-Dari, spokesman for the Muslim Ulema Council.

Wolfowitz, Paul: Deputy secretary of defense.

Yawr, Ghazi: Interim president of Iraq.

al-Zarqawi, Abu Musab: Leader of the radical Sunni Islamist group Monotheism and Jihad.

A Note on Sources

This narrative is written without academic citations, but a few sources should be acknowledged here.

Quotations in chapter 4 from the Bush–Kerry presidential debate are taken from the transcript posted by the Commission on Presidential Debates, available at https://www.debates.org/voter-education/debate-transcripts/september-30-2004-debate-transcript/.

The *New York Times* op-ed by Daniel Ellsberg quoted in chapter 4 is at https://www.nytimes.com/2004/09/28/opinion/truths-worth-telling.html, and his article in *Public Policy* can be read at https://archive.org/details/TheQuagmireMythAndTheStalemateMachine.

The *New York Times* article by Eric Schmitt discussed in chapter 6 is at https://www.nytimes.com/2004/10/31/washington/world/the-reach-of-war-outlook-in-iraq-us-officials-cite.html.

The *New York Times Magazine* profile of Laura Poitras mentioned in chapter 8 is at https://www.nytimes.com/2013/08/18/magazine/laura-poitras-snowden.html.

W. Somerset Maugham's version of "The Appointment in Samarra," a story I adapt in chapter 5 differently than he did, can be found at https://www.k-state.edu/english/baker/english320/Maugham-AS.htm.

I can no longer find a clear video of the Fallujah mosque shooting discussed in chapter 6, but the relevant text is quoted by NBC at https://www.nbcnews.com/id/wbna6496898 and the graphic video itself, with the reporter talking over it, is posted at https://www.youtube.com/watch?v=o4j5oghDeKA.

The First Cavalry Division's polls of Baghdad discussed in chapters 4, 5, and 7 are not available to my knowledge.

The Oxford Research International poll discussed in chapter 4 is not on the organization's own website, but it can be found via a bounce from https://www.google.com/url?sa=t&source=web&rct=j&opi=89978449&url=https://access.gesis.org/dbk/58736&ved=2ahUKEwicnffzk86MAxXBGTQIHSMbLSkQFnoECB8QAQ&usg=AOvVaw374OQyZSZkoHjZa9AER6LC.

The International Republican Institute's polls discussed in chapters 4 and 5 are posted on its website. July 2004 is at https://www.iri.org/resources/survey-shows-optimism-among-iraqis/, September is at https://www.iri.org/resources/iraqis-show-optimism-about-the-future-and-strong-support-for-democracy/, and October is at https://www.iri.org/resources/optimistic-outlook-on-the-future-and-support-for-democracy-continues-in-iraq/.

About the Author

Tom Mowle is the author of *Allies at Odds? The United States and the European Union*, the editor of *Hope is Not a Plan: The War in Iraq from Inside the Green Zone*, and the coauthor of *The Unipolar World: An Unbalanced Future*. He is the owner of Rampart Professional Solutions, a manuscript coaching and editing service in Colorado.